GEORGE REX GENEALOGY

Ancestry and Descendants of
George Rex First of England
to Pennsylvania in 1771

First Edition by

Leda Ferrell Rex

Privately Published in
Wichita, Kansas
1933

Second Edition by

Edward Birch Bower
Walter Scott Bower III
William David Thomas

HERITAGE BOOKS
2009

HERITAGE BOOKS

AN IMPRINT OF HERITAGE BOOKS, INC.

Books, CDs, and more—Worldwide

For our listing of thousands of titles see our website
at
www.HeritageBooks.com

Published 2009 by
HERITAGE BOOKS, INC.
Publishing Division
100 Railroad Ave. #104
Westminster, Maryland 21157

International Standard Book Numbers
Paperbound: 978-0-7884-1006-2
Clothbound: 978-0-7884-8226-7

Preface to the First Edition

To Charles Swan Rex we are indebted for the existence of this genealogy. In writing to Dr. Parks Rex under date of January 17, 1893, he says: "I have been working on the Rex genealogy for more than two years" which he continued intermittently until the time of his death, May 12, 1917. In compliance with his request, the work was then carried on by his eldest son, George B. Rex who diligently searched in all lines until some four years ago when he put the task into my hands. When it was first suggested to me I refused, but later the thought insistently recurred to my mind that if I did not do this work perhaps it might never be done. I had read in many letters written by Charles S. Rex how desirous he was to finish the book and how he feared failing health would prevent. To have his hard work lost disturbed me, and again I thought, as the father of my boy was gone, perhaps in his place it was my duty to do this work. As an offering to The House of Rex, in remembrance of the father of my boy, and for the benefit of my son and all others of the younger generations I bring my little contribution.

Tradition, history and dates are all as correct and complete as it was possible for me to obtain them. We are indebted to many members of the family for their loyal assistance, and only those who have had the experience realize what this means; also, how great the effort is at times for smallest results. For the benefit of this book, Dan and I have personally interviewed people from Seattle, Washington, to Eliot, Maine; have visited the graves of George Rex 1st and wife and of ten of their twelve children, their old homes, courthouses, and all places where records and information might be found, and have taken notes and pictures everywhere we went.

This is from the notes of Charles S. Rex:

> "I find our people all God fearing men and women; most of them warm hearted Christians holding prominent positions in all the various Protestant churches. The men the best of husbands and fathers and the women the best of wives and mothers. None exceedingly wealthy and none extremely poor. I have never known an Almshouse or prison door to shut on one of them."

At any time I will appreciate receiving corrections or additions to the family data.

Leda Ferrell Rex

Figure 1.
Charles Swan Rex
Line IX, Page 186

Preface to the Second Edition

Leda Ferrell Rex, the author of the original *Rex Genealogy*, was the wife of Loren Edgar Rex, the third child of Ross Edgar Rex. Ross Edgar Rex was the 12th child of Benjamin Rex and his second wife Martha Thompson Rex. Benjamin Rex was the 9th child of George and Margaret Kepler Rex. It was Loren's tragic death at the age of 45 that prompted Leda to complete the *Rex Genealogy*. At the time of Loren's death his only son, Daniel, was six months old.

The original edition of the *Rex Genealogy* was published privately in Wichita, Kansas by the Franklin Printery in 1933. The depression started with the stock market crash in 1929 and reached its height by 1933 when 16 million people or one third of the US workforce was unemployed. Leda Rex traveled, researched, and then published the book during this period. Two letters written by Leda Rex are reproduced below, and give insight into the problems Leda had with completing the *Rex Genealogy*.

In a letter to W. S. Bower dated September 30, 1931, Leda gives us an idea of the amount of work involved with completing the book. She writes:

"My dear friends; I thought you might be interested to know Dan and I reached home safely about 3 weeks ago. Covered a mileage of over 13,000 miles. Was very pleasant and interesting but tiresome and hard at times too. We found the Bower graves all right near where you live and Dan took pictures but as yet do not know the results as had no time yet to develop them. He is in Jr. Year High School and pretty busy with Latin, French, Math, English, and Constitution, but likes it. We often speak of our lovely visit with you all and so appreciated all you did for us. We got pictures and all safely at home and do not yet know if will copy them first or just how. If makes any difference how long we keep them may have them copied soon. Dan thinks perhaps he can do this work but will have to wait and see how he gets along if he is to do it. If you want them at any time just let me know and we will speed up. We visited the George Rex f[t] and wife Margaret Kepler graves and 10 of their 12 children's graves and took pictures of all. Went to all the courthouses and hunted records everywhere we hoped to find help. Will need lots of time and work spent on it all now to see what we really have. If you hear of anything more or anyone who might help please tell me. Dan joins me again with thanks and all best wishes to all of you."

The following letter written by Leda Rex on July 12, 1932 gives more insight as to the problems Leda had with funding the book:

"My dear friends:

As you may remember, I have been working on the Rex Family history for some time and have decided to try and publish what I have compiled. Even after reaching this stage there is yet much to do and one important matter is finance. From others who have successfully done similar work I have learned a very good way is for every family or line to pay for their own pictures used in the book and also every family contribute to the general fund whatever they can or will. According to what is needed in expense and what is contributed so the books when finished will be allotted. In other words, if you send $10 and $5 was used on your own line or family pictures then you would be contributing $5 to the general fund and when all expense counted you would get back in books however much $5 would pay for. On the other hand, if you sent $15 and your pictures cost $5, then you would get twice as many books in return, etc. Of course, I have given all my time and expenses thus far but in these times especially I could no pay for the publishing alone. From all I can learn, I think there will be little sale for the book outside of the family. For this reason and because I think little will be contributed, I will endeavor to make the expense as low as possible and yet not be ashamed of the work."

"After the book is printed, I think I could have it bound in a very good looking part leather at least for $1 per volume. I have decided it will be printed with paper back and then everybody may have bound to their taste if (they) wish a better cover. I do not have an exact figure but of course the fewer copies made the more the expense in production. 50 or 70 copies is what I think I will order. I will cut the coat according to the cloth and if you will tell me what you can contribute and if you wish any copies will be helpful. If I am not assisted in expense, I will cut down the pictures to those in which I am most interested, my family and the ones of greatest general interest, etc. In the latter class would be to my mind, the Oath of Allegiance of George Rex 1st, his home in Pa., his grave stones and of his wife Margaret Kepler, etc. Some prints are plainer than others and can be copied or half tones made of them for less money than others which must be done in Copper or etc. and also need hand retouching. I think they may average about $5 each cut of about 6 X 6 or less. In some there can be 2 or 3 small pictures in one cut where in others should just be one cut alone etc."

Leda continues the above letter with a personal note at the bottom to Mr. and Mrs. W. S. Bower:

"Dear Mr. and Mrs. Bower:

I am trying to send this letter to as many as possible of the Rex connection and learn their wishes and suggestions. In your line we have the tombstones of Elizabeth Bower and husband, the tile, the house as used to be the stone dated of it and the other stone dated which is now on the ground. The mill etc. What do you want done about them? They might not look quite so well together in group as separated but I believe would do that way and be cheaper. I think would have to be copper as so dim some of it and unless needed much hand work besides think perhaps grouped would not cost over $5. Really can not tell exactly until show all the pictures and get everything down in detail. With these hard times we are glad we took our trip last year. Hope you are all well. With best wishes and hoping to hear from you soon.

Sincerely

Leda Rex.

We do not know how many copies of the *Rex Genealogy* were actually published although we suspect that the number is between 50 and 75. We have been able to locate only three of them. The first copy and the one that we have been working from is owned by Walter Scott Bower of Fredericktown, Pennsylvania, who is descended from Elizabeth Rex Bower, the second child of George and Elizabeth Rex. The second copy is owned by William D. Thomas of Westminster, Colorado, who is descended from George Rex, II, the third child of George and Elizabeth Rex. The third copy is owned by Albert E. Moredock who is descended from Charles Rex, the twelfth child of George and Elizabeth Rex. There were approximately 2,500 names listed in the *Rex Genealogy* when it was published in 1933. It can only be speculated as to how many living descendants there are in 1996. For those interested in their own genealogy, discovery of a book like the *Rex Genealogy* is a spectacular find.

It seemed to us that it would be a tragedy to allow the work done by Leda Ferrell Rex to be lost, so the idea of updating and republishing the book was entertained. Scott and I discussed the project in early 1993 and waded into it slowly. As computer technology improved, the project became more feasible. We started with a 486 DX2 66 MHz Personal Computer and eventually finished it on a 133 MHz Pentium machine. The text was scanned with a Hewlett Packard ScanJet IIc. OmniPage Professional was then used to convert the scanned image into text format. All the photographs were also scanned using the ScanJet IIc and were 'computer enhanced' using PhotoShop. The text and the photographs were then merged into files created with Microsoft Publisher. The book was then printed using a WinJet modified HP LaserJet 4 Printer which prints at 1,200 dpi.

In order for the genealogy to be universally available, the portion of the genealogy that appeared in the First Edition was first entered using the Family Tree Maker™ and then converted to GEDCOM, a standard format for genealogies. This file was then Emailed to Bill Thomas who submitted it to the Family Search Ancestral File in Salt Lake City, Utah. This genealogy became available in 1997 via the updated Ancestral File CD-ROM disk. Because the Second Edition of the *Rex Genealogy* has been prepared in both digital and analog format, we will make it available to anyone interested in both formats. It is hoped that in this way the memory of Leda Ferrell Rex and her work will not be lost or forgotten.

In republishing Leda's book, we have made few changes leaving her writing style almost entirely intact. The modifications that we have made in the Second Edition include the following:

1. Known errors have been corrected. For example, in the original edition, Greene County Pennsylvania was incorrectly spelled Green. George Crumine listed on p. 31 should have been Daniel. The surname Schreimer listed on pp. 29-30 should have been Schreiner. The surname Mordock listed on p. 156 should have been Moredock.
2. Abbreviations of first names used extensively in the First Edition have been converted to their full spelling.
3. Several other abbreviations used in the First Edition have been converted to the full spelling. State abbreviations have been converted to standard USPS apreviations, Eg. Penna becomes PA.
4. Photographs of individuals have been added. We have also added or substituted several photographs of sites included in the First Edition with more recent photographs.
5. Corrections from the "Errata" in the First Edition have been corrected in this edition.
6. We have rewritten the section dealing with George Rex updating it with new information not available to Leda.
7. We have added one chapter dealing with Hannah Lightfoot and George III. This section originally was attached to the section dealing with Line 3.
8. We have attempted to find descendants of the various lines and have included those that were found and have added approximately 1,300 names.

We have continued to use in the Second Edition the symbols denoting generation as they were used in the First Edition. These symbols are as follows:

I. Roman Numeral	2nd generation
1. Arabic numeral	3rd generation
A. Capital letter	4th generation
a. Small letter	5th generation
(1) Parentheses	6th generationm
+ Plus sign	7th generation

We have added the following symbols:

^ Carrot	8th generation
~ Tilde	9th generation
# Number sign	10th generation

Superscript numbers by the first names also indicate generation numbers for that individual. We have also continued to use the dagger symbol † to indicate service in the military. The superscripted number associated with first or second names represents the generation of the individual.

Although we have proofread the entire book multiple times, we can guarantee that there are still errors. We will, of course, blame those errors on the computer.

Edward Birch Bower, Monroe, NC
Walter Scott Bower. Fredericktown, PA
William David Thomas, Westminster, CO

Acknowledgements

There are many people and organizations that we would like to thank for their help in the preparation of the Second Edition of the *George Rex Genealogy*. At the top of the list is Sheila Mitchell who performed two vital functions. First, she is the world's authority on Hannah Lightfoot and was gracious to review the sections dealing with Hannah Lightfoot and George Rex. Second, Sheila was instrumental in adding Bill Thomas to the authors list of this book. As it turned out, Bill owned a copy of the First Edition of the *George Rex Genealogy* and had used it in submitting his line to the Ancestral File. When Sheila consulted that database looking for Hannah Lightfoot, she found Bill's name and wrote to him. I then found Sheila by writing to the editors of the A&E Biography Series on George III which contained a segment by her on Hannah Lightfoot. She responded and gave me Bill's address. Bill and I have been communicating over the Internet on the project ever since. Sheila and I have been communicating via Royal and US mail ever since.

We would of course like to thank the A&E Biography series for introducing us to Sheila. We highly recommend the A&E Biography segment on the life of George III. We would like to thank the Thomas Cooper Library of the University of South Carolina for obtaining Mary Pendered's book *The Fair Quaker* and John Lindsey's book *The Lovely Quaker*. We are indebted to Amanda B. Bower, Ph.D. for her assistance with the book.

We thank the Rt. Hon. the Lord Sackville for giving us permission to include the image of Hannah Lightfoot (Figure 8) in this book. We thank *The National Trust for Places of Historic Interest or Natural Beauty* for providing information on the Hannah Lightfoot portrait and the introduction to the Rt. Hon. the Lord Sackville. We thank the Public Record Office who has custody of the original Hannah Lightfoot marriage certificate and will, reference number J77/44/R31, for providing copies of those documents.

We used the Internet for the majority of our search for lost descendants of George Rex. We found the most useful site for that search to be the *Roots Surname List* at http://www.rootsweb.com. We would like to thank them for providing their great service and assistance.

We would like to thank all the descendants of George Rex who have contributed information to this book. Those of the current generation whom we would especially like to thank are as follows:

- Ingrid Nelson Baillie and Wallace R. Forman helped with the descendants of Lydia Leffler, Line IX.
- Pierre E. Haver helped with the descendants of Jane Rex and John Haver, Line III.
- Ruth E. Kiser helped with the descendants of Iden Bower, Line II.
- Mike Milliken helped with Line VI.
- We especially wish to thank our wives for their help and encouragement.

The two primary sources for information about Hannah Lightfoot are as follows:

- Pendered, Mary L. *The Fair Quaker Hannah Lightfoot and Her Relations with George III*. Hurst & Blackett, Limited Paternoster House, E. C., 1910.
- Lindsey, John. *The Lovely Quaker*. Rich & Cowan, Ltd., 1939.

Other references used are sited as they appear in the book.

CONTENTS

Figure 2. Rex Ancestral home near Jefferson, Greene County Pennsylvania. Photograph taken ca. 1933 appeared in First Edition of Rex Genealogy.

Figure 3. Photograph taken in 1995 by W. S. Bower of the Rex Ancestral home. These are the same buildings that appear in Figure 2 above.

Ancestry of George Rex

"Like leaves on trees the race of man is found,
Now green in youth, now withering on the ground;
Another race the following spring supplies,
They fall successive, and successive rise
So generations in their course decay,
So flourish these, when those have passed away."

George Rex, we believe, was born at or near London, England. Although his actual birth day and month are unknown, his birth year, 1750, is calculated from an inscription on his gravestone, "George Rex Who departed this life May the 1st, A. D., 1821 in the 71st year of his age." He emigrated to America in 1771 and first settled in Pennsylvania, probably in Bucks County north of Philadelphia.

Margaret Kepler was born in Germany. Her actual birth day and month are also unknown, and her birth year, 1752, is similarly calculated from an inscription on her gravestone, "Margaret Rex Wife of George Rex who departed this life September 5, A. D., 1828 Aged 76 years."

Margaret was also living in Bucks County when she met George, and they were married in 1772 when she was 20 years old and he was 22. After their marriage and before the beginning of the Revolutionary War, George and his new wife moved to western New York State where it is likely that their first child, Mary, was born.

It was stated that George was an outspoken Tory, and possibly for a brief time an officer in the British Army. In a letter written in 1913 by Boyd Crumrine, one of George Rex's great-grandsons, George was described as such an enthusiastic Tory that "on the occasion of a reverse of the American forces in some important engagement, he (George) roasted a white ox whole, and fed it to the people as a triumph for the British victory." This behavior did not go well with the loyal Americans in the area who were described in Boyd Crumrine's letter as 'American Cowboys'. Arrangements were made to put George on a vessel for England where George's detractors said that he belonged. George learned of the plot and arranged for his young wife and daughter to travel alone in a canoe down the Susquehanna River from their home to Harrisburg, Pennsylvania, approximately 130 miles in the dead of winter through hostile Indian territory. George bribed some officers of the seagoing vessel when it left New York to stop in

Philadelphia allowing him to disembark. George then traveled from Philadelphia to Harrisburg and there met his wife and children.

It is not known when the family moved from New York state to Pennsylvania, although it was most likely prior to 1777. It was in that year that George signed an oath of Allegiance and Fidelity which was required by an Act of the General Assembly of Pennsylvania. If he had still been living in New York, it is unlikely that he would have signed the oath.

The oath is reproduced below. It is a pre-printed form that has added the handwritten names of Rex and Allen, the dates, and the Northumberland Co.

"Lancaster printed by Frank Bailey
Northumbdt-

I do hereby certify that George Rex Worthy has voluntarily taken and subscribed the oath of Allegiance and Fidelity as directed by an Act of General Assembly of Pennsylvania, passed the 13th day of June, A. D. 1777 as Witness my Hand and Seal the 8th Day of December Anno Domini 1777 Sam'el Allen (L. S.)"

Note that the old English long S. and double S. are used.
George and Margaret settled next in Cumberland County in Central Pennsylvania in the Valley of the Juniata River. The area in which they settled would eventually become Mifflin County which was formed from Cumberland and North Cumberland Counties on Septem-

Figure 4. Oath of Allegiance of George Rex 1st.

ber 19, 1789. Living in close proximity to the Rex family in the Juniata River Valley were Benjamin Kepler, brother of Margaret, and the Bower family. There are deeds on record (Deed Book D page 471, dated March 14, 1785) at Lewistown, Mifflin County, Pennsylvania in which Benjamin Kepler sold some land to George Rex. Records found in the Pennsylvania Archives, Volume XIX p. 63 and 54, note George Rex, farmer, tax £4. 8D. George Rex 1779, 1 horse 2 cattle, Cumberland Co. 1780, 2 horses 8 cattle, Cumberland Co. Vol. 20, 1781, 2 horse 3 cattle. The 1790 U. S. Census has George Rex listed as 1-3-6 (meaning 1 male head, 3 sons, 5 daughters and a wife). Cumberland County was formed in 1750 and extended back to the Western limits of PA; Bedford County was formed in 1771 out of Cumberland County, and in 1773 Westmoreland County was formed out of Bedford. Westmoreland County then became Washington county in 1781.

The George Rex family probably moved from Mifflin County to Washington County, Pennsylvania around 1790. The area of Washington county where they moved would eventually become Greene County. Mifflin County Deed Book D. page 466, dated November 11, 1790 states that "George Rexworthy and wife Margaret sell their land in Mifflin County to Nathaniel Hart in consideration of 265 pounds." When George and Margaret left Mifflin County they had eight children. Their ninth child, Benjamin, was born in Washington County on January 9, 1792.

The Greene County Patent Book, P, Vol. 27, pg. 432, shows that on March 21, 1796 George Rex patented 252 ½ acres of land called the William Harrod "Drowl" near Jefferson, Pa. This land then became known as the ancestral homestead of the Rex family. There were members of the fam-

Figure 5. Original log portion of George Rex 1st home near Jefferson, PA. 1932. Described in 1798 direct tax list as "2-story log dwelling 20 x 17, 2 windows of 12 lites each."

ily who remember this original document which was sheepskin. Another four acre tract near the larger one had a warrant granted January 6, 1819, and was patented to George Rexworthy. It should be noted that there are many spellings of the family surname all of which reflect the family name: Rix, Rax, Rex, and Rex Worthy. As reported in the 1931 edition of this book, this 252 acres was divided many years ago among the heirs who may yet own parts of it. The homestead portion, however, was sold outside the family in 1907, and the present owner (1931) was D. D. Thistlewaite. The last member of the Rex family to be born at the old home was Ernest Walton Rex on May 23, 1885. The home is where Margaret and George Rex died, and were buried in the family plot. In 1895 their bodies were removed by their grandson, George Rex, (son of Charles) to the New Jefferson, Pennsylvania cemetery. The exact inscriptions are given here as appear on their very quaint large flat stones. These death records were confirmed by markings on the tombstones and have been seen by Dan and Leda Rex, August 4, 1931, and by W. S. Bower in 1995 (Figure 6).

In
Memory
of
George Rex
Who departed this life May the 1st, A D., 1821 in the 71st
year of his age.
This stone was erected by his executors, A. D., 1822

Remember man as you pass by
As you are now so once was I
As I am now so you must be
Prepare for death and follow me.

In
Memory
of
Margaret Rex
Wife of George Rex
Who departed this life
September 5, A. D., 1828
Aged 76 years

Called from these scenes of pain and woe,
From every sorrow risen,
Hope bids the bosom fondly glow,
And whispers she's in heaven.

Figure 6. Photograph of the Rex Family Plot near Jefferson PA taken by W. S. Bower in 1995. The first flat slab marks the grave of George Rex I, while the second flat slab marks that of his wife, Margaret Kepler Rex. The next tall white stone marks the grave of their son, Charles Rex, and the next short dark stone marks the grave of their daughter, Margaret Rex-McCullough.

Margaret was described as very dark, heavy, and short of statue although her age at which these observations were made is not known. George Rex 1st is described as a tall man of slight build, very quiet and unassuming and a devout Episcopalian. A man of influence in the community in which he lived, successful in a business way, but owing to his extreme reticence only the actual monuments he left behind tell the story of his life. He built a chapel on his farm near Jefferson and left quite an estate when he died. To every one of his twelve children he gave a large Bible and a prayer book (see his will) subscribing in each of them some admonition for right living. The following is from the Benjamin Rex Bible, line 9:

"The gift of George Rex, Senior, to his son Benjamin, June 10, 1817. It is also his sincere desire that this his most valuable and last bequest shall be preserved and the precepts therein laid down be strictly followed."

George Rex

In an Episcopal church paper called *The Church News*, for March, 1926, is a copy of a letter signed G. D. H. to Bishop Mann, where the writer tells of this Will of George Rex and giving these bibles to his children. Countless church records have been searched but to no avail, hoping to find the marriage bond of Margaret and George Rex and even the archives in London were appealed to because many of the old churches until the Revolution were operated under the missionaries of the S.P.G. The twelve children of Margaret Kepler and George Rex 1st are as follows:

Mary Rex (Polly) b. 1773, d. 1847, m. John Hughes 1795.
Elizabeth (Betty) b. 4-2-1775, d. 1852, m. John Bower 1794.
George 2nd, b. 10-14-1778, d. 1856, m. Jane Black 1806.
Martha, b. 7-15-1780, d. 1853, m. William Winter.
Edward (Ned) b. 11-24-1782, d. 1843, m. Hetty Huffdale, 1821.
Jonas, b. 2-4-1785, d. 1841, m. Rhoda Milliken, 1808.
Hannah, b. 7-16-1787, d. 1866, m. Isaac Shane 1805.
Margaret, b. 11-8-1789, d. 1808, m. William McCullough 1807.
Benjamin, b. 1-9-1792, d. 1854, m. Anna Barclay 1816, Martha
    Thompson, 1839.
Catherine, b. 12-2-1793, d. 1873, m. Joseph Burson.
Sarah (Sally) b___ m. Day and Cloaky. No issue.
Charles, b. 1-1801, d. 9-13-1854, m. Mary Hickman 10-2-1831.
All married and all had families except Sarah Rex.

WILL AND TESTAMENT
The Last Will and Testament

I, George Rex, of Jefferson Township, Greene County, Pennsylvania, being of sound and disposing mind and memory do make, declare and publish this to be my last will and Testament, hereby revoking all former ones by me made.

First: It is my will and desire that I be buried as soon after my decease as convenient in a decent manner—(by the north side of my daughter, Margaret,) under a tombstone with my name, age, etc., to be provided as soon as convenient by my Executors.

Item: It is my will that all my real and personal estate, after my decease, be and remain in the possession and under the control of my Dear Wife Margaret, during her natural life, to be assisted therein by her sons, Benjamin and Charles.

Item: Will and direct that my son, Benjamin, have one-half of all the profits made annually on the place during the life of his Mother; the other half to her and his brother, Charles, and so to continue to Charles after his Mother's decease until Charles is of age.

Item: I also will and direct that my wife and her son, Charles, keep possession of the dwelling house and one-half the barn and stabling during her life. And at her death, if Charles, my son, will be of age I hereby will and direct all equal division of all real and personal estate so left by my wife, between Benjamin and Charles, their heirs and assigns forever. And shall Charles not be of age on the death of my wife, I hereby direct that he and his brother, Benjamin, may farm or work the place together, dividing annually the profits until Charles is of full age, at which time I wish one to buy up the other's right if they choose to separate.

Item: I give and bequeath unto my son, George Rex, One Hundred and Fifty Dollars of monies which may be found of my Estate; also a piece off the north-west side of my land which is separated by a jut or run from the bridge on the road to Jefferson to follow the meander of the said run to Ten Mile Creek, also the two lots in Jefferson whereon his home is erected and which he now occupies to him and his heirs forever.

Item: I give and bequeath unto my son, Jonas Rex, One Hundred and Fifty Dollars to be paid to him in full of all my Estate–real and personal mixed.

Item: I give and bequeath unto my son, Edward Rex, One silver dollar, also all the bonds, writings obligatory, or any accounts which may be found against him in my possession in full of his share also.

Item: I give and bequeath unto each of my daughters, who are now married, One Hundred and Fifty Dollars, viz:–To Betsy Bower, to Polly Hughs, to Martha Winters, to Hannah Shane and to Catherine Burson to be paid to them or their legal representative after my decease out of monies which may be found in my possession or of debts due to me, and the legacies to my sons to be paid in like manner.

Item: I give and bequeath unto my daughter; Sarah Rex, when she becomes of age, Three Hundred Dollars and a sorrel year old colt now in my possession, two good cows, and six sheep of the stock on the farm, besides over and above what her mother may please to give her at her marriage or at her mother's decease.

Item: I give and bequeath unto my grandson, George McCullough, One Hundred Dollars when he is of age, and I also direct that he may be put to a trade at the age of fourteen.

Item: I order and direct my Executors immediately after my decease, (if it is not done before) to purchase out of the money of my Estate, twelve Quarto Bibles of as good print and paper as can be conveniently found, not to exceed four dollars each, also twelve books "of Common Prayer" of the rites and ceremonies of the Episcopal Church. Eleven of the said Bibles and prayer books to be given to my eleven children, and one each to my grandson, George McCullough as a memorial of my affection to them and their children that their names may be written therein as the bequest of their father.

Lastly I constitute and appoint my wife, Margaret Rex, Executrix and my son Benjamin Rex, and Hugh Barclay Executors of this my last Will and Testament given under my hand and seal this twenty-ninth day of April Anno Domino, One Thousand, Eight Hundred and Seventeen. 1817.

GEORGE REX.

Will Book I pg. 232 Waynesburg, PA.

Signed, sealed, publish and declared by said Testator as his last Will and Testament, in the presence of us, who in his presence and at his request, and in presence of each other, have subscribed as Witnesses.

Thomas Fletcher,
William Fletcher,
Richard Hughs.

Greene County, PA.,

I, William T. Hays, Register for the Probate of Wills and granting letters of Administration in and for the County of Greene aforesaid, do certify the annexed to be a true copy taken from and compared with the Original remaining in the Register's office in Waynesburg. In testimony whereof I have hereunto set my hand and the seal of office this 15th day of November, A. D., 1822.

William. T. Hays, Register.

Letters of administration were granted to Benjamin Rex and Hugh Barclay on May 8-1821.

Waynesburg, PA

William. T. Hays, Register.

Proof of Will.   Waynesburg, PA
    November 15, 1822   William. T. Hays, Register

Inventory and Appraisment

Inventory and appraisment of the goods and Chattles rights and credits of George Rex of Greene County, deceased, taken this 17th day of May, 1821 by Hugh Barclay and Benjamin Rex, administrators.

Wearing apparel, horse, saddle, and bridle of the Intestator.................$ 58.25
Cash in the purse...954.70
Samuel Black's note dated 29th of June, 1819 for..................................91.00
Samuel Haulsworth's note 22nd of June, 1820 for..................................75.00
Samuel Haulsworth's note 23rd of June, 1820 for..................................70.00
Edmond Burson, two notes 6th of Sept., 1819
    with interest from date, 6th, 1820..130.00
Thomas Coleman, Pittsburg, 17th of Mar., 1817......................................80.00
Isan Cysander, note dated 28th of Jan. 1820...5.00
John Bower, Esq., back account cattle...60.00
John Young, blacksmith, account...18.33
William. McCadden, hides and skins to tan on shoes...................................9.64
Peter Sharpnack, shoemaker...3.25
John Miliken, Cooper...3.12½
William Ketcham, flour..2.50
George Rex for 2 steers and 5 bushels of oats...33.25
Chest and money box...2.00
Trundle bed-stead and cradle...1.00
Five hundred, sixty swin bushels of wheat in the mill and barn (32¢)...181.67
Twenty-eight barrels of flour in G. H. Mill ($1.50)..............................42.00

47 flour barrels in barn..12.00
43 gallons of whiskey and barrel...11.25
A Wagon..60.00
A sorrel mare...40.00
An old gray horse..16.00
4 sets gears..12.00
2 beds and bedding below...32.00
A clock...16.00
A cupboard...10.00
2 beds and bedding up-stairs...40.00
1 bed and bedding up-stairs...15.00
2 double coverlets..11.00
8 new blankets...12.00
4 old blankets..5.00
A set of curtains...5.00
2 bed quilts..2.00
16 bags...6.00
2 old bed quilts..1.50
(End of first page in C. S. Rex's copy of Original Inventory).......$2,153.30½

A loom and gears...12.00
A bay mare...38.00
14 sheep and six lambs..16.00
4 swine...9.00
7 swine...12.25
A large sow..3.00
A harrow..5.00
4 yards brown cloth, 8 yards drab...12.00
1 red stag steer..10.00
1 black and white cow...8.00
1 red cow...8.00
1 brown cow..7.00
1 yellow cow..7.00
1 speckled cow..8.00
1 spotted heifer...6.50
1 red and white steer...8.00
1 black and white steer...7.50
1 red steer...7.00
1 black steer..6.50
1 red and white steer...6.00
1 white faced brindle steer..5.50
1 yearling bull...4.00
1 heifer..4.50
1 yearling calf...2.50
2 small calves..4.00

17 geese.. 3.00
Old wagon irons.. 2.40
1 plow.. 3.00
3 old plows... 3.00
125 bushels of corn (30¢)..37.50
2 large and 1 small clevishes... 1.50
A bureau.. 9.00
14 yds. check tow cloth... 3.50
A wagon cover... 2.00
Thread for linen cloth.. 7.00
12 yards toweling.. 3.00
6 yards flax linen.. 2.25
4 yards fulled linsey... 2.00
300 pounds of sugar (6¢).. 18.75
A new woman's saddle and bridle.. 15.00
An old saddle... 6.00

$2,452.01½

The end of second page

5 course sheets.. 4.00
2 fine sheets.. 4.00
14 pillow cases.. 3.00
1 counterpane.. 1.00
2 towels... .25
5 huckaback table cloths... 5.00
5 plain twilled table cloths.. 5.00
A frying pan... 1.00
A sifter.. .25
An old chest.. .50
4 old scythes.. 4.25
A cradle... 1.25
2 lots of wool.. 8.50
11 split bottom chairs... 3.00
A pair of steel yards (155 lbs)... 2.00
A shot gun... 4.50
4 candle sticks... 1.75
A pair andirons.. 1.26
A lot of old books.. 2.00
2 tables in the kitchen... 3.00
A stand.. .60
A lot of pewter.. 3.00
2 salvers.. .37½
A large table.. 2.75
A bench... 1.00

George Rex

A reel.. .50
A looking glass... 2.00
An old chest... .75
Old breakfast table up-stairs... .50
One yoke.. .50
A pair of sheep sheers.. 1.00
A cradling scythe... 1.25
2 hackles... 2.50
A spinning wheel.. .50
Furniture.. 5.00
6 pieces pot metal.. 4.00
3 large kettles.. 7.00
1 copper kettle... 3.50
A tea kettle and small copper kettle................................... 3.00
A shovel and tongs.. 1.50
2 flat irons... 1.25
3 buckets... 1.00
A kneading trough.. 1.50
A lot of carpenter's tools... 1.50
4 hoes.. .25
3 bee hives.. 3.00
3 empty hives.. .37½
A grind stone... 2.00
A spade and shovel.. 1.00
2 sets of double trees (vioned)...1.00
A log chain...2.00
2 dung forks and dray..1.25
4 hay forks...1.25
A cutting box (old bad knife).. 1.60
A fan or wind mill..7.00
2 meat tubs - 4 rakes, old..1.25
A sow and seven young pigs..3.00
6 shoats...4.00
A set of old gears and halter chain....................................3.00
A tar and water bucket... .75
A half bushel..1.00
100 old sugar crocks..3.00
A small tub... .37
A churn... .75
2 old whiskey barrels..1.00
4 old sickles... .50
A grubbing hoe...1.25
3 axes and iron wedge..3.00
1 fifth chain..2.50
A wheel barrow...1.50

A cross cut saw..6.61

$2,610.00

March 17, 1821. Benjamin Rex and Hugh Barclay Administrators.

Chapter 2

One of the most fascinating elements of George Rex's genealogy lies in the mystery of the identity of his parents. Specifically, the evidence suggests George Rex may have been the result of a morganatic marriage between Hannah Lightfoot, a beautiful commoner, and George, Prince of Wales, soon to become George III, King of England. Much has been written about the relationship between Hannah Lightfoot and George III, but most of this writing was done after the death of George III and almost 75 years after the events allegedly took place. Several documents remain that prove that Hannah existed, but there is little objective evidence to prove the relationship between George and Hannah. It was as noted by Mary Pendered in *The Fair Quaker*, the "enormous amount of hearsay evidence" of the relationship between Hannah and the eventual King of England might logically lead one to conclude that such evidence may have arisen from basis in fact.

George III

The German House of Hanover, of whom George III was a member, ascended to the British throne because the British preferred a king who was Protestant and German to a monarch who was Catholic and British. The dislike towards Catholicism began when Tudor King Henry VIII ousted the Catholic Church from England and persecuted all Catholics. This dislike turned to overt animosity when Mary I, Henry VIII's daughter, a Roman Catholic, reestablished the Catholic Church in England and persecuted and killed Protestants, earning the name 'Bloody Mary.' Over 100 years later, in 1688, the Stuart king, James II, a Catholic, fled the country. Parliament then replaced

Figure 7. George William Frederick, George III.

James II with his Protestant daughter, Mary and her husband, William of Orange. Because of the distrust of Catholicism, Parliament passed the Act of Settlement in 1701 that barred a Roman Catholic from ever ascending the throne of Britain. When Queen Anne, sister of Mary and the last Protestant member of the House of Stuart, passed away in 1714 without any heirs (despite having been pregnant 19 times), her closest Protestant relative rose to the throne. That relative was Prince George Elector of Hanover, Germany, and he became George I. George I's son, George II, and his son Fredrick were all born in Germany and spoke German as their primary language.

On June 4, 1738 (N.S.)*, George III, son of Frederick, was born prematurely in London at Norfolk House, St. James' Square to the nineteen year old Princess Augusta of Saxe-Gotha, Princess of Wales. George was baptized on July 2, 1738 as George William Frederick. George III was the first of the Hanoverian kings to be born in England and speak English as his primary language. On March 31, 1751 (N.S.), Frederick, Prince of Wales, died as a result of being hit by a tennis ball. Consequently, on April 20, 1751 Prince George who was not yet 13 years old became the Prince of Wales, direct heir to the Throne. His grandfather, George II King of England, was then sixty-eight years old.

Hannah Lightfoot

Hannah Lightfoot's immediate family belonged to the Society of Friends (Quakers) and was described as God-fearing, honest people. Her father Matthew Lightfoot was born February 1, 1689 or 1690 in Yorkshire and worked as a shoemaker. He married Mary Wheeler on August 3, 1728 and they had two children: Hannah, born October 12, 1730 in the Parish of St. John's, Wapping; and John born July 1, 1732. Matthew died of asthma on February 1, 1732 before the birth of his son, who in turn died October 28, 1733. Henry Wheeler, Mary Wheeler Lightfoot's brother, invited his widowed sister and her young daughter to live with his family. Henry was a prosperous linendraper, and his home was located above his shop on the east corner of the St. James' Market. While Hannah was living with the Wheelers, she signed as a witness a certificate showing the birth of a cousin, one of

* The Gregorian calendar which is used today was introduced by Pope Gregory XIII in 1582 to correct an error in the Julian calendar. The date Oct. 5, 1582 was called October 15, 1582. Because of the British distrust of Catholicism, the Gregorian calendar was not adopted in England until 1752 and was known as New Style (N.S.) of dating. George III was born May 24, 1738 using the Old Style (O.S.) of dating and June 4, 1738 using the New Style (N.S.) of dating.

the documents that survives today and helps support the existence of Hannah.

Henry Wheeler's house and linendraper's shop abutted Market Lane, a narrow street that ran out of Pall Mall at the back of the Opera House (now renamed His Majesty's Theater). One theory as to how the Prince of Wales first saw Hannah is related to this theater and its proximity to the Wheeler house. When the Royal Family attended the Opera House, they went by way of Market Lane, passing by the Wheeler house and shop, and entered the theater through its back door. The Royal Family was preceded by footmen, followed by the Family in theater chairs, and concluded with about twelve Yeomen of the Guard. On these occasions when the Royal Family attended the theater, the linens were taken out of the eastern window of the Wheeler house so that Hannah could watch the procession. This may have allowed the young Prince of Wales to reciprocate and observe the beautiful Hannah.

During this period of British history, smallpox was endemic, and few people were spared the facial scarring that the disease produced. Those who were spared and possessed a fair, unsullied face were quite noticeable. Hannah was such a person, and that fact coupled with her own natural beauty led to the title that was given her, 'The Fair Quaker.' One correspondent observed that, "She indeed was one of the most beautiful women of her time."

Hannah and George Meet.

Prince George lived for a time with his widowed mother at Leicester House in close proximity to the Wheeler home and shop. Many versions of the story of how the Prince arranged to meet Hannah were printed. The most popular version appeared in the *Monthly Magazine*, July 1821. This story used the formula of boy sees girl, boy has someone arrange for a meeting with girl, and finally boy arranges for a place to meet. In this case, the boy was soon to become The Prince of Wales, direct heir to the throne of Great Britain. The other principal players in this story were: Miss Elizabeth Chudleigh, soon to become Duchess of Kingston, who arranged the meeting, and a man named Perryn of Knightsbridge, who may have been Hannah's uncle and who provided the house for the frequent meetings.

Several authors including Sheila Mitchell have suggested that the Prince met Hannah in 1749 when he was only 11 years old, and she was 19 years old. It is not known why the Prince would choose a woman significantly older than himself. Beckles Willson in his book, *George III as Man, Monarch, Statesman* gives the best explanation of how such a relationship could develop. He suggested that the boy was quite unhappy during his stays with his grandfather. Apparently, George II detested young George's mother, and levelled continual insults at her. This led to feelings of loneliness and humiliation for young George. During the period when the alleged relationship between George and Hannah took place, George was separated from his mother for varying periods and became associated with men of "little principle." It was suggested that once freed from the restraints of Leicester House and his mother, he may have met his first temptation and displayed his "budding manliness in an amour." It was further suggested that because of his young age he would seek a girl of much lower social rank, and that he found her in the lovely Quaker who was older but probably just as naïve as the younger George.

The Royal Family Interferes.

Upon discovering the relationship between George and Hannah, the Royal Family set out to terminate it. The plot was simple enough and consisted largely of getting rid of Hannah by having her marry someone of her own class and age. The problem was to find someone who would discretely make all the arrangements including finding a suitable volunteer to marry Hannah. Miss Elizabeth Chudleigh once again stepped forward to offer her services, this time to undo the relationship, which she had reportedly started.

Elizabeth went to work and with the aid of a handsome dowry was able to find a man named Isaac Axford and convinced him to marry Hannah. Not much is known about Isaac except that he probably was a Quaker, lived at Ludgate Hill, and knew the Lightfoot family. The wedding took place on December 11, 1753 not in a church but at Dr. Keith's Marriage Chapel in Mayfair. The actual record of that marriage can be found in The Registers of the Mayfair Chapel for that date with the simple entry, "Dec. 11, 1753. Isaac Axford of St. Martin's, Ludgate, to Hannah Lightfoot, of St. James's, Westminster."

These marriage chapels were quite popular in London during this period but were in direct competition with the Church of England. Eventually enough pressure was placed on Parliament and Hardwicke's Marriage Act was passed outlawing these business-stealing chapels. The significance of this law lies in the fact that it was passed in June 1753 but did not get embodied in the Statute Book until 1754. Hannah and Isaac's marriage occurred between these two dates. This meant that the validity of marriages occurring between these dates was left open to liberal interpretation. This may have been the loophole that George, Hannah, Isaac, and Isaac's future second wife took advantage of in 1759.

Hannah Disappears.

There are several versions of the story of what happened next. All versions have the common thread of Hannah's disappearing in a closed carriage either immediately after the wedding or sometime thereafter. One version of the story was reported in *The Aristocracy of England: a History for the People* by John Hampden. "Soon after the return of the bridal party from the ceremony, Hannah Lightfoot was observed to be restless, went to the window several times, and appeared to be in an absent state, or as if listening for something. A man playing a pipe and tabor appeared in the street, stopped and played awhile before it, and scarcely had it ceased when Hannah Lightfoot was found to have disappeared. On making search for her, her friends learned that she had left the house and been seen to enter a closed carriage which stood in the next street, and then drove rapidly away." A second version suggested that the couple did live together following the wedding. However, after approximately six weeks of marriage, a coach with four horses came to her house when Isaac was away, and Miss Chudleigh carried Hannah off at a gallop as was described in the first version.

After Hannah disappeared, Isaac Axford tried to find his wife, presenting a petition to both Weymouth and The St. James Court. Both courts ignored him. Isaac never found Hannah, but did remarry a Miss Bartlett six years later in 1759 and lived another 60 years dying at the age of 86 on April 14, 1816.

According to reports in John Lindsey's book, Hannah was taken to Knightsbridge to a farm hidden from the road that supplied milk to the Royal Family. The owner or tenant of the farm was a man named Perryn who was thought in other reports to have been related to Hannah. On April 4, 1757, the will of a Robert Pearne of Isleworth was probated giving "Mrs. Hannah Axford, formerly Miss Hannah Lightfoot a yearly payment of £40." John Lindsey in his book suggested that Robert Pearne was the Mr. Perryn of Knightsbridge, Lindsey's argument was based on the state of literacy in England in 1760 and 1820, that since Pearne and Perryn are phonetically very similar, the different names could easily be referring to the same person. If this theory that Pearne and Perryn are the same person, that will then suggests that Hannah was taken to Knightsbridge and that she was still alive in 1757.

Other Evidence Supporting the Hannah and George Relationship.

Other verifiable events suggest a link between Hannah and George. On March 3, 1756, Hannah was expelled from the Quaker church for marrying someone who was not a Quaker. Lindsey in his book suggested that Hannah's expulsion was a result of her marriage to George and not to Isaac Axford as Isaac was a Quaker. In the proceedings of the Westminster Friends, no mention was ever made of Hannah Lightfoot's husband's name. Lindsey noted that names of husbands were always recorded in the Minutes of the Meeting and this implied that the name was omitted because of who it was namely, George, Prince of Wales.

Another intriguing piece of evidence exists that not only supports a relationship between George and Hannah but also that Hannah was still alive in 1757. This evidence, a portrait, hangs in Knole Castle and is catalogued by The National Trust as *'Miss Axford'*, reputedly *Hannah Lightfoot, Mrs. Axford, and 'the Fair Quaker.'* Sir Joshua Reynolds, a famous portraitist of his day whose work was

Figure 8. Hannah Lightfoot portrait painted by Joshua Reynolds.

usually reserved for the aristocracy, painted this alleged portrait of Hannah. The 3rd Duke of Dorset acquired the painting before 1778 but the Rt. Hon. The Lord Sackville is now the owner. According to The National Trust, the painting was dated c. 1756 but that conclusion was based on little physical evidence as the portrait is badly damaged with little of the original paint remaining. The portrait is 29½" x 24½", painted as an oval and depicts a lady dressed in "white satin edged with lace and decorated with pink bows, and white headdress," which certainly was not the dress of a Quaker. The painting appears to be that of a lady around 30 years old. Therefore, if the subject were in fact Hannah, the portrait would have been painted between 1759 and 1763 after Hannah had been expelled from The Society of Friends.

Lindsey stated in his book that ownership of Reynolds' paintings is usually well documented, but this portrait had no history until it appeared in Knole Castle. Sheila Mitchell suggests that the Reynold's journals are complete save for a few which have been lost. Unfortunately, the one covering the period when it is believed the painting of Hannah Lightfoot was done is one of the journals which has been lost. The mystery then is who introduced Sir Joshua Reynolds to Mrs. Axford, who commissioned the work, and who owned it after it was painted? John Lindsey's hypothesis is that the person that did all of these things was the same person that removed Hannah from the door of Keith's Chapel seven years before.

The marriage of Hannah Lightfoot to George III was first mentioned in print in 1831 in *the Authentic Records of the Court of England*. Why George III chose 1759 or ten years after he met Hannah, and six years after he was reported to have abducted her from Isaac Axford to finally marry her is not known. Lindsey suggests that George and Hannah waited until Isaac had remarried Miss Bartlett. As will be presented later, there is evidence that Hannah and the Prince already had children. Lindsey also suggested that George was an honorable man and married Hannah because that was the honorable thing to do. Remembering that Hardwicke's Marriage Act was passed in 1753 outlawing marriages solemnized in marriage chapels, we can theorize that George and Hannah waited until it could legally be assumed that Hannah's and Isaac's marriage was not legally binding. Sheila Mitchell gives the explanation that if Prince George did marry Hannah in 1759 he probably felt that he could get Hannah acknowledged as his wife once he became King. The problem was that he did not know that he would actually become King the next year.

George and Charlotte: An Acceptable Marriage.

George William Fredrick became George III on October 25, 1760 when his grandfather, George II, passed away. George III's priorities immediately changed from loyalty to his morganatic wife and family to loyalty and concern for the greater good of his country. In short, his wife and family were made to disappear. Later in 1760 it was decided that George should have a proper marriage to a spouse of royal lineage. Early in 1761 he was persuaded to allow a search for a potential bride. A Colonel David Graham was dispatched to the courts of Europe and according to Lindsey was instructed to find someone royal, Protestant, and a "good breeder." He found Princess Charlotte at the German Court of Mecklenburg-Strelitz, the youngest daughter of the Duke. When the Princess arrived in London September 8, 1761, she spoke no English, and was married that night to a man that she had never met.

At the time of the marriage between Charlotte and George, it was apparently against the law to speak of the relationship between Hannah and the King. In April 1761 in the city of Westminster, a man named Green was fined twenty marks for speaking of the King and the Quakers. In May of the same year a man was hanged at Newgate because he "spoke words of the King and his doings with the people called Quakers." Lindsey reported that a woman was tortured a year after the wedding at St. Albans who "spoke against the King and the Quakers." No reference could ever be found as to what was said about the King and the Quakers. Things changed in the nineteenth century with regard to writing about George and Hannah. H. Barton Baker in his *Stories of the Streets of London* wrote, "In 1759, George marries the pretty Quakeress. Alas! Two years later he is forced to forsake his charming wife for 'the ugliest woman in Europe,' Charlotte of Mecklenburg Strelitz."

The reign of George III was the second longest in British history, second only to his granddaughter Victoria's, but unfortunately not altogether enjoyed by the king. He began having periodic bouts of insanity probably secondary to acute intermittent porphyria starting as early as 1765. These episodes of insanity became more frequent, totally incapacitating the King. Finally, on February 5, 1811, Parliament passed the Regency Act that authorized the Prince of Wales to reign in place of his father. George III lived, blind and insane, until January 29,1820.

Intriguing evidence: The Serres/Ryves Papers.

The evidence presented thus far supports Hannah's existence, but only suggests the relationship between Hannah and George. The evidence that we shall present now, namely a marriage certificate between Hannah and George and a last will and testament of Hannah, not only proves that relationship but also suggests they had children. It should be noted, however, that the veracity of the documents has been questioned because of the convoluted manner in which they came to light. Therefore, in order for us to have a better understanding of the documents, it is necessary to present the history of those documents in some detail. Two people, Olivia Serres and her daughter Lavinia Ryves, who had nothing to do with either George III or Hannah Lightfoot, produced the documents in their efforts to establish a claim to royal lineage. Their adventure culminated in the 'Great Trial of 1866' after which the documents were impounded for 100 years.

Olivia Wilmot was born April 3rd, 1772 to the wife of Robert Wilmot, a house painter of Warwick. Olivia's mother died when Olivia was quite young leaving Olivia initially in the care of her father. Robert Wilmot had a brother James who, as it turned out, is central to judging the authenticity of these documents. James Wilmot received the degree of Doctor of Divinity from, and became a Fellow of Trinity College, Oxford. He gained a considerable reputation as a learned clergyman and was assigned to the rectory of Barton-on-the-Heath, Warwickshire. It was at Barton where James Wilmot eventually "enjoyed the exclusive confidence of George III." James was a lifelong bachelor and lived by himself comfortably in the rectory.

It is not known why, but he invited his niece Olivia to Barton where she began her early education. It had been suggested that James Wilmot was trying to help the family of his somewhat impoverished brother. In any case, by the time Olivia left Dr. Wilmot, she was better educated than most young ladies of her time. In 1789, Olivia's father moved to London, and Olivia joined him. After moving to London, she began to study art under the painter John Thomas Serres whose seascapes at the time were in vogue. Olivia fell in love with him and they were married in 1791 at her uncle's church. Because Olivia was underage at the time of her wedding, it was necessary under the terms of the Marriage Act passed in 1753 for her father to swear an affidavit stating that he was her natural and lawful father. This affidavit was the first of several that would come to haunt Olivia in her quest to prove royal lineage.

After her wedding, she continued her studies but soon discovered that her husband was a "dreadful sort of artist" and she left his classes to paint on her own. She was quite successful and exhibited regularly at the Royal Academy and the British Institution. She eventually was appointed landscape painter to the Prince of Wales, soon to become George IV, a particularly great honor for a woman artist.

Olivia's other talent was writing. She produced large volumes of literary works including romance writings, opera librettos, poems, didactic essays, and theological dissertations. Throughout her life she was a voluminous letter writer. As John Lindsey stated, "Neither her books nor her pictures appear attractive to us today. They have no mark of genius. The pictures are, perhaps, the less second-rate of the two. But both pictures and books were obviously pot-boilers, serving the useful purpose of keeping Olivia in the foreground of the public scene until she was ready to make her claim."

In 1804, Olivia obtained a deed of separation from her husband. When her Uncle Dr. Wilmot died in 1808, she was comforted in her distress by Edward Duke of Kent, younger brother of George III and father of Queen Victoria. Edward became one of her few supporters, and was reported to have paid her £400 a year while he lived.

In 1813 Olivia launched into a new and curious career, publishing a book *A Memorial to James Wilmot, D. D.* In *Memorial*, she declared that the theologian was the author of *Letters to Junius,* a very controversial expose revealing state secrets. Although it was eventually shown that James Wilmot did not write *Letters*, Olivia convinced the public that he had written it by producing a hand-written note from his diary implicating his authorship. The book created a great stir and was completely believable since Dr. Wilmot had spent many years near his Sovereign.

In 1817, Olivia began her quest to convince the world she was of royal birth. Olivia presented a petition to the King declaring herself to be the natural daughter of the Duke of Cumberland, the King's youngest brother, and that her mother was a Mrs. Payne, a married woman. The petition she submitted was ignored but she followed it with another claiming that she was again the daughter of the Duke but this time by her mother's unmarried sister. This claim too was rebuffed. Undaunted, she elaborated her case and changed her story once more. This time she claimed to be the legitimate daughter of the Duke of Cumberland and the illegitimate daughter of Dr. Wilmot also named Olivia (Olive) whom the Duke had secretly married. Olivia worked out her story in great detail with names, dates, and places, supporting her thesis with multiple signed documents. She even had reasonable explanations to why the story should have been concealed until after the only person who could have verified her parentage, Dr. Wilmot, was dead. Olivia believed in her story with such fervor that she was able to persuade many other people that it was true.

Because Olivia's claims and petitions were consistently rebuffed, she stopped sending them and waited for her next move. After the death of George III in 1820, she assumed the title, Princess of Cumberland and had herself re-christened at Islington Parish Church in September 1821 as "Olive, daughter of the Duke of Cumberland, and of Olive his wife." After giving herself the title, she lived extravagantly but without the funding to support that lifestyle. She went into debt, and was promptly arrested according to the laws of the time. Her defense for the debtor charge was based on a plea of royal birth, which, if true, would have protected her. To prove her case, she produced what appeared to be an early will of George III, witnessed by the Earl of Chatham, Solicitor General to the King, and John Dunning, Chancellor of the Duchy of Lancaster. In that will £15,000 were bequeathed to "Olive, the daughter of our brother of Cumberland." This claim was set aside on the grounds that the prerogative court (ecclesiastical probate) had no jurisdiction to grant probate of a will of the sovereign.

Olivia was very convincing and was able to gain some support from friends. One of those was a man named O'Brien who owned a newspaper, *The British Luminary and Weekly Intelligencer*. In 1821, the paper took up her cause with yellow journalistic fervor convincing even more people of her story. As Mary Pendered stated in her book, "For, if it could be proved that she was, as the *British Luminary* obviously believed, a much injured and maligned woman, the marriage of Prince George and Hannah would be established on her testimony." This observation will become more obvious as we will see in the great trial of 1866.

Olivia's last years were unhappy. Her ex-husband repudiated her claims of royal birth to his death in 1825. Her father, Robert Wilmot, likewise persisted to his deathbed that Olivia was his daughter. Her debts accumulated and she eventually did go to prison where she died on November 21, 1834. She left two daughters. The younger daughter accepted her father's theory, and repudiated all claims to royal birth. The older daughter, Lavinia Janetta Horton Ryves, or as she called herself, Lavinia Janetta Horton de Serres, assumed the title of Princess of Cumberland and Duchess of Lancaster eventually taking up where her mother had been stopped.

Lavinia was born in 1797. Like her mother, she married, could not live with, and divorced an artist. At the time of her divorce in 1841, she was 44 years old, had six children, and lived in destitution. In 1844, ten years after her mother's death, Lavinia, supported by Sir Gerard Noel, filed a bill against the Duke of Wellington who was the executor of the will of King George IV. She asked for £15,000, which is what her mother had claimed under the alleged will of George III. Once again the Court of Chancery declared that it held no power to give relief.

Lavinia did not capitulate as her mother did. In 1858 Mrs. Ryves published a letter titled *An Appeal for Royalty,* addressed to Queen Victoria and signed "Lavinia, Princess of Cumberland and Duchess of Lancaster." Included in this appeal to Queen Victoria were facsimiles of a number of documents, attested to by royal signatures. The first document stated the following:

"George R. Whereas it is our royal command that the birth of Olive the Duke of Cumberland's daughter is never made known to the nation during our reign, but from a sense of religious duty we will that she be acknowledged by the royal family after our death, should she survive ourselves, in return for the confidential service rendered ourselves by Dr. Wilmot in the year 1759.

> Kew Palace, May 2nd, 1773
> Endorsed – London, 1815
> Delivered to Mrs. Olive Serres by Warwick
> Witness: Edward."

In other words, Olivia Serres was to be recognized as the daughter of the Duke of Cumberland in repayment for a service provided by Dr. Wilmot. According to *Appeal*, the phrase "confidential service" referred to the marriage of Hannah Lightfoot to George Prince of Wales. Two additional documents in *Appeal* were marriage certificates. The certificates, dated April 17, 1759 and May 27, 1759 (Figure 9) affirmed the marriage between Hannah Lightfoot and George Prince of Wales and were signed by J. Wilmot. A third document included in *Appeal* was a copy of Hannah's last Will and Testament (Figure 10.)

As Mary Pendered stated in her book, "the boldness of this publication [*Appeal*] takes one's breath away." But because there was so much other scandal at that time and "the Press was young," the Press seemed to bypass the story. Queen Victoria, of course, also quietly ignored it. Queen Victoria's motivation may have been due to the fact that the allegations would have set up a claim to the very throne upon which she was seated.

Parliament passed the Declaration of Legitimacy Act in 1861, requiring people to declare their parentage. Because of the new law, Lavinia filed a petition in that year stating that the marriage between her mother and Mr. Serres was valid. To gain this petition she had to renounce her claim of royal descent. According to the Royal Marriage Act, her mother could not have married without the consent of the reigning sovereign if she had been of royal descent. Obtaining that decree then was another document that weakened her case when she tried to prove royal descent in the trial of 1866. The need to declare her parents in the Act of 1861 clearly conflicted with her desire to prove royal birth, a goal that she would continue to pursue.

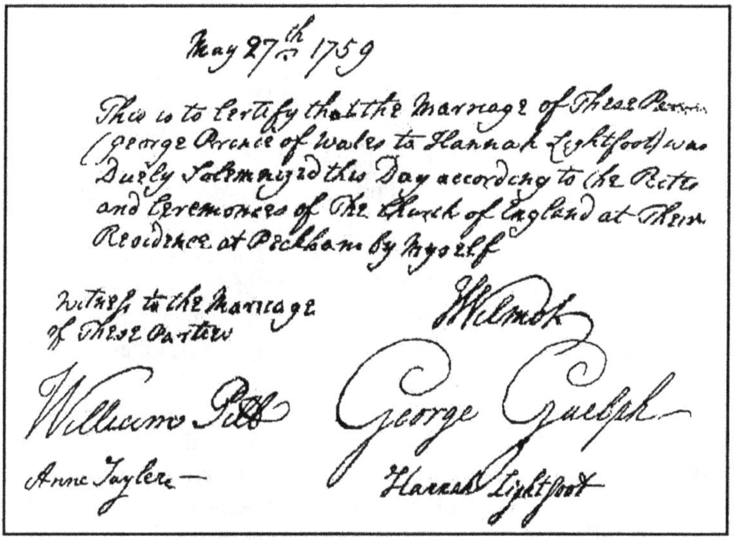
May 27th 1759

This is to Certify that the Marriage of These Parties (George Prince of Wales to Hannah Lightfoot) was Duly Solemnized this Day according to the Rites and Ceremonies of The Church of England at Their Residence at Peckham by Myself

J Wilmot

Witness to the Marriage of These Parties

William Pitt

George Guelph

Anne Tayler

Hannah Lightfoot

Figure 9. Marriage Certificate between Hannah Lightfoot and George III impounded until 1966.

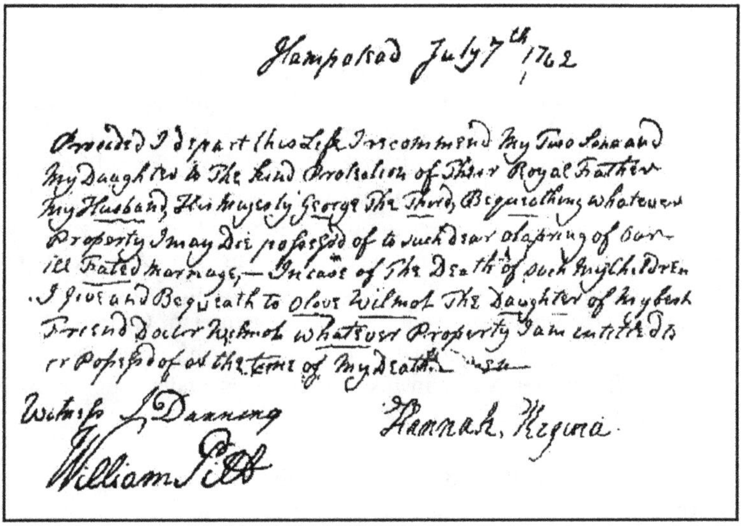
Hampstead July 7th 1762

Provided I depart this Life I recommend My Two Sons and My Daughter to The kind Protection of Their Royal Father My Husband His Majesty George The Third, Bequeathing whatever Property I may die possessed of to such dear offspring of Our ill Fated marriage,— In case of The Death of each my Children I give and Bequeath to Olive Wilmot The Daughter of my best Friend Doctor Wilmot whatever Property I am entitled to or Possessed of at the time of My death

Witness J Dunning

William Pitt

Hannah Regina

Figure 10. Last will and testament of Hannah Lightfoot. Impounded until 1966.

The Trial of 1866.

Lavinia petitioned the Court of Probate and Divorce in 1866 to declare that the Duke of Cumberland and Olive Wilmot were married, and that Olivia Wilmot Serres was their legitimate daughter. The case was heard before Lord Chief Baron Pollock, the Lord Chief Justice; Sir J. P. Wilde, Judge Ordinary; and a special jury. The Attorney General was represented by the top legal minds of that department and was described as "a strong force" by *The American Law Review*. Because Lavinia was living in destitution, she could not engage the "highest known legal ability in her cause." According to Mary Pendered, her case was handled "with little ability and ingenuity."

Mr. J. W. Smith, Levinia's attorney's explained to the jury the provisions of the Declaration of Legitimacy Act and outlined that the main question was whether the Duke of Cumberland, younger brother of George III, was married to Olive Wilmot. Two certificates of marriage between the Duke of Cumberland and Olive Wilmot were produced. On the back of these two documents were the two variations of the Lightfoot marriage certificates (Figure 9). It seemed absurd that two seemingly unrelated documents were written on the backs of each other on odd shaped bits of paper.

Seventy documents in all were produced containing 43 signatures of Dr. Wilmot, 36 of Lord Chatham, 12 of Mr. Dunning, 12 of King George III, 32 of Lord Warwick, and 18 of the Duke of Kent. The most interesting part of the trial came when a Mr. Netherclift, one of the greatest handwriting expert of the time, was called to testify. He was asked to examine and test the documents written and signed by Dr. Wilmot including the marriage certificates of Hannah and George III. His conclusion was that these were indeed in the handwriting of Dr. Wilmot. He was also certain that the signatures of George III on the documents in question were the same as those on Treasury warrants. He did not waver in his opinion even under tough cross-examination.

Mrs. Ryves was called to the stand after the favorable expert's evidence was given. Apparently she was ill advised and began speaking of Hannah Lightfoot from the start. She was immediately stopped and the Chief Justice declared all the documents forgeries and ended the trial. In summary, the trial was conducted in a prejudicial manner putatively because the throne of England was at stake. Had the trial been conducted in a less prejudicial manner, the entire question about Hannah Lightfoot and her relationship with George III might have been answered.

John Lindsey suggested that the certificates dealing with George III and Hannah Lightfoot were genuine and were only written on scrap pieces of paper because they were written probably in haste under clandestine circumstances. All the signatures on them were authenticated by the greatest handwriting expert of the day. One of the signatories, Edward Duke of Kent, gave warm friendship and support to Olivia, the owner of the documents. The authenticity of the documents on their reverse side is less secure and it is possible that they may have been forged in the ill-conceived notion that pairing forgeries with genuine documents might have made them seem more authentic. In all probability, the Court was not concerned with Mrs. Ryves claim to royal descent, but was concerned with the implication that the documents made to royal succession itself.

At the end of the trial, all the documents were impounded for 100 years. Mrs. Ryves lived five more years dying in 1871. Her documents were locked up in 1866 but eventually were released in 1966.

If the marriage certificate and will are genuine, Hannah was married to George III and they had at least two boys and a girl. It is not known when Hannah died. A letter in 1909 that appeared in the *London Daily Mail* reported that she did not die until 1829, but there is no proof of this. The significance of how long Hannah lived, as it relates to royal descent is summarized by John Lindsey, "If Hannah was alive in 1768, and the will is not a forgery, all children of George III and Queen Charlotte who were born before that date were illegitimate. If she was still alive in 1829, the whole family was likewise illegitimate."

Could George Rex Be the Son of George III and Hannah?

The question then arises if George III and Hannah Lightfoot were married and had children, could George Rex have been one of the two boys? If George Rex's birth year was 1750, and if the above cited documents are correct, then George III and Hannah Lightfoot were married 9 years after the birth of George Rex. Since George III was born in 1738, he would have been only 11 or 12 years old when George Rex was conceived. Boyd Crumrine in Helen Vogt's book, *Westward of Ye Laurel Hills* in 1976, suggested that George Rex's birth date may have been falsified for 'state reasons' to make it appear less likely that George Rex was the son of George III. As noted above, the Prince was probably seeing Hannah well before her marriage to Isaac Axford in 1753. Since no dates can be confirmed in the historical record, it is still possible that George III could be the father of George Rex.

As was noted in Chapter 1, the surname Rex Worthy was used synonymously with the surname Rex. As Crumrine stated in Helen Vogt's book, the name 'Worthy' was not part of the family name, but was a distinctive appellation to denote that George was of noble descent. Crumrine, an attorney and competent historian, considered the naturalization papers made out in Lancaster County December 8, 1777 (Figure 4), as the most important evidence for the link with George III as the name used was clearly 'George Rex Worthy.' Crumrine also found the name Rex Worthy used in a summons dated January 1, 1800, in Greene county records, naming "George Rex Worthy, otherwise called George Rex." Crumrine felt that since the summons was written by the English-born John Boreman, who would have also known the significance of the title 'worthy,' that it indicated Boreman supported the story of George's ancestry.

Sheila Mitchell also felt that the name Worthy had significance not fully explained. Worthy was not a title conveyed by a Sovereign or Parliament but was used at a more local level to denote someone 'worth while' and who has done worthy deeds over many years. If worthy deeds done over many years are required for the name Worthy to be given, it is not clear why George Rex was given that title at such a young age in America when he was loyal to Britain. The argument could be made that George Rex was given the title in England before coming to America and that it denoted his Royal heritage without actually suggesting who his parents were.

In his book, John Lindsey stated that he heard from nine families that could purportedly trace their descent in the unbroken line from the son or daughter of George and Hannah. Each of these sons and daughters had no known father or mother, as was the case with George Rex. "Sometimes he or she suddenly appeared in a certain place with no ascertainable background, but around whom there grew legend and tradition that he or she was the son or daughter of Prince George and Hannah Lightfoot." Lindsey goes on by saying, "These persons all appear as moderately wealthy and moderately influential. They were on terms of intimacy with royalty. Nobility feted them. They refused or were not able to give any account of their parentage; and they refused or could not give any reason as to why they would be wealthy or why they should be influential." This description of families tracing their descent from George and Hannah given by Lindsey fits well into the history of the descendants of George Rex as we shall see below in the section taken from the First Edition of *The Rex Genealogy*.

Evidence of George Rex's Parentage Presented in the First Edition of *The Rex Genealogy*.

Many second and third generation children of George Rex held the belief that George III and Hannah Lightfoot were the parents of George Rex. Sarah J. Beggs (Line III, pp. 73-74) and the Kelly family have assisted much in the preparation of the First Edition of *The Rex Genealogy* and are among those believing the family descends from Hannah Lightfoot and George III, King of England. Mrs. Beggs so firmly believed this that July 17, 1929 she took an oath subscribed and sworn on this date at Ogden, Utah, as follows:

"That I, Sarah Jane Rex-Kelly-Beggs, was born July 17, 1840, and being of sound mind on this 17th day of July, 1929, do hereby make the following statement for the information and benefit of all whom it may concern, that according to my best knowledge and belief I have known by common conversation, within my father's household, and family history of the Rex family from the years of my childhood, through youth and maturity, that I am a direct descendent of Prince George William Frederick, who was later crowned George III of England and Hannah Lightfoot, 'The Fair Quakeress' and of George Rex and Margaret Kepler and of George Rex and Jane Black and of William Winters Rex and Mary Ann Mesler."

She states further that the other members of the family have this same knowledge and then says, "The story as I have always known it is that for reasons of State, Hannah Lightfoot and her son George were brought to America accompanied by a colony of people, among whom were relatives who located in N. Y. State. She was well provided for with cattle, horses, servants, material necessities and luxury, silver plate, etc. which has been treasured and handed down in the Rex family. That during trouble with the Indians they left N. Y. and part or all of the colony went by boat down the Susquehanna River and later settled in Western Pennsylvania." The casket of Mrs. Beggs gives her name and descent as given above. There are members of the family who do not believe this story at all and others who feel this book would be entirely remiss without mention of it.

As was reported in the First Edition, Mrs. Aline Shane Devin, (Line 7, p. 178) a writer and traveler, wrote to Lord Sackville-West years ago to learn about the Sir Joshua Reynolds portrait of Hannah. She corresponded with a daughter of Lord Sackville in regard to the picture. Although the date of the letter that Mrs. Aline Shane-Devin wrote to Lord Sackville is unknown, the letter itself was shared with Mary Pendered, who quoted it in *The Fair Quaker*:

> "My father's mother was Hannah Lightfoot Rex, and her father was a son of the third George of the Hanoverian line, and of Hannah Lightfoot, the Quakeress. My great-grandfather, George Rex, came to America during the Revolutionary war, and was, from first to last, a devoted Royalist. He married in Pennsylvania a woman of German birth, and by her had a large family. His oldest son was called George, his oldest daughter, my grandmother, receiving her grandmother's name. The origin of the family has always been known and accepted by its members, though the circumstances connected with it were felt to be of so discreditable a nature to both sides that it was very seldom mentioned, and then as something to be deplored and concealed.

> We of this generation, however, are far enough removed from the scandal to appreciate the romantic interest that in most minds, attaches to the love affairs of a Prince, even when they reach their consummation 'without benefit of clergy,' a con-

clusion which, in this particular, is open to question.

The very little confirmatory evidence obtainable on this point, however, does not seem to me to be of a convincing character, even though one may heartily wish to be persuaded. Therefore, in asking for information concerning the reputed portrait of Hannah Lightfoot, I do so only to gratify a natural interest which you will, I hope, appreciate, in an ancestress whose charms are said to have equaled her misfortunes, as well as conduced to them, and the mystery of whose fate must still arouse compassion."

Mary Pendered wrote to Mrs. Shane-Devin at the address that was on the letter but received her letter back with the statement that there was no such person to be found at the address.

Perhaps one of the most intriguing pieces of evidence suggesting a link between the George Rex family and Hannah Lightfoot is found in the above letter. The seventh child of George and Margaret Rex was Hannah Lightfoot Rex who was born July 16, 1787. At that time the name Lightfoot was not the household name that it would become in the later half of the 19th century. As was already noted, prior to the death of George III virtually nothing was printed concerning any reputed relationship between Hannah Lightfoot and George III. People in England who did talk about it were hanged and tortured. Why would George Rex have named his seventh child with the middle name Lightfoot? The only suitable explanation is that the name Lightfoot was a family surname and may very likely have been George Rex's mother's maiden name.

Anne Rex Vale (p. 195) wrote in The First Edition of *The Rex Genealogy*, "I have heard my father, Benjamin Rex and Aunt Sarah Day Cloaky, talk many times of Grandfather George Rex 1st having received a pension from King George III to the day of his death." Parks Rex also remembered having heard aunt Burson and his father speak at different times of the Grandfather George Rex pension from King George III and these boys did not then know of the relationship to King George III but they fully believed the same from family history and family resemblance. Aunt Kitty Burson and Lib. Rex daughter of Benjamin were the very picture of Queen Victoria, and as

Parks said later, Ross E. is the very likeness of Edward VII." Aline Shane Devin wrote that after Walter Besant saw the picture of her Grandmother Hannah Rex Shane he said that there was a strong resemblance to the royal family in it. Mrs. Devin also wrote, "When I was in England the first time and having my hair dressed, the attendant said to me, 'Pardon me, Miss, but may I say that you resemble our dear queen very strongly,' to which I replied, 'Oh, mercy, do you really think so?' For as you remember Victoria was not very easy on the eyes, for that matter neither am I, still I did think rather better of my own looks." Mrs. Stevens of line 12 wrote, "You know Hannah Lightfoot and King George III both had red hair and so did my great grandfather, my grandfather and also his oldest brother. The toot-mouth comes down for generations in the Rex family, being very strong in our own line the same as that of George III."

Following is an article from the Chicago Tribune Published in the 1880's:

> **"OF ROYAL DESCENT**–A granddaughter of George III lives in Chicago. George Rex, the son of George III, and the Quakeress, Hannah Lightfoot, came to America to reside. The Chicago woman, who refuses to give her name, traces her relationship to him through both her father and mother. Some bits of historical information.

> Following is an extract from a letter received Yesterday from the Tribune:

> "Chicago, Ill., Jan. 16. (Editor of the Tribune)–In view of the recent death of the heir apparent to the throne of Great Britain and the discussions it has evoked in the daily journals concerning the genealogies of the members of the reigning House of Hanover it has occurred to the undersigned that you might consider it of interest to your readers to interview a direct descendent of the third George through his morganatic marriage with the fair Quakeress, Hannah Lightfoot. It is not the desire to achieve a brief newspaper fame that prompts this suggestion, and the one consideration of the interview would be that your reporter should not make public the present name of the great-granddaughter of the obstinate and narrow-minded

but kindly George III of Hanover."

"In response to the foregoing a Tribune reporter called at a pleasant apartment house on Warren Avenue yesterday afternoon and after a few preliminary questions and answers, in which the inevitable speaking tube acted as intermediary, was ushered directly into the presence of a thoroughly American cousin of the Queen of England. A blue-eyed, fresh-looking woman of perhaps 35, with a refined, agreeable voice and cordial manner–such is the descendent of the "Third George," who finds herself living in Chicago just 133 years after her royal ancestor fell in love with and was married to pretty Hannah Lightfoot in Curzon Street Chapel, Mayfair, England."

"One seems to see in her dignity of carriage, in her directness of speech, even in her complexion and her regular features, traces of her kinship but in her surroundings there is nothing of the pomp and ceremony that is popularly supposed to hedge about kings and the daughters of kings, although all the furnishings of the little flat bespeak good taste and comparative prosperity."

"There are good pictures on the walls and books in abundance on the shelves and tables. The rugs and draperies are quiet in tone, selected with evident care. Although it is plain that America has been faithful to what ever tactic charge England laid upon her when George Rex, eldest son of King George III and Hannah Lightfoot, came over to this country shortly after the end of the Revolutionary War and proceeded to identify his interests with those of the young Republic by marrying a Philadelphian, and has dealt kindly with the members of the family thus established."

George's Granddaughter Talks

"I haven't much of a story to tell you, after all," said George III's granddaughter. "I have found it difficult to trace the career of the various branches of my family, on account of the extreme reticence of the older people to talk of our origin.

They feel that it is in someway a stain upon our fair name, and in reply to questions they always say: 'Let sleeping disgrace lie.' It is only within the last ten years that I and some of my cousins have begun investigating the matter for our own satisfaction. Perhaps what we have found out may be of interest just now."

"Of course you know that George III married quite legally Hannah Lightfoot, a Quakeress, two years before he was persuaded by his Ministers into marriage with Princess Charlotte of Mecklenburg-Strelitz. By his morganatic wife three children were born to him, one of whom married an East Indian officer, a second died insane, and the third, George Rex, when he was in his early twenties, came to America. I don't know much about him, save that he was a pronounced Tory, that he never mentioned his parentage, and that he had a small income, presumably supplied by the King. He brought with him some Church of England prayer books and some silver marked 'G. R.', which were afterwards distributed among his children and which are still in existence, treasured by some of my cousins, although I do not happen to have any. His eldest child was a son named George, the second a daughter, Hannah. She was my grandmother. My grandfather was Isaac Shane, a wealthy farmer, who lived near Steubenville, in Jefferson County, Ohio. My father was the third of twelve children, and, after he married, he settled in Iowa, where he has been a Judge of the Circuit Court. He also enjoys the rank of colonel, which he won by his services in the late war."

Doubly Related to the King

"My mother too, was a descendent of George the Third, as my father's aunt married her father. She has been dead a great many years, but my father is still living. I have only one sister, who lives in Dakota. She is married and has children, one a son, so the family will not die out. I have no children myself, unfortunately. I think that is really all I can tell you. Some time I hope to know more of the details of the family history."

"Asked for photographs, the descendent of the House of
Hanover very willingly loaned that of her grandmother, Mrs.
Isaac Shane, and rather reluctantly, those of her mother and
father, but refused positively to allow her own to appear in the
Tribune."

"In connection with her story it is interesting to know that
shortly after King George's marriage with Princess Charlotte,
Hannah Lightfoot disappeared. It is supposed she died. At all
events nothing more was ever heard of her. According to the
Rt. Hon. Lady Anne Hamilton, who has chronicled some
matters pertaining to the Court of England not always found in
other histories, says the King was greatly distressed to ascer-
tain the fate of his much-beloved and legally-married wife, the
Quakeress, and intrusted Lord Chatham to go in disguise and
endeavor to trace her abode; but the search proved fruitless.
Whatever became of her the children seem to have been left in
charge of an old nurse, to depend upon the rather unstable and
uncertain assistance the court might give them. They were
brought up by the nurse near London, apparently receiving
some recognition from their father, although naturally of the
slightest nature."

Conclusions.

It is highly likely that Hannah Lightfoot existed and that she suddenly
disappeared. Whether she ever had a liaison, marriage, or children
with George III will probably never be satisfactorily supported without additional information. Since finding eyewitnesses is out of the
question, two areas of scientific investigation might be productive. An
examination of the Serres/Ryves documents using modern handwriting experts and scientific technique might determine whether the
marriage certificates of George and Hannah and Hannah's will are
genuine. Now that these documents are less of a threat to the monar-
chy, an examination of these documents might be possible.

Another possible method of determining the veracity of the story of
Hannah and George is through the use of genetic testing between the
known descendants of George III and members of those who suspect
royal descent. This DNA testing would not necessarily prove the

relationship between Hannah and George III but could serve to support it. Further, the genetic testing could also serve to indicate that the descendants of George Rex are *not* of royal descent. This, in turn, would eliminate the possibility that George Rex was a descendent of George III. The most likely conclusion is that we will never know.

Chapter 3

Mary[2] Rex (1st child of George Rex and Margaret Kepler Rex) was b. in PA in 1773. Bates History of Greene Co. PA states that Mary Rex was a native of Lancaster Co., PA having been born before her father came to Westmoreland Co. She was commonly called "Polly." There is very little known of her girlhood. On August 27, 1795, she married John Hughes at the family home near Jefferson in Greene Co., PA. They both lived and d. in Greene Co. near the family home. Mary Rex Hughes d. in January, 1849. John Hughes d. 7-23-1844. They were the parents of 12 children, 6 boys and 6 girls. John Hughes was b. 1774; he and his wife are buried in Old Presbyterian Church Cemetery at Jefferson, Greene Co., PA. A brick church is in same yard and says "Dedicated to the worship of God by the Presbyterian Church, 1845."

Both gravestones (Figure 11) are large flat slabs (much like a casket above the ground). Hers reads, "In memory of Mary Hughes, Consort of John, who departed this life 1-11-1849, 72 yrs. and 1 mo." At her left is the same kind of flat table, sort of white gray sandstone, and reads "In memory of John Hughes who departed this life July 23,

Figure 11. Gravestones of Mary Rex and husband, John Hughes.

1844, aged 70 yrs., 2 mo., and 16 days." (Copied by Leda Rex 8-5-1931, while Dan took pictures of the stones.) The mother of John Hughes was Elizabeth Swan who traces her history back to Charlemagne, A. D. 742, through the Swans. John †Swan was a Major in the Revolutionary War. Waynesburg, PA Deed Book I, p. 661, deeds Thomas Hughes to George Rex, 1802, lots 10 and 18, town of Jefferson, PA on Washington and Green Streets. Marie Prine O'Brien-Lemley's notes (which we acknowledge with thanks) say these lots were given to Thomas Hughes, father-in-law of Mary Rex-Hughes, for his Rev. War services. The deed reads "Said lots being a part of a tract of land granted unto said Thomas Hughes by the Commonwealth of

Pa., by patent bearing date 4-17-1795." Patent Book 25, p. 50. Mrs. O'B-L further says that the father of Thomas Felix Hughes was a soldier in the Revolution. Also says that Thomas Hughes was the founder of Jefferson Borough, PA, coming there from Carmichael Valley, and built a stone house near the home of the widow Stephens.

1. Elizabeth[3] Hughes (1st child of John and Mary[2] Rex Hughes, George[1]) was b. in Greene Co., PA 7-26-1796. She m. John Bucking-ham about 1816. She d. 8-29-1865. Both she and her husband are buried at North Yam Hill, OR. They moved to Oregon from Pike Co., MO, in 1846 and most of their children went with them and still live there. They were the parents of ten children, 4 boys and 6 girls.
   A. George[4] Buckingham b. 11-17-1817 m. Elizabeth Campbell.
   B. Mary[4] Buckingham b. 1-3-1820 m.Thomas H. Heines.
   C. Hiram[4] Buckingham b. 7-13-1821 m. Margaret Kincaid 2-24-1844.
   D. John[4] Buckingham b. 1-1824 m. girl in TX.
   E. Nancy[4] Buckingham b. 10-1827 m. Louis Ray Kimes.
   F. Elizabeth[4] Buckingham b. 1-1829 m. Riley in MO.
   G. Mariah[4] Buckingham 4-1831 m. Robert Pittock, OR, 1853.
   H. Hanna[4] Buckingham, 3-1833 d. in 1845.
   I. Charles[4] Buckingham 5-7-1835 m. Adaline Landers 10-2-1862, later Effie Trowbridge.
   J. Melissa[4]Buckingham b. 11-1837 m. Vincent Roberts.

2. Margaret[3] Hughes (2nd child of John and Mary[2] Rex Hughes, George.[1]) was born in Greene Co., PA 1-12-1798. She m. John Hyatt Virgin, 12-8-1818. They moved to IL and the town of Virginia is named for them. She d. 12-8-1863, aged 65 yrs. 10 mo. 27 days. Her monument of marble at Indian Point Cemetery has the following inscription:

> "Remember friends as you pass by
> As you are now, so once was I,
> As I am now, soon you will be
> Prepare for death and follow me."

John Hyatt Virgin, husband of Margaret Hughes, b. Fayette Co., PA 4-19-1798. He d. at Petersburg, Manard Co., IL 10-14-1858. John Hyatt Virgin was the eldest of Eli and Nacka Hyatt Virgin and grandson of Capt. Rezin (of Rev. War) and Jemima Arnold Virgin, great grandson of Jeremiah and Lucy Virgin, who were among the first settlers west of the Allegheny mountains in Northwestern VA and Southwestern PA about 1750. Their six children are:

A. Mary[4] Jane Virgin, d. unmarried, dates unavailable.

B. Eli[4] Virgin, b. 1821 d. unmarried 7-29-1868.

C. George[4] Virgin (Figure 12) b. 5-10-1827 Fayette Co., PA. d. 9-1907 Virginia, IL. m. 2-16-1852 to Eliza Ann Enslow b. 12-19-1833 in Scioto, Co., OH. d. 1-21-1914, Virginia, IL. Children:

Figure 12. George Virgin.

  a. John[5] W. Virgin (Figure 13) b. Menard Co., IL 1-21-1854 m. 3-8-1881 Lou M. Stribling, Virginia, IL. b. 2-18-1856. 14 yrs. cattle ranching in NM where his 4 children were b.

    (1) Dorothy[6] Eliza Virgin b. 4-10-1886, San Marcial, NM. Chief Technician, Physiotheropy Dept., Beekman St. Hospital, N. Y. City.

    (2) Norma[6] Lucile Virgin b. 9-2-1888. m. 1924 Benjamin S. (Van) Sweringen. Womens College, Chicago Art Institute, Art Students League of NY. Post Grad. F. R. Gruger. Specialty Portraits. Lived in Santa Fe, NM. No children.

    (3) †Eli[6] Horace Virgin b. Ft. Craig, NM 9-7-1890 m. Rachael Rexroot, b. 4-20-1920 at Virginia, IL. 2 yrs. in Agriculture College, University of IL, Urbana, IL. 1 yr. with A. E. F. in France as a volunteer in 20th Reg. Engineer. In 1932, a farmer in IL, Cass Co., P. O. Virginia, IL. 4 children.

Figure 13. John W. Virgin.

    +Robert[7] Horace Virgin b. 6-13-1921.

    +George[7] Eugene Virgin b. 5-26-1924.

    +Alice[7] Lou Virgin b. 10-22-1926.

+Rachael[7] Dorothy Virgin b. 6-19-1929.

(4) Emma[6] Louise Virgin b. San Marcial, NM 12-31-1893. Student at IL Womens College, Jacksonville, and at IL University, Urbana. Home Virginia, IL.

b. Ida[5] Amelia Virgin b. 7-20-1856 m. 10-6-1889 George A. Aldridge. 1 child.

(1) George[6] Virgin Aldridge b. 6-5-1895 m. Josephine Hanschu. Live 708 Springfield Ave., Chicago, IL. 2 children.

+Albert[7] Virgin Aldridge b. 10-31-1923.

+Virginia[7] E. Aldridge b. 2-3-1927.

c. Eli[5] Thompson Virgin b. 10-9-1858 m. Nellie Warmuth. Resided near Junction City, OR. 7 children.

(1) Ida[6] Virgin m. Allen.

(2) Grace[6] Virgin m. McBee.

(3) Maud[6] Virgin m. Richardson.

(4) Lester[6] Virgin m. Velma ——.

(5) George[6] Glen Virgin b. 2-22-1900 m. Leila Bast, 6-6-1925.

(6) Cora[6] Virgin m. C. Stapleton.

(7) Guy[6] Virgin b. 5-19-1909.

d. George[5] M. Virgin b. 7-29-1862 m. May Shaw, San Marcial, N. M. 1 daughter.

(1) Marguerite[6] Virgin, lived in CA near Los Angeles.

e. Frank[5] Virgin b. 9-6-1866 m. Apilene Graves, Virginia, IL 12-21-1910. She was born 8-10-1871. 1 daughter.

(1) Helen[6] Virgin b. 2-14-1913.

f. Orland[5] Virgin b. 8-25-1871 m. Nettie Ater. Orland d. 4-11-1914. 6 children.

(1) Mabel[6] Virgin b. 10-6-1896 m. E. A. Baylor.

(2) George[6] Virgin b. 12-27-1898 m. Minnie Cook. 1 daughter.

+Evadine[7] Virgin.

(3) Edith[6] Virgin b. 1-27-1901.

(4) John[6] H. Virgin b. 4-12-1903 m. Mary Ellison.

(5) Myrtle[6] Virgin b. 7-15-1905 m. Carl Adkins 7-10-1923.

(6) Frances[6] Virgin b. 1-22-1908 m. P. McLeod, 1 daughter.

g. Fred[5] E. Virgin b. 3-14-1878 m. Nellie Conover 12-31-1901. 3 children.

(1) Louise[6] May Virgin b. 1-14-1904.

(2) Hazel[6] Irene Virgin b. 2-22-1907.

(3) John[6] Conover Virgin b. 12-2-1915.

D. John[4] Virgin b. 9-16-1830 d. 11-18-1898. b. in Greenup Co., KY.

m. Mary Emily Gibbs 4-28-1838, Newberg, NY. 11 children.
  a. Charles[5] Franklin Virgin, b. 8-26-1857 m. 2-2-1888 Harriet
  Ellen Latham b. 4-4-1869. 8 children.
    (1) L.[6] J. Latham Virgin b. 5-29-1889 m. 2-18-1914 Ella B.
    Wilson.
    (2) Bessie[6] Gibbs Virgin b. 6-18-1891 m. 12-1913 Benjamin
    Arthur Smith b. 1-29-1892.
    (3) John[6] W. Virgin b. 6-4-1893 m. 12-16-1914 Ella Mae Smith
    b. 8-18-1893. 1 son.
      +Charles[7] Walker Virgin b. 1915.
    (4) Anna[6] Irene Virgin b. 6-16-1895.
    (5) Charles[6] Franklin Virgin, Jr. b. 8-14-1901.
    (6) Helen[6] Harriet Virgin b. 12-22-1906 d.7-31-1909.
    (7) George[6] Raymond Virgin b. 12-29-1909.
    (8) Bernice[6] Lynn Virgin b. 9-15-1912.
  b. Harriet[5] Emily Virgin b. 12-6-1858 m. 11-10-1887 George E.
  Dewees. 1 daughter.
    (1) Lee[6] Lorine Dewees b. 7-30-1889.
  c. Clara[5] May Virgin b. 9-15-1865 m. 2-20-1889 Samuel J. Willet
  b. 8-28-1865. 2 daughters.
    (1) Clara[6] Virgin Willet b. 3-1-1890 m. 2-13-1916 Noah Gullett
    (Atty. of Springfield, IL.) 2 sons.
      +John[7] Hungerford Gullett b. 2-14-1920.
      +William[7] Waltman Gullett b. 10-11-1922.
    (2) Mary[6] Emily Willet b. 9-14-1892 m. 11-4-1919 Dr. Robert
    Emmett Smith. 1 daughter.
      +Elizabeth[7] Locke Smith b. 9-10-1920
  d. Maria[5] Lee Virgin b. 8-2-1867 d. 8-22-1868.
  e. Annie[5] Leila Virgin b. 6-10-1869 m. 7-26-1896 to Dr. Frank P.
  Martin d._____.
  f. Evelyn[5] Irene Virgin b. 4-6-1872 d. 10-31-1875.
  g. Luella[5] Florence Virgin b. 1-1-1875 d. 10-16-1900.
  h. John[5] Hughes Virgin m. 3-16-1898 to Maude Fife. 2 daughters.
    (1) Mary[6] Catherine Virgin b. 2-28-1911.
    (2) Anna[6] Margaret Virgin b. 10-20-1916.
  i. Byron[5] Lionell Virgin b. 1-13-1879 m. 4-18-1899 to Daisy May
  Caldwell. 1 daughter.
    (1) Dorothy[6] Maxine Virgin b. 7-1900 d. 6-1901.
  j. Leon[5] Clyde Virgin b. 10-15-1881 m. Emma Schwab on 10-12-
  1910. She d. 10-1913. 1 son.

(1) Edward[6] Leon Virgin b. 8-1-1911.

k. Inez[5] Minon Virgin b. 3-20-1883 m. 4-24-1907 to Ernest H. Zircle. 1 son.

(1) Ernest[6] Virgin Zircle b. 8-31-1911.

E. Maria[4] Virgin b. Knox Co., OH 2-10-1834 m. Lewis Bonnett at Lincoln, IL 12-12 1859, d. 3-17-1890 at Chariton, IA. Lewis Bonnett d. 6-10-1899. 5 children.

a. John[5] Virgin Bonnett b. 9-26-1863 at Leroy, IL. d. 10-18-1908 at Chariton, IA. 6 children.

(1) Ruth[6] E. Bonnett b. 10-21-1891.

(2) Lewis[6] B. Bonnett b. 9-15-1893.

(3) John[6] V. Bonnett, Jr. b. 6-16-1896.

(4) Gene[6] Bonnett b. 9-15-1900.

(5) Willard[6] Bonnett b. 12-5-1902.

(6) Eunice[6] Bonnett b. 3-5-1906.

b. Isaac[5] Bonnett b. 12-17-1865 at Chariton, IA. 5 children.

(1) Mary[6] Bonnett b. 6-21-1898.

(2) Pearl[6] M. Bonnett b. 4-5-1900.

(3) Lewis[6] J. Bonnett b. 12-27-1901.

(4) Jessie[6] W. Bonnett b. 10-31-1904.

(5) Helen[6] Bonnett b. 12-21-1906. m. Dillow.

c. George[5] Bonnett b. 12-6-1868. 3 children.

(1) Paul[6] Bonnett b. 5-22-1901.

(2) Dean[6] Bonnett b. 5-31-1905.

(3) James[6] Bonnett b. 8-18-1907.

d. Lewis[5] Rex Bonnett b. 6-21-1873. No children.

e. Ruth[5] Bonnett b. 1-13-1875 m. Alfred Trump. 3 children.

(1) Elizabeth[6] Trump b. 9-5-1898, Kahokia, MO.

(2) Donald[6] Trump b. 5-26-1902, Kahokia, MO.

(3) Alfred[6] G. Trump b. 4-26-1907, Kahokia, MO.

F. Ruth[4] Virgin b. about 1836. Exact dates not available.

3. Thomas[3] Hughes (3rd child of John and Mary[2] Rex Hughes, George[1]) b. in Greene Co., PA 4-16-1800. m. Elizabeth Hickman 12-13-1821 at Clarksville, PA. They lived there all their lives and d. within a month of each other at Clarksville, PA. Thomas d. 6-3-1872, Elizabeth d. 7-3-1872. 9 children.

A. Mary[4] Ann Hughes b. 10-7-1822 m. Uriah Zollers 2-10-1839. d. 7-5-1904 at Oskaloosa, IA.

B. Elizabeth[4] Hughes b. 1824, m. Thomas Odbert 1845 d. 2-27-

1910, Mt. Vernon, OH.

C. Margaret[4] Hughes b. 1-7-1827 m. William Buckingham 1-27-1851.

D. Alexandria[4] Lindsey Hughes b. 1831 m. 1st Martha Webb, m. 2nd Barbara Huff, he d. 1-2-1898, Hamilton Co., IA.

E. William[4] F. Hughes b. 3-20-1834 m. Margaret Rex 11-25-1857 d. 12-28-1896, Mt. Pleasant, IA.

F. John[4] Lincoln Hughes b. 6-19-1835 m. Jennie Michener 1-31-1864. Completed his education at Academy, Beallsville, PA where he met Sarah Jane Michener, daughter of William and Mary Michener of Carmichaels, PA. whom he married. Moved to Mt. Vernon, IL and later to Mt. Pleasant, IA. She d. 4-1926, he d. 11-1913. 7 children.

  a. Edgar[5] Allen Hughes, manufacturer of Mandolins and Banjos. Invented the Panorama Camera and other instruments.   m. Susan Wats. 6 children.

   (1) Thadeous[6] William Hughes, m. Florence Pierce, Aurora, IL. 1 son.

   (2) Helen[6] Virginia Hughes m. Robert Shaw, Chicago, IL. 2 children.

     +Robert[7] Shaw, Jr.

     +Sally[7] Shaw.

   (3) Maxwell[6] Hughes m. Mildred Clark, Chicago, IL.

   (4) Marshall[6] Hughes m. in Chicago, IL.

   (5) Ruth[6] Hughes, Chicago, IL. Single.

   (6) Rowena[6] Hughes, single.

  b. Thadeous[5] Hughes m. Harriett Shepenson of Greencastle, PA. 4 children.

   (1) Walter[6] Dell Hughes.

   (2) Annette[6] Hughes.

   (3) Emma[6] Hughes.

   (4) Benna[6] Hughes, deceased.

  c. Walter[5] Hughes m. Nyietti Crouse of Chicago, IL.

  d. Alice[5] May Hughes, grad. of Weslyn University, Mt. P. IA. m. Dr. C. W. Payne of Mt. P., IA.

  e. Helen[5] Beatrice Hughes, grad. of Weslyn University, Mt. P., IA. m. Del Mar Milton Reynolds of Pasadena, CA. 2 children.

   (1) Del Mar[6] Milton Reynolds, Jr.

   (2) Mary[6] Jane Reynolds.

  f. Myrtle[5] L. Hughes, grad. of Seattle General Hospital Training

School for Nurses.
  g. Adella[5] L. Hughes, m. Willetts Hawery Fisher of Chicago, IL.
  1 daughter.
    (1) Dorothy[6] Jane Fisher m. Allen Crabb of Chicago, IL.
     +Allyne[7] Crabb.

4. Anne[3] Nancy Hughes (4th child of John and Mary[4] Rex Hughes, George[1]) b. in Greene Co., PA 3-23-1802. Nancy Hughes m. Benjamin Montrose. We have no additional information on this branch of the family except that Nancy died young.

5. John[3] Hughes 2nd (5th child of John and Mary[2] Rex Hughes, George[1]) b. in Greene Co., PA 2-1-1805. m. Mary Ann Haver (no date). They moved to Mt. Vernon, OH and are probably buried there, Rich Hill Cemetery. Extensive stock shipper. 4 children. Children all lived at Mt. Vernon, OH.
  A. George[4] Hughes m. Amanda Bell.
  B. Mary[4] A. Hughes b. 1-1-1836 m. Hiram Bell 12-17-1856, Rich Hill, OH.
  C. Percilla[4] Hughes m. G. W. Porterfield, Bladenburg, OH.
  D. Elizabeth[4] Hughes m. Virgil Mitchell, Utica, OH.

6. George[3] Hughes (6th child of John and Mary[2] Rex Hughes, George[1]) b. in Greene Co., PA 12-9-1807. m. 1st Sarah Ellston of Jefferson, PA. She d. 9-7-1850. m. 2nd Margaret Weaver b. in Licking Co., VA 7-23-1827. 7 children all by the first wife.
  A. Mary[4] Hughes b. 1831 m. Carey Bell. d. 3-1908.
  B. Carrie[4] Hughes (Kate) b. 1835 m. Scott Vance.
  C. John[4] O. Hughes b. 1837 never married. d. 1867.
  D. Thomas[4] O. Hughes b. 7-20-1838 m. Elizabeth Davis 8-1-1887.
  E. Hugh[4] Hughes.
  F. Amelia[4] Hughes.
  G. Sarah[4] Hughes b. 1850 m. Ulery, Eagle Lake, TX.

7. Mary[3] Hughes (7th child of John and Mary[2] Rex Hughes, George[1]) b. in Greene Co., PA 9-25-1809. d. 1825. We have no further record of Mary.

8. Catherine[3] Hughes (8th child of John and Mary[2] Rex Hughes, George[1]) b. in Greene Co., PA 12-27-1811. She m. Amos Gordon. 2

children.

   A. Elizabeth[4] Gordon, in IA.

   B. Malissa[4] Gordon, in IA. We have no other information.

9. Lindsey[3] Hughes (9th child of John and Mary[2] Rex Hughes, George[1]) b. in Greene Co., PA 2-26-1814. Prior to his death at Hapster, OH, 9-30-1844, he m. and had 3 children.

   A. Mary[4] Hughes b. 7-1839.

   B. Maria[4] Hughes.

   C. John[4] Hughes. No other information.

10. Charles[3] Rex Hughes (10th child of John and Mary[2] Rex Hughes, George[1]) b. in Greene Co., PA 8-22-1816. He first m. Catherine Sharp (whose parents came from New Jersey) 9-21-1843. She d. 6-13-1856. m. 2nd Elizabeth Hill 5-26-1858. She b. 1829 d. 11-28-1887 at Jefferson, PA. 6 children by first marriage, 2 by 2nd, all b. at Jefferson, PA. Farmer and Cumberland Presbyterian.

   A. John[4] Swan Hughes b. 7-4-1844 m. Lizzie Babbitt 4-22-1869. d. 11-29-1912, Chiepley, FL. 4 children.

      a. Charles[5] Hughes d. single.

      b. Stanley[5] Hughes d. single.

      c. Rex[5] Hughes m. and has 3 children.

         (1) Lenois[6] Hughes, m.

         (2) Shirley[6] Hughes m. Walter H. Warren 5-3-1931, Huron, SD.

      d. Augusta[5] Hughes, single, Pasadena, CA.

   B. George[4] Hughes b. 7-22-1846 d. at age of 7 years.

   C. Mary[4] Elizabeth Hughes b. 2-19-1848 m. Hamilton Riggle 10-14-1868, Webb, ID. m. 2nd Noah Emerick, 9-1883. Had 9 children. She d. 1-31-1916.

   D. Pamelia[4] (Amie) Hughes b. 7-23-1850.

   E. (Millie)[4] Hughes b. 9-6-1854 m. D. A. Bumgardner 12-25-1879. Delaware, OK. She d. 2-16-1929. 2 children. Charles and Cecil.

   F. Mariah[4] Catherine Hughes b. 2-23-1856 m. Dr. Frank Kendall 3-29-1822. d. 5-3-1930. 1 daughter, Ruby Kendall.

   G. Hannah[4] Margaret Hughes b. 5-31-1863. (See Figure 14)

   H. Anna[4] May Hughes b. 7-9-1866 d. 3-1932.

11. Barnett[3] Hughes (11th child of John and Mary[2] Rex Hughes, George[1]) b. in Greene Co., PA 10-12-1819. He lived on his father's farm near Jefferson, PA until he d. 3-30-1884. He m. Pamelia Young,

daughter of Christopher and Rachael Young of Clarksville. No dates.
3 children.
  A. John[4] H. Hughes m. Mary Bell, had 2 children, Barhey and
  Lettetia.
  B. George[4] Hughes m. Anna Crayne, Morgantown, WV. She d.
  1930.
  C. Rachael[4] Hughes d. young.

12. Mariah[3] Hughes (12th child of John and Mary[2] Rex Hughes,
George[1]) b. in Greene Co., PA 2-2-1822, d. 1900. Buried in New
Cemetery, Jefferson, PA. (On the same stone are listed Zelma
McNeeley Dean 1851-1888, and Lemorne McNeeley 1859-1898)
She m. Joseph McNeeley, also of Greene Co. who d. 1870. 5
children.
  A. Nancy[4] McNeeley.
  B. George[4] McNeeley m. Sarah Dean.
  C. Charles[4] McNeeley m. Martha Lancaster of Clarksville, PA. 3
  children.
    a. John[5] McNeeley, single.
    b. Zelma[5] McNeeley m. Ray Lewis.
    c. Earl[5] McNeeley m. Lena Dowlin.
  D. Zelma[4] McNeeley b. 1851 m. Isaac Dean.
  E. Lemorne[3] McNeeley b. 1859. d. single. Of the McNeeley's, Anna
  Davis is the only living one (1933).

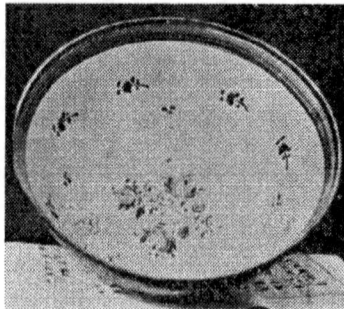

Figure 14.   Rare old bowl
(Chinese Lowes Loft) of Hannah
Margaret Hughes, many years a
family treasure and used as a
mush bowl.

Chapter 4

Our records say that Elizabeth[2] (called Betsy, second child of Margaret Kepler and George[1] Rex) was born in Mifflin County, PA. April 20, 1775. At the family home near Jefferson, Greene Co., PA July 15, 1794 she married John Bower. He was born Apr. 23, 1772, Lancaster Co., PA. He came there and settled in Fredericktown, PA. where they lived and died. She died Oct. 11, 1852 and he died July 29, 1836.

John Bower was a boat builder, distiller, and had a mill and pottery business. There are pictures of the Old Mill built in 1828 and Distillery, first in the town. We made a very pleasant stop at Fredericktown, spent the night as guests at the Bower Hotel, owned and operated by Walter S. Bower, grandson of Betsy Rex Bower. We saw

Figure 16. Cornerstone of the Bower barn in 1995.

Figure 15. Bower barn. Incorrectly labeled as Mill in the First Edition of *George Rex Genealogy*. Photograph was taken around 1904.

and have pictures of an old tile bearing his name and date. We also saw the old corner stones (Figure 17), one of which is still in place, in the lovely old stone house built by John and Betsy Bower (Figure 19). This is also where they died. The doorways and outside chimneys of this house are as beautiful as any to be found. We also visited the Millsboro Cemetery, a mile above Fredericktown, where there are 16 of the Bower family buried. The Betsy and John Bower stones are slabs in good repair (as Figure 18 shows). Hers reads "In memory of Elizabeth, wife

Figure 17. Cornerstone of the Bower home.

of John Bower, died Oct. 11, 1852, aged 77 yrs."
The old mill burned in 1929. There was a runway
right from the Mill to the river.

John Bower built the first boat to run on the
Monongahela River–Adriadne by name–of which
his son Charles was Captain. Around 1835 John
Bower discovered and mined the first coal along
the Monongahela Valley in what was then known
as "Apple Bottom."

From the History of Washington Co., PA, p.
767, published 1882: "John Bower, the ancestor of
the family of that name, was a son of Andrew
Bower of York Co., PA who was a son of Michael
Bower (Bower 1st records pg. 2), a German emi-

Figure 18. Grave-
stone of Elizabeth
Rex Bower as it ap-
peared in 1987.

grant. John Bower was born April 23, 1772 and on July 15, 1794
married Elizabeth, daughter of George Rexworthy who moved west-
ward in about 1793 and settled near Jefferson, Greene County. John
Bower with his wife followed in March and April 1796 and settled at
Fredericktown then lately laid out on the Monongahela River. On
Aug. 18, 1801, he received a deed from David Blair for a tract of 52½
acres, patented to Blair, May 13, 1789, and called "Apple Bottom."
This tract formed part of the homestead of Mr. Bower and upon it he
erected the large stone residence at the lower end of Front St., in
Fredericktown, where he lived till his death, July 29, 1836. His widow
survived him and died Oct. 11 1852. Mr. Bower was commissioned a

Figure 19. Photograph of the Bower House taken around 1900.

justice of the Peace under the constitution of 1790 on Dec. 10, 1813, which position he held at or near the time of his death."

Mr. W. S. Bower, Fredericktown, has the original letter written by his grandfather John in 1818, from which I copied the following: "Flat Boat in the mouth of Big Kenaway at Point Pleasant 300 Miles below Pittsburgh, Sunday, Dec. 20, 1818. I expect your waters are closed with ice, you will wonder how it is with us; I will therefore inform you that we are here blocked up until the weather changes, etc. etc.

John Bower."

The Friday Evening Call, Vol. 1. No. 2, Monesson, PA Dec. 11, 1808.

"Discovery of Coal in this Valley"

David Blair, sly old fox, would have kept a great fuel field to feed his Blacksmith Forge had not the Miller of Apple Bottom discovered his secret.

By Mrs. John Risbeck.

"The richest coal producing valley in the world was discovered quite by accident in the person of David Blair. Somewhere previous to 1835 this was made known to the world by John Bower, Miller O'Apple Bottom, according to the honor and justice to him keeping his mill right merely at Fredericktown on the bank of the deeply rolling Monongahela River. Now be it remembered that the Monongahela River is most unlovely, most dark, etc. It is an old busybody of a river, plodding away in the prosaic rut our fathers knew; it has seen the rise and fall of empires, the decline and growth of races, the curled periwig of Lafayette and the fevered nose of Washington. It can recite history by the mile and knows more than anybody could ever guess, but it won't tell. Its valley is the only possible modern prototype of Sinbad's valley of diamonds. Nor is the finding of it without romance since it has to deal with the miserliness of one Blacksmith to whom little credit is due for happening upon this Valley of diamonds, and seeking to keep its riches for himself and one Miller who discovered to the race at once the perfidy of the Blacksmith and our common inheritance from the mother of us all. As for the manner of this man, John Bower, he was a strong fellow, frugal and enterprising to a degree that made his memory a tradition of the town among its people who speak of him even now as one who lived nearly a century before the world was ready for his kind. With head and hand he worked and planned always to the advantage of the town and his fellows. He had no manner of patience with the spendthrift or the droan (sic). In addition to his many business enterprises he allowed his townsmen to elect him Squire and 'tis said he handed out justice with Brutus like impartiality.

John Bower left impress of his practical nature upon Fredericktown. He was Justice of the Peace 23 years of his life, he organized and successfully conducted the business of boat building, pottery and tannery. He began making redware very early in the 19th century and some of the tile he made may be seen yet in the neighborhood of Apple Bottom which is a part of Fredericktown wherein are located the old Bower buildings. David Blair was hunting in vicinity of Dan Ther Den Hollow, chased a fox into a shallow cave and in poking it with a stick, dislodged a lump of coal. He tried to keep the find a secret and have for only his own use. John Bower also discovered where he got it and soon opened a mine near Blair's shop and everybody had coal."

Elizabeth[2] Rex and John Bower were the parents of the following twelve children.
1. George[3] Bower b. 6-5-1795 d. 7-7-1796.
2. Phillip[3] Bower b. 8-5-1796 d. infant.
3. Jonah[3] Rex Bower b. 12-26-1797 d.1825.
4. Hannah[3] Bower b. 10-14-1799 d. 2-4-1835 m. Joseph Woodfill. Moved to Indiana.
   A. Martha[4] Adelaide Woodfill b. 12-26-1834 Washington Co., PA d. in Maton Co., MO 9-7-1916 m. Rene Smith Goodrich 9-27-1860 at New Albany, IN. 2 children.
      a. Nathaniel[5] L. Goodrich b. 9-24-1864 Madison, IN. m. Lena Stolp 9-25-1889. 2 children. Twins.
         (1) Rene[6] Goodrich b. 9-19-1897 m. in 1918 Pauline Ruth Novinger. 2 children.
             +Betty[7] Jean Goodrich b. 1-16-1919.
             +Marianne[7] Goodrich b. 4-6-1928.
         (2) Roland[6] N. Goodrich b. 9-19-1897 m. 11-23-1922 Marjorie Ware Jackson. 1 daughter.
             +Peggy[7] Ware Goodrich b. 10-9-1923.
      b. Alice[5] R. Goodrich b. 11-23-1868 m. Tyson N. McCully 12-24-1890. 7 children.
         (1) Inez[6] A. McCully b. 2-17-1892 d. 12-19-1928 m. Herbert V. Cook 10-21-1914. 4 children.
             +Herbert[7] V. Cook, Jr. b. 6-1-1918.

+William[7] Tyson Cook b. 12-24-1919 d. 11-9-1925.

+Dorothy[7] M. Cook b. 11-6-1921.

+Howard[7] Wade Cook b. 12-16-1928.

(2) Leslie[6] T. McCully b. 7-6-1901.

(3) William[6] Lloyd McCully b. 11-20-1903.

(4) Vivian[6] Irene McCully b. 1-27-1906 m. Elmer H. Bennett 12-22-1930.

(5) Allen[6] Rene McCully b. 12-17-1909.

(6) Margaret[6] A. McCully b. 11-27-1912.

(7) Harold[6] Eugene McCully b. 3-10-1899 m. 3-1921 Mabel B. Jones. Have 4 children.

+Creola[7] Maxine McCully b. 5-5-1922.

+Ines[7] Blanch McCully b. 5-8-1923.

+Shirley[7] Gene McCully b. 7-15-1925.

+Ruthelma[7] McCully b. 7-17-1928.

B. Andrew[4] Bower Woodfill m. and left 5 children.

a. Richard[5] Woodfill.

b. Warren[5] Woodfill.

c. Laura[5] Woodfill.

d. Hannah Louise[5] Woodfill.

e. Hattie Corrine[5] Woodfill.

5. Andrew[3] Bower (5th child of John and Elizabeth[2] Rex Bower, George[1]) b. 4-10-1802 d. Feb. 28, 1845. Elected Justice of the Peace 1836 which office he held until his death. m. Tirzah Roberts b. ? d. 7-2-1840. 4 children.

A. Francis[4] Marian Bower b. 9-2-1834 Fredericktown, PA., m. 1-22-1862 Greene Co., PA. Agnes Elizabeth Cree b. 2-10-1834 Carmichaels, PA d. 1-3-1923, Moravia, IA. He d. 5-2-1892. Came from PA to Moravia, IA in 1869 and settled on a farm. Cumberland Presbyterians.

a. John[5] J. C. Bower 11-5-1862 Heisterburg, PA. Merchant at Jefferson, IA. m. 12-9-1885 Addie Louise Horner (daughter of Elizabeth Horner) b. 11-30-1864 Moravia, IA. 3 children.

(1) Marie[6] Brandon Bower m. 1912 Edward L. Martin. Lives in Cedar Rapids, IA. She was a P. E. O. 2 children.

+Earl[7] Eugene Bower.

+Jack[7] Martin Bower.

(2) Edna[6] Lorraine Bower, Supervisor of music in schools, Ames, IA. P. E. O.

(3) Frances[6] (Frank) Eugene Bower m. 11-2-1929 Charlotte Butler, Billings, MT.

b. Dorcas[5] Virginia Bower called "Prose" b. 4-3-1867 at Heister-burg, PA. m. 10-22-1895 Clinton, IA Jacob H. Schreimer, Merchant of Moravia, IA. 2 children.

(1) Kenneth[6] Bower Schreimer m. 5-12-1923 Elenor Broshar, Waterloo, IA.

(2) Dale[6] Gutensohn Schreimer, student Iowa State College. Lives in Moravia, IA.

B. Mary[4] Elizabeth Bower b. 7-2-1838 Fredericktown, PA. d. 1-17-1924, Colorado Springs, CO. m. Fayette Co., PA 3-20-1861 George Alex Miller b. 2-18-1837 Morristown, PA. d. 12-19-1887 Shennandoah, IA. 2 children.

a. Annie[5] Bell Miller b. 7-12-1862 m. Henry Ross, lives in Farragut, IA. 7 children.

(1) †Howard[6] Ross, 4 yrs. in Navy, Denver.

(2) Curtis[6] Ross.

(3) Fred[6] Ross, Hill City, Dakota.

(4) Edith[6] Ross, Farragut, IA.

(5) George[6] Ross, Sioux City, IA.

(6) Leah[6] Ross, Chicago m. and has 3 children.

(7) Nellie[6] Ross, m. Omaha, NE.

b. Idesta[5] Althea Miller b. 5-10-1868. Married. 3 children.

(1) Fannie[6] Miller d. in infancy.

(2) Willie[6] Miller d. in infancy.

(3) Myra[6] Miller m. Al Powers, had several children. Lived in Unionville, IA.

C. Tirzah[4] Virginia Bower m. Sam Jennings. Came to IA with Francis and Mary Bower, miller in 1869. 4 children.

D. John[4] R. Bower b. 1837 d. 9-5-1858. d. at age 21 just a few weeks before his graduation as a lawyer from Waynesburg college. Was very intelligent.

6. (Hiram) Theron[3] Rex Bower b. 10-18-1804 d. 8-18-1832.

7. Charles[3] Worthy Bower (7th child of Elizabeth[2] and John Bower, George[1]) b. Washington Co., PA 12-23-1806 m. 4-2-1841 Charlotte Hook of Waynesburg, PA. d. 1884. Was an engineer on a U.S. Steamer, Tennessee River, during the (Civil) war. Also Capt. of boat built by his father, John Bower, "The Adriadne."

A. Charles[4] Edward Bower b. 4-11-1849 at Waynesburg, PA. m. Josephine Gordon in 1872. 2 sons.
    a. Jerome[5] Bower (in Kansas?) In U. S. Gov. Service.
    b. Oliver[5] Bower d. in 1924 at Waynesburg, PA.

8. John[3] K. Bower (Figure 20) (8th child of Elizabeth[2] and John Bower, George[1]) b. in Washington Co., PA 3-7-1809. m. Lucinda Wise 9-5-1830. She b. 8-22-1809 and d. 2-15-1891 in Cincinnati, OH. She was daughter of Jacob and Martha Wise. 5 children (Figure 21).

Figure 20. John Kepner Bower.

Figure 21. J. K. Bower children (left to right) William Knoffsinger Bower, Scottsville, KA, Frank Heaton Bower, Cincinnatti, OH, Mary Bower Burgess, MA, Lafayette Quincy Bower, Silverton, OR, and Charles Columbus Bower, Reading, PA.

A. Martha[4] Maria Bower b. 5-17-1831 d. 9-18-1834.
B. Charles[4] Columbus Bower (Figure 22) b. 12-31-1833 in Fredericktown, PA. As a young man, he worked as an itinerate teacher in Pittsburgh. He became a potter and moved to Reading PA in 1872 where he was the proprietor of the Centennial Pottery for many years. He then was employed by the Boyd Directory Company for 20 yrs. He was a prominent Mason for 52 yrs. d. 4-25-1907 in Mt. Gretna. Married Philipiann Park 6-9-1855. She b. 11-7-1836 d. 9-3-1919 in Reading, PA. 8 children
    a. David[5] Edwin Bower b. 6-26-1856. He was apprenticed to his

Figure 22. Charles Columbus Bower Family. first row: Charles Columbus Bower, Anna Bower, Philipiann Bower. Second row: Lyttle Eddie Bower, Andrew Park Bower, William Lafayette Bower, and Charles Franklin Bower.

father as a potter. While going to work on 1-25-1873, he took a shortcut across a frozen canal and slipped, striking his head developing a subdural hematoma. He died 3 days later. Entry in the Family Bible: "David Edwin Bower died of brain fever after the most intense suffering of three days although possessing the faculties of his mind up to within four hours of his death which occurred at 7 o'clock PM Jan. 28th 1873." Edwin's parents were devastated, but at the time of Edwin's death, Edwin's mother was pregnant with her last child. Charles consoled his wife, Philipiann, by telling her not to worry that Little Eddie would soon be here. This then was the origin of Lyttle Eddie's name.

b. Elizabeth⁵ Ellen Bower b. 6-13-1858 d. 10-5-1859.

c. Mary⁵ Evaline Bower b. 1-5-1860 d. 5-29-1860.

d. Charles⁵ Franklin Bower b. 5-5-1861 m. Emily R. Mueller 10-17-1893. 4 children.

  (1) Marie⁶ Bower.

  (2) †Edwin⁶ Bower. Trained as a machinist with Reading Railroad Shops. Served during WW I in Navy and reached rank of CWO serving in Pacific. Retired in San Diego, CA.

Several children.

+Edith[7] (Sunshine) Bower

(3) †Leroy[6] Bower. Enlisted in Army making it a career and reaching rank of Corporal. Found murdered along the Mexican border.

(4) Josephia[6] Bower. m. Kohl. Lived in family home on Pear St., Reading, PA before it was sold outside the family. 2 sons.

e. William[5] Laffayette Bower b. 3-23-1865 d. 2-18-1934. m. Ellanora Freeman. Financially successful, Owned several hotels in Berks Co., PA. 1 daughter.

(1) Anna[6] Bower m. James Plunkett. 2 sons.

+Joseph[7] Donald Plunkett.

+William[7] James Plunkett.

f. Andrew[5] Park Bower b. 5-14-1869 Apollo, PA. d. 10-24-1949 Reading, PA. Became cigar maker at an early age. Joined the Cigar Maker's International Union of America in 1886 and was secretary-treasurer of the Reading local union from 1904 until his death. In 1942 was elected president of the Cigar Maker's International Union of America. His work as a labor leader and mediator in the tobacco industry took him to many parts of the US. He was VP of the PA Federation of Labor from 1909 until his death.

His civic interests included founding a sanitarium association which built the first county TB hospital in Berks Co. From its founding until his death, Andrew served as president or chairman of the institution's Advisory board. He served 6 yrs. as trustee of the Welfare Federation of Reading. He was active in the Reading and Berks Co. Welfare Federation and Social Agencies Council. He was superintendent of Old Age Pensions and was on the Board of Public Assistance for Berks Co. He served 15 years as VP of the Berks Co. Council, Boy Scouts of America receiving their Silver Beaver Award. m. Maude Estella Weightman. She b. 5-28-1874 in Girardville, PA. d. 7-30-1968 Reading, PA. 3 children.

(1) Esther[6] Weightman Bower. (Figure 23) b. 10-29-1900 in Reading, PA. Educated: Girls' High School, Reading 1906-1918. Millersville State Normal School, Diploma 1920. West Virginia U., BS 1927. PA. State College, MS (Child Development) 1940. Taught in Public School in Reading, PA 1921-1924. From 1940-1945 Director Child Care Centers, Camden,

NJ and Grumman Aircraft
Corp. Taught Kindergarten
at Red Bank, NJ Public
Schools from 1945 until her
retirement in 1965. d. 1-31-
1994.

(2) Julia[6] Wells Bower.
(Figure 23) b. 12-27-1903
in Reading PA. Graduated:
Valedictorian, Girls' HS,
Reading, PA 1921; Summa

Figure 23. Esther and Julia Bower (left
to right.) Photograph taken in 1982 at
Ormand Beach, FL.

Cum Laude, Syracuse U., AB 1925; AM 1926; U. of Chicago
Ph.D. 1933. Title of Dissertation: "The Problem of Lagrange
with Finite Side Conditions." Honor Societies: Phi Beta
Kappa, Sigma Xi, Sigma Delta Epsilon, Phi Mu Epsilon, Phi
Lambda Theta, Phi Kappa Phi, Sigma. Teaching positions:
Vassar College 1926-1927, Sweet Briar College 1927-1930,
Syracuse U. 1927-1931, Connecticut College 1933-1969
where she was Chairman of Dept. of Mathematics, 1943-1969.
Retired in Central FL. She assisted in the preparation of this
book.

(3) Philippa[6] Ann Bower. d. young of Diphtheria.

g. Eva[5] Ann Bower b. 12-30-1870 d. 1-11-1955 in Reading, PA.
m. Mr. Scotten. No children.

h. Lyttle[5] Eddie Bower b. 2-27-1873 d. 6-26-1934. Educated to 8th
grade. Worked for minstrel company in black face. When minstrel company folded, he worked for bicycle company in Reading, PA as a machinist apprentice although he maintained an
interest in the theatre and local minstrel shows for the rest of his
life. He then worked for the Reading Railroad in the locomotive
shops. Following this, he worked in sales for the Bell Telephone
Co. When WW I started, he returned to the Reading RR shops
where he remained until he retired in 1933. Lived in 1000 block
of N. 5th St. Reading. Member of the Knights of Malta. m.
Amanda Catherine Stuber Fields 2-27-1901. 2 children.

(1) Stillborn Daughter.

(2) †John[6] Roehrich Bower (Figure 24). b. 10-23-1904 Reading, PA. Graduated 5th in class at Reading HS. Worked for 2
yrs for Reading RR in their offices. Attended Bucknell U. for
3 yrs maintaining an A average, then went to Jefferson Medi-

cal School receiving MD degree in 1933. Elected to Alpha Omega Alpha honorary fraternity. Internship at Reading Hosp. Set up General practice in Kutztown, PA until he entered Army after WW II started. Stationed at Camp Hood, Texas until end of war. Returned to Reading where he practiced Neuro Psychiatry until he retired at age of 80. Was Chief of Dept of Psychiatry at Reading Hosp. for many years. d. 9-23-1996. He was a great Dad.

Figure 24. John Roehrich Bower.

m Haidee I. Wilson (Figure 25) 11-23-1933. She b. 7-27-1906 Reading, Pa. d. 2-15-1994. Graduated Girls' HS Reading. Received BS Degree from Cedar Crest College, Allentown, PA. Taught Biology there for 2 yrs. Raised her family. Then Received MS Degree from Temple U. and taught Biology at Kutztown U. 3 sons. She was a great Mom.

Figure 25. Haidee I. Wilson Bower.

+John[7] Robert Bower (Figure 26) b. 8-3-1940 Reading, PA. BS Degree Haverford College, MD Degree Jefferson Medical School. Member Alpha Omega Alpha. Residency in OB/Gyn Thomas Jefferson U. Hospital. Chief of Gynecology Reading Hospital, Reading PA. m. Jill Louise Simpson 8-8-1970 Pittsburgh, PA. 2 Children.

Figure 26 John Robert Bower Family. (Left to right) John Roehrich Bower II, John Robert Bower, Jill Louise Simpson Bower, and William Edward Bower.

^John[8] Roehrich Bower, II b. 8-5-1971 in Reading, PA. Graduated Haverford College. Lives in Chicago. IL. Employed as an actuary.

^William[8] Edward Bower b. 6-8-1973 in Reading, PA. Graduated Western Maryland U.

+ †Edward[7] Birch Bower (Figure 27) b. 9-30-1942 Reading

PA BS, MS Degrees
Bucknell U., MD
Degree   Jefferson
Medical School, In-
terned   U.   VA,
Surgery Residency
Thomas Jefferson U.
Hospital.   Chief
Surgery US Army
Hospital Ft Stewart,
GA 1975-77. Prac-
tices General and Pe-
ripheral   Vascular

Figure 27. Edward Birch Bower family. (Left to right) Curtis Edward Bower, Angela Thomas Bower, Amanda Birch Bower, and Edward Birch Bower. Photograph taken 1991 at Amanda's graduation from University of Richmond.

Surgery at Monroe, NC. One of the co-author/editors of
Second Edition, *Rex Genealogy*. m. Angela Winfree
Thomas of Ridgewood, NJ 7-30-1966. She b. 11-12-1944
Knoxville, TN. B.S. Degree Bucknell U. She is administra-
tor for her husbands surgical practice and does much volun-
teer work for United Way. She was named 1996 Union
County Citizen of the Year. 2 Children.

   ^Amanda[8] Birch Bower (Figure 27) b. 8-20-1969 Philadelphia, PA. BS Degree in BA from U. of Richmond *Cum
   Laude*. Ph.D. from USC 1997. Now an Assistant Professor of Marketing at Louisana State University.

   ^Curtis[8] Edward Bower b. 12-26-1973 Philadelphia, PA.
   BS Degree UNC, Chapel Hill, Second year medical student at Jefferson Medical School Philadelphia, PA.

+James[7] Richard Bower (Figure 28). b. 2-16-1947 Reading,
PA. BA Degree Haverford College.
Employed by a consulting company
doing database management. m.
Joyce Lennea Carlson. She b. 10-26-
1948 Cleveland, OH. Grad. *Magna
cum Laude* U. Minnesota. She is a
social worker. The family lives in
South Hadley, MA. 1 daughter.

   ^Lennea[8] Rose Bower b. 2-24-1985
   in MA.

Figure 28. James Bower family. James Richard Bower, Joyce Lennea Carlson, and Lennea Rose Bower.

C. †William[4] Knoffsinger Bower (Figure
29) b. 7-13-1836 in Washington Co., PA.

d. 1915 in Scottsville, KS. m. Margaretta W. Werts 9-8-1860 in Mt Paletine, IL. She b. 5-28-1837 in New Jersey and d. 8-20-1903 in Scottesville, KS. They lived in Magnolia, IL where he worked as a farmer. Their first son was born 6-11-1861, 29 days after the first shots were fired on Ft Sumpter. He enlisted as a Private into Co. E 94th Regiment Illinois Infantry 8-7-1862 and was discharged 7-17-1865 at Galveston TX. He fought in the following engagements: (1) *Battle of Prairie Grove, AR* 12-7-1862; (2) *Seige of Vicksburg, MS* June and July 1863; (3) *Expedition to Brownsville, TX* 11-6-1863; (4) Siege of Fort Morgan, AL August 1864; (5) *Skirmish at Fiti, MS* 12-22-1864; (6) *Siege of Spanish Fort, AL* March and April 1865.

He returned to his family and in the Spring of 1872 moved to his new home about one and one half miles west of Scottsville, KS. They had 5 children, two of whom did not survive beyond infancy. He eventually became Postmaster of Scottsville, KS. In 1913, at the age of 77, he was given a pension of $30 per month for his service during the Civil War. Sometime after the death of his wife, his daughter, Virginia, who had never married, and he moved to Topeka, KS where they lived together until his death.

Figure 29. William Knofsinger Bower Family. 1. John F. Bower. 2. William Clinton Bower, MD. 3. Nicholas Werts. 4. Frank Heaton Bower. 5. William Knofsinger Bower. 6. Ralph L. Bower. 7. Harriet Keeler Bower. 8. Paul H. Bower. 9 ?Maud Kerns Bower. 10. ?Earl or Lyle Bower. 11 Margaret Werts Bower. 12. Mary Virginia Bower. Photo taken Summer 1900 outside of the house in Scottsville, KS.

a. William[5] Clinton Bower b. 6-11-1861 in Magnolia IL. d. 12-13-1928 in St. Frances Hospital Topeka, KS. m. Maud Kerns 5-17-1886. In 1876, he began carrying the US Mail between

Concordia and Beloit, KS, a job he held for several years. He completed a course in a private normal school in Concordia and then received his MD Degree from the Rush Medical School in Chicago. After their marriage, he and his wife moved to Lebanon, KS where he resided for 25 years practicing medicine. In 1888 he joined the Independent Order of Odd Fellows and eventually filled all the chairs of the state order of that lodge. In 1913 he and his wife moved to Topeka, KS where they resided until his death.

(1) Earl[6] V. Bower lived in Lebanon, KS.

(2) Lyle[6] C. Bower lived in Los Angeles, CA.

b. Mary[5] Virginia Bower b. 1863 d. 1961.

c. John[5] F. Bower b. 1886 in IL. m. Harriet Keeler 6-5-1890. They lived in Scottsville, KS until the death of their 2nd son in 1913 when they moved to St. Paul, MN. 2 children.

(1) †Paul[6] H. Bower b. May 20, 1892 in Scottsville KS. He enlisted in the army as a private April 8, 1918 at Beloit, KS. He served as a Private in the 3rd Co. 1st Bn. 164th Depot Brigade. On his enlistment papers his vocation was listed as Draftsman. He eventually settled in St. Paul, MN where he owned a microscope repair business. He owned the Family Bible and eventually passed it on to John[6] R. Bower, M.D. of Wyomissing PA. Paul died in May 6, 1974 of heart disease.

(2) Ralph[6] L. Bower b. 7-3-1900 in Scottsville, KS. d. April 21, 1913. He most likely had tuberculosis and his mother took him to Sinton, TX in the "hope of restoring his health which had been failing for some time." His father came to Sinton, about one month before Ralph died. Ralph was described in his obituary as "though old for his years and of a quiet, retiring disposition, was a cheerful little fellow and even during his hours of suffering and reflected a large measure of God's sunlight upon his surroundings. At school he was earnest and studious, taking great pride in the accomplishment of the tasks assigned him and ever considerate of his companions and teachers. The last thoughts he expressed were not of himself but for those who would mourn his departure. These traits endeared him to all who knew him."

d. Laura[5] Della Bower b. 7-17-1873 d. 4-28-1900. She was an invalid for 21 years, "shut off from the pleasures that have been bestowed by God to his children."

D. Frank[4] Heaton Bower b. 3-4-1839. m. 6-3-1874 to Sarah L. McGonigle in Cincinnati, Ohio.

E. Lafayet[4] Quincey Bower (Figure 30) b. 3-21-1842. m. 3-1866 Mary Kistler in IL. Lived in Silverton, OR. 9 children.

Figure 30. Lafayet Quincey Bower family. Photo taken 1907 on front porch of home in Silverton, Oregon. 1,2. Bob and Bert, 3. L. Q. Bower, 4. Dick C., 5. Edna or Lillian, 6. Son of #5, 7. Husband of #5, 8. Edna orLillian, 9, 10, 11. unknown, 12. Lloyd Ivan, 13. Flossie Etta, 14. Esther Julia, 15. Rex, 16. Iden Lee Bower.

a. Iden[5] L. Bower. (Figure 30) b. 1-27-1869 in Golden City, MO and d. 5-2-1949. He owned a 3,000 acre ranch located about 45 miles south of Great Falls, MT. He was a well liked and respected rancher running one of the finest ranches in the area. He raised white-faced Herefords, and later sheep. He also grew wheat and mustard. He d. 5-2-1949 in Great Falls, MT. m. Esther Julia Wyland. She b. 10-9-1868 in Oregon and d. 10-15-1930 in Great Falls, MT. She first m. Alfred E. Smith 7-6-1887 but no children from her 1st marriage. 3 children from 2nd marriage.

  (1) Lloyd[6] Bower b. 2-14-1891. d. 9-6-1983 in Spokane, WA. m. 1st Nona McCartney but no children. m. 2nd Annabel Bailey She b. 7-17-1915. 3 children.

    +Vern[7] Bower b. 1-23-19?? Bremerton, WA. 2 children

      ^James[8] Lee Bower b. 8-18-1974.

      ^Timothy[8] Bower b. 11-19-1975.

    +Glen[7] Bower b. 7-11-1948 Spokane, WA. 1 daughter.

      ^Julie[8] Ann Bower b. 4-26-1973.

+Carolyn[7] Bower b. 12-13-1949 Spokane, WA. m. Dale
Oens. Live in Vancouver, WA. 2 children.

^Ruth[8] Ellen Oens b. 9-3-1972.

^Christian[8] Gene Oens b. 3-22-1977. d. 4-18-1977 of crib
death.

(2) Flossie[6] Etta Bower b. 6-11-1893 in Hubbard OR d. 1-21-
1956 Great Falls, MT. m. George Theodore Overose on
10-16-1918 at Helena, MT. He b. 3-23-1886 in Minneapolis,
MN and d. 3-5-1960 near San Diego, CA. 5 children.

+Donald[7] George Overose b. 8-30-1919. St. Peter, MT. m. 1st
Alice Ripplinger later divorced. m. 2nd Vickie ? 1 son.

^Keith[8] Steven Overose b. 12-16-1947. Lives in Broken
Arrow, OK.

+Ruth[7] E. Overose b. 7-24-1920 (twin) in Cascade MT. m.
Ervin G. Kiser 8-8-1942 in Great Falls, MT. He was a
master carpenter. Ruth has contributed greatly to the information about her line. 4 children.

^Grant[8] Eugene Kiser b. 10-1-1946 Great Falls, MT. Postmaster in Clancy, MT. m. 1st Candice Helen Hanson
4-13-1968 but later divorced. m. 2nd Nancy Zendron. 3
sons from 1st marriage.

~Scott[9] Michael Kiser b. 2-13-1969 Everett, WA.

~Gregory[9] E. Kiser b. 11-10-1970 Whitefish MT.

~Timothy[9] Grant Kiser b. 9-23-1976 Kalispell, MT.

^Crystal[8] Ann Kiser b. 6-24-1948 Great Falls, MT. m. 1st
Neil Raymond 7-26-1969 but then divorced. m. 2nd Kelly
Ferguson 2-14-1992. She is the housekeeper for a retired
Anaconda Aluminum official and his family. They live on
Whitefish Lake, Whitefish, MT. 5 children from 1st mar-
riage.

~Eric[9] N. Raymond b. 6-11-1971 Kalispell, MT.

~Joelle[9] A. Raymond b. 8-31-1973 Kalispell, MT.

~Angelee[9] Brooke Raymond b. 6-3-1975 Kalispell, MT.

~Jon[9] M. Raymond b. 8-12-1979 Kalispell, MT.

~Lee[9] C. Raymond b. 5-7-1983 Kalispell, MT.

^Kenneth[8] Leigh Kiser b. 7-3-1950 Great Falls, MT. M.S.
Degree in Public Administration from BYU and in Computer Science from Michigan State. He is a systems
analyst for the US Forest Service Regional Hdqtrs in
Ogden, UT. m. Lorraine Velasquez in Delta, CO. 7-18-

1981. She is employed by the IRS. 1 daughter.

~Allison[9] Leigh Kiser b 9-3-1984.

^Russell[8] Thomas Kiser b. 12-19-1953 Kalispell, MT. Works at a body shop in Columbia Falls, MT. m. 1st Norma McMichael in Provo, UT later divorced. m. 2nd Robin Griffis of Delta, CO. She works as scrub nurse for ophthalmologist in Kalispell, MT. 2 daughters.

~Chelsea[9] Jewel Kiser b. 10-15-1989.

~McKenzie[9] Rose Kiser b. 7-9-1983.

+Robert[7] Iden Overose b. 7-24-1920 (twin). m. Evelyn Baker 5-18-1941 in Great Falls, MT. She b. 2-6-1918. 1 daughter.

^Cheryl[8] Overose b. 5-15-1943 in Portland, OR.

+Shirley[7] Theodore Overose b. 7-15-1922. Great Falls, MT. m. Willo Jean Popovich 2-14-1947 in Great Falls, MT. 1 son.

^George[8] Terrell Overose.

+Mabel[7] Marjorie Overose b. 5-19-1925. Great Falls, MT. m. L. Clark MacDonald 12-1-1946 in Great Falls, MT but later divorced. 3 daughters.

^Denise[8] Eileen MacDonald b. 3-15-1949.

^Janice[8] Sue MacDonald b. 7-28-1951.

^Beverly[8] Jean MacDonald b. 7-6-1955.

(3) Rex[6] Bower b. 5-1-1895 in Needy, OR. d. 5-16-1960 in Great Falls, MT. m. Ona Harris from Clarksburg, MO. 3 children.

+Betty[7] Ann Bower b. 1-3-1925 Cascade, MT.

+Jean[7] Elinor Bower b. 3-5-1926 Great Falls, MT.

+Richard[7] Carroll Bower b. 2-1-1929 Great Falls, MT. d. of leukemia at age 53.

b. Edna[5] Bower (Figure 26) d. of tuberculosis. 2 children.

c. Dick[5] C. Bower (Figure 26) wife's name was Gertrude. 2 sons, one killed 1939 while learning to fly airplane.

d. Lillian[5] Bower (Figure 26) d.of tuberculosis. 2 children.

e. Bob[5] Bower (Figure 26).

f. Bert[5] Bower (Figure 26).

F. Hiram[4] Rex Bower b. 10-25-1844 d. 7-2-1847 near Pittsburgh.

G. Mary[4] Matilda Bower b. 3-18-1847. m. George F. Burgess 1-30-1867. Lived in Massachusetts.

9. Margaret[3] Bower (9th child of Elizabeth[2] and John Bower, George[1])

b. 3-25-1812, Washington Co., PA. She died Oct. 14, 1849. m.
12-26-1830 Daniel Crumrine. Mr. Crumrine weighs over 200, a fine
specimen of physical manhood. (Taken from Biographical album of
prominent Pennsylvanians, published at Phila. in 1889). *Hist. Wash.
Co.*, PA. p. 768. Daniel Crumrine b. 4-25-1805, by trade a mill-
wright. In 1831, with Ephriam L. Blaine (father of James G. Blaine),
erected the saw mill now occupied by John S. Pringle in West
Brownsville. m. Margaret, daughter of John Bower, Esq. of Fredericktown 12-26-1830. She d. 10-1849. Their children are all living
excepting 2 who d. in infancy.

A. Elizabeth[4] Crumrine, still at home with her father, single.

B. Boyd[4] Crumrine, Atty. Wash. Co., PA. b. 2-9-1838. *Hist. of
Wash. Co.*, PA. p. 206-10 (Beers and Co. 1893) Boyd Crumrine,
prominent in PA, in East Bethlehem Twp. Son of Daniel and
Margaret Bower Crumrine. Excepting for his great grandfather on
maternal side who was an Englishman, George Rex, by name, his
blood is all German from the Upper Rhine. Graduated from
Jefferson College, Canonsburg. Chose law the next year. m. Harriet J. daughter of George A. and Jane B. Kirk. 4 children.

  a. Ernest[5] Ethelbert Crumrine partner of his father in law office.
  m. Gertrude daughter of Rev. J. F. Magill, Fairfield, IA. Have 1
  son.

  b. Louise[5] Celeste Crumrine m. J. P. Patterson, Esq. of Pittsburgh
  Bar.

  c. Roland[5] Thompson Crumrine, d. very young.

  d. Hattie[5] J. Crumrine, d. very young.

C. Bishop[4] Crumrine, Atty. Topeka, KS.

D. Lesage[4] Crumrine b. 1844 d. 3-20-1926 at Beallsville, PA. Had a
son and daughter as follows:

  a. Russell[5] Crumrine living at Ben Avon, PA.

  b. Irma[5] Crumrine, m. W. G. Carl, Baptist Minister of 603
  Hampton St., Wilkinsburg, PA.

E. Alonzo[4] Crumrine, deceased. m. Ellen Weaver and had sons as
follows:

  a. Hon. Judge Boyd[5] Crumrine, Washington, PA. (m. and has
  son).

  b. Dr. Clyde[5] Crumrine m. and had a son. Now dead.

10. Elizabeth[3] Bower (10th child of Elizabeth[2] Rex and John Bower,
George[1]) b. 11-29-1816 d. 1900.

11. Benjamin[3] F. Bower (Figure 31) (11th child of Elizabeth[2] Rex and John Bower, George[1]) b. 1-28-1818 in Fredericktown, Washington Co., PA and was the last son of John and Elizabeth Bower to live in the family homestead at Apple Bottom from which, after the death of his father, he conducted the family businesses of coal mining, distilling, farming, boat-building, and pottery. He was a skilled horseman and had several teams and wagons for hire. He was a Justice of the Peace for East Bethlehem Township, PA, and went to the Gold Rush in California in 1852 via the Isthmus of Panama. He d.

Figure 31. Benjamin F. Bower. ca. 1900.

12-8-1900 at Fredericktown, PA; buried at Millsboro, PA. He m. first Narcissa Craft of Fayette Co., PA 2-23-1842, she b. 1817 d. 12-9-1848. 3 children.

  A. †Lawrence[4] (Larry) W. Bower b. 8-13-1843 d. 3-1897. He enlisted in the Civil War in 1862 and served until the end of the war. He was twice married but left no children.

  B. †George[4] Rex Bower (Figure 32) b. 8-17-1845 d. 8-5-1864. Enlisted in the Civil war and was shot from his horse and killed.

  C. John[4] Morgan Bower b. 11-26-1848 m. Susan Bowell of Millsboro, PA 1872 and he d. 4-1-1916. 6 children.

    a. George[5] Rex Bower, 2nd, b. 12-28-1873. Located at St. Louis, MO. Employed in U. S. Civil Service d. 2-21-1928. m. Maude L. Baker 4-9-1922.

    b. Jessie[5] M. Bower b. 10-20-1875 d. 12-24-1893. m. Wooda H. Lange 10-28-1893.

Figure 32. George Rex Bower was the second son of B. F. Bower, and died in 1864 during a battle of the Civil War.

    c. Sarah[5] Elizabeth Bower b. 2-19-1878 m. Arthur Neal 2-22-1905 engaged in coal business, Springfield, IL.

    d. Helen[5] Bower b. 1-12-1881 m. Merlin A. Maze, Pittsburgh, PA. Have 2 fine boys.

      (1) Morgan[6] Bower Maze b. 10-17-1908.

      (2) Merlin[6] A. Maze, Jr. b. 12-4-1912.

    e. Benjamin[5] F. Bower b. 7-24-1888 (named for his grandfather) m. Marian Jeffries. Resides in Pittsburgh, PA.

    f. Mary[5] Edna Bower kept house for her father b. 9-26-1884 and d. 8-7-1922.

Benjamin[3] F. Bower m. 2nd Elizabeth Horner of Millsboro, PA 3-1866. She d. 11-15-1876 and they had one son.

D. Walter[4] Scott Bower (Figure 33) b. 5-29-1867. Later a partner in his father's horse business, he operated a hotel and livery in Fredericktown, PA before building the Hotel Bower there in 1903 which he successfully operated with his wife until his death in 1933. He was a director of the First National Bank of Fredericktown and an East Bethlehem Township Commissioner. He m. Mar-

Figure 33. Walter Scott Bower ca. 1930

Figure 34. Margaret Stathers Bower ca. 1940.

garet E. Stathers (Figure 34) 1-5-1895. She was a daughter of George and Charlotta Reeves Stathers; b. 1865 d. 1953. She attended California (PA) Normal School and was an elementary teacher in East Bethlehem Township prior to marriage. Are Methodists. Have 1 daughter and 2 sons.

a. Elizabeth[5] Bower b. 3-23-1904 d. 8-14-1904.

b. †John[5] Edward Bower (Figure 35) b. 9-18-1903; d. 3-13-1977. Attended Waynesburg (PA) College where he played football. Jointly operated the Hotel Bower with his mother, brother, and sister-in-law until his death, following the passing of his father. He was an enlisted man in the U.S. Coast Guard with stateside duty during WW II. He earned a mate's license for steam and motor vessels on the inland rivers. His extensive collection of antique steamboat artifacts, formerly on display in the Hotel Bower barroom is now owned by the Pittsburgh History and Landmarks Foundation.

Figure 35. John Edward Bower and Walter Scott Bower, Jr. ca. 1909

c. †Walter[5] S. Bower, Jr. (Figures 35, 36), known as "Babe." b. 11-5-1906; d. 8-27-1973. B.S. in Education, 1930, Waynesburg (PA) College, where he assisted with the football team. High school and college football official in Southwestern PA for over 30 years. Sales representative, Seagram's Distillers, Pittsburgh, PA, then English teacher, football and baseball coach, East

Bethlehem Township High School. He was later elected school director of East Bethlehem Township Schools. He served as director of the First National Bank of Fredericktown. He was an enlisted man in the U.S. Army Air Corps with stateside duty during WW II. Along with his brother and mother, he jointly operated the Hotel Bower. m. Lois Dulaney Stephens of Waynesburg, PA 8-27-1930. She b. 6-10-1907; d. 5-23-1981. She was the daughter of Captain Homer E. and Carrie Call Stephens. She was an X-Ray technician at Waynesburgh, PA prior to her marriage. Have 1 daughter and 1 son.

Figure 36. Walter Scott Bower, Jr. ca. 1938.

(1) Elizabeth[6] Anne Bower b. 6-9-1931. Attended California (PA) State Teachers College prior to her marriage on 7-7-1951 to †Richard M. Ames of Beallsville, PA. He b. 6-1-1929, a U.S. Navy veteran, factory worker, and retired lockman on several U.S. Army Corps of Engineer, Ohio Valley Locks. 2 children.

+Janet[7] D. Ames. b. 3-9-1961 m. 9-18-1995 David C. Flinn.

+David[7] A. Ames. b. 10-22-1962 m. 5-23-1992 Ann M. Woods. 1 daughter.

^Ashley[8] N. Ames, b. 10-31-1993.

(2) †Walter[6] Scott Bower, III. b. 2-9-1938. Formerly employed by Battelle Memorial Institute and the Ohio Geological Survey, Columbus Ohio, English teacher, Latrobe (PA) public schools and teaching/research associate, Ohio State U. Now associate Professor of Education, West Va. U., Morgantown, WV. B.S. in Geology, Waynesburgh (PA) College, 1959; M.A. in Education, 1965, and Ph.D., Education and History, 1972, both at Ohio State U. Enlisted man, U.S. Army National Guard, Vietnam era. One of the co-authors/editors of Second Edition of the *Rex Genealogy*. m. Barbara Ellen Henneke 4-20-1962 at Columbus Ohio. She b. 5-26-1941, a daughter of Henry J. and Mary E. Henneke. She attended Ohio State U. and worked as a lab technician, teacher's aide, and geriatric aide before and after her marriage. Mr. and Mrs. Bower reside in the original John and Elizabeth Rex Bower homestead at Apple Bottom, Fredericktown, PA (Fig. 19). 2 daughters and 2 sons.

+Lois[7] Ellen Bower b. 8-20-1965. B.A. in Dance, West Virginia. U, 1988; private dance instructor, Pittsburgh, PA.

+Rena[7] Kathleen Bower b. 3-25-1966. B.S. in Mathematics, Ohio State U., 1994; office manager, Super Duper Markets, Columbus, Ohio.

+Walter[7] Scott Bower, IV b. 1-30-1974. B.S. in Mathematics, Waynesburg (PA) College, 1996. Math teacher, Cumberland County Schools, Fayetteville, NC.

+John[7] Andrew Bower b. 1-22-1976. Employed at Sunset Marina, Millsboro, PA.

12. Mary[3] Bower b. 1-3-1821 d. 5-1-1845.

Chapter 5

George[2] Rex, (third child and oldest son of
Margaret Kepler and George[1] Rex) b. in Mifflin
Co., Pa. 10-14-1778, d. Jefferson, PA 10-18-1856.
m. Jane Black early in 1806 who was b. 8-18-1785,
d. 1850. Are buried side by side in Presbyterian
Cemetery, Jefferson, which exact inscriptions I
give as copied by myself (Leda R.) August 5, 1931,
at which time Dan Rex took pictures of the stones
(Figure 37). They are white slabs with foot stones
"George Rex, died Oct. 18, 1856, aged 78 years, 4
days; Jane, wife of George Rex, died Dec. 27,
1850, aged 65 years, 4 mo. and 11 days." are the
parents of 12 children all born in Greene Co.,
PA.

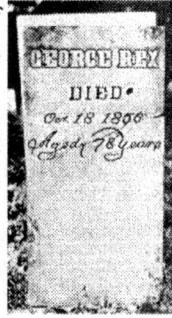

Figure 37. Gravestone of George Rex II.

1. William[3] Winters Rex (1st child of George[2]
and Jane Rex, George[1]) (Figure 38) b. 1-8-
1802. (Named for William Winters, husband of
his aunt Martha Rex Winters) Oct. 29, 1837 at
Beaver, PA. m. Mary Ann Messler, b. 11-14-
1819, d. 7-27-1895 daughter of John and
Rachael Messler. M. A. M. joined Methodist
Ch. 1832 and Christian 1878. Spring of 1838
they located on government land Ripley Co.,
IN 1845 he was elected sheriff and moved to
County seat, Versailles. 1858 moved on farm
near Clinton. Moved to Virginia, IL. 1865 and
1867 to Blue Ridge, 12 miles south of Kansas
City, MO, where William Winters Rex d. 7-6-1877. Is buried at Blue
Ridge church. His wife d. 7-27-1895, and is buried at Sharon Church
near Drexel, MO. Parents of 7 children. The first three listed died
without issue:

Figure 38. William Winters Rex.

   A. Samuel[4] Rex, b. 10-5-1838, d. 7-29-1839.

   E. John[4] Maglen Rex, b. 8-26-1847, d. 4-27-1857.

   G. William[4] Winters Rex, 2nd, b. 10-4-1851, d. 4-24-1857.

   B. Sarah[4] Jane Rex, (Figure 39) b. 7-17-1840, Ripley Co., IN. d.
      8-2-1929, Ogden, Utah, m. 1st Peter Lostutter Kelly, 1-11-1856.
      She lived at Ashland, IL until 12-11-1908. Sarah J. Rex Kelly had

two sons by first marriage.

   a. George[5] Johnson Kelly, b. 2-26-1857, Versailles, IN d. Ogden, Utah, 2-10-1929. Both he and his mother buried in Mt. View Cemetery. Taught school in Ill. seven years, moving in 1884 to Stockville, NE where in a period of 7 years he was County Clerk, V. Pres. of a bank and managed his 1,000 acre ranch. Moved to Ogden in 1891 where he was in the Real Estate and Insurance business for 38 years. A member of Weber Lodge No. 6, A.F. and A.M.,

Figure 39. Sarah Jane Rex-Kelly, Beggs.

Ogden Chpt. Royal Arch Masons, El Monte Commandry No. 2 Knights Templar, Utah Consistory No. 1 Scottish Rite and El Kalah Temple, Order Mystic Shrine, B.P.O. Elks No. 719, Ogden Real Estate Board and Chamber of Commerce. Was an active Republican and served as State Senator in 1911. m. 5-6-1888 Emma Mathis (daughter of John and St. Helena Hand Mathis) at Phila., IL. Parents of two children.

   (1) Dana[6] Kelly, b. 3-24-1887, Stockville, NE Grad. University of Chicago. Taught many years in Ogden schools and now principal State School for Blind, Ogden. Past Pres. Ogden Art Society, Past Matron Marian Chpt. No. 14, O.E.S., Grand Marshal Grand Chpt. O.E.S. for State of Utah. Charter member Drama Club, Past Pres. Women's University Club, Ogden. Traveled extensively in Europe and America.

   (2) †Rex[6] Mathis Kelly, b. 8-29-1890, Phila., IL. Grad. Ogden H. S. In World War, 79th Div. Battery A, 312 Field Artillery, in France a year. Discharged Ft. Russell, Wyo. 6-6-1919. Weber Lodge No. 6 A. F. and A.M., B.P.O.E. Lodge No. 719, Ogden. m. Mable France 6-10-1927 d. 11-11-1931 after a week's illness with pneumonia. Always lived in Ogden but the first year of his life. Pres. of Real Estate Board at time of his death, took prominent part in organizing the Archery Club in which he was an officer. Member Herman Baker Post No. 9 American Legion. Services in Masonic Temple, interment Mountain View Cemetery, Ogden.

   b. William[5] Henry Kelly, b. 3-14-1859, Versailles, IN. Was an orchardist, d. 5-19-1917, Ogden, Utah.

m. 2nd, William Harvey Beggs, 3-5-1867 and they had two sons.
c. Carey[5] Temple Beggs b. 9-10-1868 in Jacksonville, IL Lived at
Mytor, UT. m. Emma Laura Bartlett, 8-12-1890 at Stockville,
NE where both their children were born.
  (1) Dorothy[6] Marie Beggs, b. 8-16-1891, m. Harold King-
  Palmer 7-31-1918.
  (2) Robert[6] Harvey Beggs, b. 5-3-1893, d. 11-2-1914.
d. Charles[5] Harvey Beggs, b. 4-27-1871, Jacksonville, IL. Mgr.
Kelly-Beggs Orchards, Ogden, UT. Single. (For Revolutionary
line see Thomas Beggs *The Book O'Begs*).
C. †George[4] Washington Rex (Figure 40) b. 8-29-1842, Ripley Co.,
IN. m. by Rev. Wilmot at Hickman Mills, MO to Anna Bryant,
12-28-1869, who was b. 3-2-1852, daughter of Isaac and Anna
Edmond Bryant. He d. 9-11-1819, Drexel, MO buried Sharon
Church. She d. 5-21-1927. G.W.R. enlisted 8-19-1862 Co. D. 85th
Reg. Ind Vol. Infantry. Discharged 6-21-1865 at Indianapolis, IN.
Parents of seven children. First 5 b. Hickman Mills, MO. Other 2
Lisle, MO.

Figure 40. George Washington Rex and Wife, Anna Bryant, and family. Standing ,left
to right, William T., Cam D., Frank M. Nettie, George S., Fred Band, C. Vivian.

a. Cam[5] D. Rex (Figure 40) b. 1-9-1871, m. 3-18-1902, Holden,
MO by Rev. Boulton to M. Bess L. Bass who was born 12-12-
1879, daughter of James H. and Scynthia Elizabeth Woolfolk
Bass. Parents of 1 child.
  (1) Anna[6] Elizabeth Rex b. 11-19-1904, Drexel, MO. m. F.
  Clifton Broadhurst 5-29-1920.
b. William[5] T. Rex (Figure 40) b. 7-8-1872, m. Esther H. Noble

2-26-1900, Drexel, MO. Had 2 children.

(1) William[6] Harold Rex b. 1-1-1903, Geologist with Shell Co., Eldorado, KS.

(2) Helen[6] Esther Rex b. 7-31-1908, MO. U. 1929.

c. Ethel[5] Velnetti Rex b. 1-10-1874. Single.

d. Frank[5] Merritt Rex (Figure 40) b. 7-14-1875, m. Nell M. Jackson 10-14-1902, Kansas City, MO. Parents of 2 children.

(1) Harriett[6] Frances Rex b. 10-2-1905, Lisle, MO.

(2) Mildred[6] Nell Rex b. 11-21-1910, Lisle, MO. m 10-6-1932 Robert O. Reich, Kansas City, MO.

e. George[5] S. Rex b. 12-5-1877, d. 11-4-1925, Des Moines, IA. Held responsible position for 30 yrs with Swift and Co. m. Chicago, IL, Bess Moore 2-10-1910. No issue.

f. Fred[5] B. Rex b. 6-24-1880. Farmer and Stockman, single.

g. Vivian[5] Rex b. 8-8-1896, m. Jewel Jeans, Paola, KS.

D. Elizabeth[4] Avaline Rex b. 3-16-1846, Ripley Co., IN (near Versailles) d. Peoria, IL 7-13-1913, husband d. 7-4-1915, both buried Ashland, IL. m. 9-28-1869 near Hickmans Mills, MO. Marion H. Pritchett who was b. 9-21-1842. Parents of 6 children.

a. Carl[5] Templeton Pritchett b. 9-26-1870, Springfield, IL where he has always lived. m. Anna Mathens, Springfield, IL, 1887. Parents of seven children and ten living grandchildren (1931).

b. Mary[5] Vintonel Pritchett b. Toronto, IN 10-13-1872 and d. 3-5-1928. She buried Ashland, IL. m. Edward Bockemuehl of Peoria, IL. He b. 8-16-1860, Baltimore, MD and d. 6-26-1904. No issue.

c. Charles[5] Rex Pritchett b. Toronto, IN 11-13-1874. d. 6-6-1898, Peoria, IL and buried Ashland. Was single.

d. George[5] Vivian Pritchett b. Virginia, IL 7-13-1877, m. Virginia A. Wires, Peoria. Widower and lived with his sister, Mrs. Kocian. (He had the William Winters Rex Bible).

e. Florence[5] Bussell Pritchett, b. Ashland, IL 6-29-1882, m. George E. Kocian 8-23-1900. 1 son.

(1) George[6] Herbert Kocian b. 3-23-1902, Peoria, IL. m. Idabell Vonhonter, 10-23-1924.

F. Mary[4] Ann Rex (Mollie) b. Versailles, IN 7-11-1860, d. 1887, Pasadena, CA. m. Charles Newton Stanley 2-26-1874 who was b. 3-4-1846. 1 daughter.

a. Eva[5] Rex Stanley b. 1-6-1876, Indianapolis, IN. On 9-19-1901 m. Charles Edwards Rice, dentist, who was b. 1-12-1876, San

Francisco, CA. (Son of Sarah Gideon Edwards and Hugh Brown Rice, he b. 10-1840 d. 10-30-1905 and she b. 4-15-1846). Three children, all born at 1341 W. 25th St., Los Angeles, CA.

(1) Charles[6] Stenley Rice, b. 10-26-1902, m. 11-24-1926, Mina Cecelia Norton, daughter of Mary Agnes Curran and Charles Warren Norton.

(2) Marian[6] Elizabeth Rice b. 8-18-1906 d. 6-1909.

(3) William[6] Theron Rice b. 7-25-1910, m. Annabelle Kaltenbach. 1 son.

  +William[7] Frederick Rice b. 2-12-1932.

2. Margaret[3] Rex (2nd child of Jane and George[2] Rex, George[1]) b. 3-28-1808, m. Samuel Harper 6-4-1835. She is buried in Sharon Cemetery near Drexel, MO. Had a daughter Elizabeth Margaret Harper (Lizzie) d. 4-18-1896, who wrote a letter to Mrs. Beggs from Versailles, IN, 2-23-1891, in which she tells family data as her mother is telling it to her. There was another daughter Isabel Harper Durbin who had a daughter Fannie Durbin Dickenson.

3. Samuel[3] Rex (3rd child of Jane and George[2] Rex, George[1]) b. 1-17-1810 d. 9-20-1836. No issue.

4. Mary[3] Rex, (4th child of Jane and George[2] Rex, George[1]) b. 8-17-1811, d. 2-20-1869. m. Alexander Dunlap on 9-10-1835 who was b. in PA 2-1-1810, d. Kansas 8-23-1879. Parents 11 children.

A. Martha[4] Jane Dunlap, b. 6-7-1836, d. 9-3-1859 Washington, PA. Single.

B. Hannah[4] Lacky Dunlap b. 9-27-1838, d. 4-29-1880 near Howard, Kansas. Single.

C. †John[4] Randolph Dunlap b. 8-12-1840, d. about 1910. Buried in Los Angeles. Civil War veteran (carried a bullet in his side till his death). m. Lavina Faddis, Jefferson, PA. Parents of 6 children.

  a. William[5] Dunlap b. in PA d. Los Angeles, CA 1911. Widow and children in Los Angeles. One daughter has large family near Battleford, Saskatchewan., Canada.

  b. Charles[5] Dunlap, m. twice. (Children are by 1st wife) as follows

  (1) Frances[6] Dunlap.

  (2) John[6] Dunlap, married.

  (3) Mary[6] Dunlap.

  (4) Alma[6] Dunlap, died young.

    c. Frances[5] Dunlap, m. Stog Smith, M. D., died Jefferson, PA. Had 2 children.

      (1) Frank[6] Smith, living in PA.

      (2) John[6] Smith, married and has children, San Bernardino, CA.

    d. John[5] Mead Dunlap, b. near Howard, KS and d. Los Angeles, CA. m. 1st at St. Louis, MO. 2 children. Children of 2nd wife also in Los Angeles, CA.

      (1) Elmer[6] Dunlap, Los Angeles, CA.

      (2) Dorothy[6] Dunlap, Los Angeles, CA.

    e. Clara[5] Dunlap, b. 8-13-1877, d. 10-16-1912, Los Angeles, CA. m. Elga Bruckner 10-16-1903. 3 children.

      (1) LaVenia[6] Bruckner b. 10-17-1904, PA. m. Graydon Randolph 12-1923. 1 daughter.

      +Clara[7] Victoria Randolph b. 9-1924, S. Mt., PA.

      (2) Frances[6] Bruckner b. 2-22-1905. Supt. Nurses, Hospital, Los Angeles, CA.

      (3) Harry[6] Bruckner b. 3-20-1911, Los Angeles, CA.

    f. Andrew[5] Dunlap b. near Howard, Kansas has several children, lived Chicago.

D. Mary[4] Margaret Dunlap b. 6-11-1842, d. 10-13-1891. m. at Henderson, IL 9-5-1867, Alex. Shannon who was b. 2-28-1828, Billingsville, IN d. 1-15-1887. Had 5 sons all born near Henderson, Ill. and 4 buried there with their parents.

    a. John[5] Shannon b. 8-3-1868, d. 8-30-1870.

    b. Charles[5] N. Shannon b. 10-14-1870, d. 9-20-1922.

    c. George[5] Dunlap Shannon b. 64-1872, m. 11-11-1903, Ida A. Pemnan who was b. 6-14-1880, Brazil, IN. Parents of two children. G. D. S., Atty. Terre Haute, where he resided for the past 30 years, had a letter written by Grandfather Alex Dunlap to his mother, dated 1-24-1871, which gives much of this family data.

      (1) William[6] Rex Shannon b. 6-3-1906, Terre Haute, IN. m. 4-4-1928, Elma Marie Holdaway b. 2-10-1912, New Goshen, IN.

      (2) Helen[6] Shannon b. 3-27-1909, Terre Haute, IN.

    d. Fred[5] W. Shannon b. 12-10-1874, d. 4-3-1905. Single.

    e. Alex[5] Rex Shannon b. 9-1-1877, d. 10-25-1902, Single.

E. †Samuel[4] Rex Dunlap b. 4-3-1844, d. 1-13-1863 in Civil War. Buried Fort Schyler.

F. Sara[4] Ann Dunlap b. 8-6-1846, d. 5-8-1877. m. Houston Kerr near Carmichaels, PA. Buried there. 2 children.

    a. George[5] Kerr, Cumberland Presbyterian Minister.

    b. Louise[5] Kerr d. young.

G. George[4] Washington Dunlap b. Uniontown, PA 2-13-1848, d. near Howard, KS. 1894. Bur. Forrest School. m. Anna Shriver, IL about 1874. 6 children.

    a. Mary[5] Ellen Dunlap.

    b. Alex[5] Henderson Dunlap b. Elk Co., KS 12-16-1876. m. 1st Jessie Easley 1903, Piedmont, KS. d- 8-24-1913- m. 2nd Eulah Jenkins 1-17-1917, Piedmont. By 1st wife, 2 children.

      (1) Clifford[6] Thomas Dunlap b. Piedmont 1-1-1909, d. 4-23-1918.

      (2) Madaline[6] Mardell Dunlap b. 3-23-1912, Granite City, IL. Teacher. m. John M. Bennett, Madison, KS. Are Methodists. 1 daughter.

        +Barbara[7] Jean Bennett b. 1-1932.

    By 2nd wife, 2 children.

      (3) Clara[6] Frances Dunlap b. 3-2-1918, Piedmont, KS.

      (4) Gertrude[6] Estelle Dunlap b. 5-13-1921, Springfield, MO.

    c. Elizabeth[5] Dunlap d. in infancy.

    d. John[5] Collie Dunlap b. 9-23-1881, Elk Co., KS m. Bertha St. Louis, MO. 1 child.

      (1) Leona[6] Dunlap b. Granite City, IL 1907. m. Hugh Rahinson 6-1925. 2 daughters:

        +Betty[7] Lee Rahinson.

        +Alice[7] Ann Rahinson.

    e. Clara[5] Frances Dunlap b. 2-1888. m. Jess Moss, 1918.

    f. George[5] Rex Dunlap.

H. Joseph[4] Alexander Dunlap b. 3-7-1850 Fayette Co., PA. d. near Howard, KS 4-2-1911. Bur. Forrest School. m. Harriett Samantha Billingly b. 1-30-1848 near California, Wash. Co., PA. 8 children.

    a. Mary[5] Elizabeth Dunlap b. 10-12-1871, Calif. PA. d. 10-23-1926 and bur. Leavenworth, KS. At Howard, KS. 2-11-1899, m. Harmon Allen, M. E. Minister. Grad. Kansas State Teachers College, 1898. 6 children.

      (1) Joseph[6] Levi Dunlap Allen b. 12-2-1899, Evanston, IL Grad. Kans. State Agricultural College, 1923. m. Agnita Ellis (teacher) 6-19-1926. Manufacturer of Creamery Products. 3 children.

        +Joseph[7] Ellis Allen b. 4-22-1928.

+Phillip[7] Edward Allen b. 9-1930, d. 2-1931.

+Virginia[7] Ann Allen b. 11-1932.

(2) Harriett[6] Jane Allen b. Evanston, IL 11-28-1902. Grad.
K.U. 1925. m. 10-19 Forrest Lee Noll teacher at
Leavenworth, KS. 2 children.

+Lewis[7] Harmon Noll b. 10-30-1925, Easton, KS.

+Forrest[7] Lee Noll, Jr. b. 3-6-1929, Lawrence, KS. Teacher,
Lawrence, KS. 1 child.

(3) Edward[6] Harmon Allen b. 1-16-1906, Mound, KS. Grad. K.
U. 1928, Teacher. m. 3-30-1929 Willardean Harner, teacher,
Lawrence, KS. 1 child.

+Phyllis[7] Joan Allen b. 2-1932.

(4) Mary[6] Frances Allen b. 2-1907 Mound City, KS. Teacher m.
Lawrence, KS. 6-7-1930 Gustav Geiger, K. City, KS.

(5) George[6] Hadley Allen b. 8-16-1912, Caney, KS.

(6) Elizabeth[6] Louise Allen b. 11-20-1917, Lansing, KS.

b. Emma[5] May Dunlap (teacher) b. 11-9-1873, Calif, PA Grad.
Kans. State Teachers College 1902. Miss D. and her sister, Mrs.
Allen, furnished much of the Dunlap data.

c. Anna[5] G. Dunlap b. Calif. PA. 7-23-1876 m. George Crawford
Harrison 4-8-1903, Howard, KS. Parents of 4 children.

(1) Burnace[6] Dunlap Harrison b. 3-13-1904, Marion Kansas.
Grad. Southwestern College. Chicago Sales Dept. Donnelly
Pub. Co. Single.

(2) Dorace[6] Dunlap Harrison b. 11-17-1906, Quinlan, OK.
Salesman. m. Louise Miller 8-27-1927, Winfield, KS. 1
daughter.

+Betty[7] Louise Miller b. 4-13-1929, Winfield, KS.

(3) Eva[6] LaVerne Harrison b. 7-14-1908, Quinlan, OK. m.
12-21-1929, Alfred Lee Price. 1 son.

+Alfred[7] Lee Price, Jr. b. 1-8-1931.

(4) George[6] Verrel Harrison b and d. 7-23-1910, Quinlan, OK.

d. Sierra[5] Nevara Dunlap b. 11-13-1878, Howard, KS. d. 2-26-
1920, m. Claud B. Taylo 3-26-1904, Howard, KS. 2 daughters.

(1) Mary[6] Margaret Taylo b. 12-21-1904, Howard, KS..
Teacher. Grad. Phillips U., Enid, OK 1928.

(2) Julia[6] Agnes Taylo b. 8-26-1906, Howard, KS.

e. James[5] Harrison Dunlap b. 3-25-1882, Howard, m. Ruth
Armstrong 3-14-1906 at Howard. Fruit grower. 2 children.

(1) Harry[6] Carl Dunlap b. 5-24-1907, Howard, m. Emma Lee

Waldrop 11-20-1928 at Shawnee, OK. A draftsman, Amarillo, TX.

(2) Alma[6] Ruth Dunlap b. Howard 10-26-1911. m. Howard Wilson 9-23-1929, Fayetteville, AR. 1 son.

+Harry[7] Howard Wilson b. 7-26-1930.

f. Ernest[5] Charles Dunlap b. 7-29-1885, Howard, KS. m. Bertha Aaron 6-23-1909 Leavenworth, KS. Advertising Mgr. Enid Daily Eagle. Parents 3 children.

(1) Emma[6] Jane Dunlap b. 6-10-1912, Sedgwick, KS.

(2) Margaret[6] Ellen Dunlap b. 1-17-1916, Enid, OK.

(3) Mary[6] Alice Dunlap b. 9-23-1918, Enid, OK.

g. Earl[5] George Dunlap b. 7-29-1885, Howard, KS d. 12-31-1886.

h. Zirn[5] Norwell Dunlap b. 7-2-1888, Howard, KS. m. Bess Alderson 11-28-1911, Sedgwick, KS. 4 children.

(1) Helen[6] Kathlen Dunlap b. 11-1-1914, Winfield, KS.

(2) Dona[6] Belle Dunlap b. 7-28-1918 d. same day.

(3) Barbara[6] Rex Dunlap b. 8-8-1920, Winfield, KS.

(4) Betty[6] Jo Dunlap b. 12-2-1923, Winfield, KS.

The greater portion of the Dunlaps are Methodists.

I. Andrew[4] Jackson Dunlap b. 5-5-1852 d. 9-12-1877 near Howard, KS. m. Elizabeth Southerland who also died. No issue.

J. Elizabeth[4] Katherine Dunlap b. 12-25-1854 d. 11-18-1877, Tripolet, MO. m. Cyrus Sillibaugh, Uniontown, PA. 2 children.

K. Louise[4] Dunlap b. 1-1-1857 d. 1-26-1897. m. David Henderson b. 1-16-1845 d. 5-31-1924. Killed by train, Tripolet, MO 9 children.

a. Sparks[5] Dunlap Henderson b. 11-5-1880, near Henderson, IL.

b. Stewart[5] McKinley Henderson b. 9-21-1891, Engle, MO.

c. Sam[5] J. Henderson b. 8-27-1881.

d. Mary[5] Skinner Henderson b. 7-11-1884.

e. Amanda[5] Henderson b. 4-15-1885 m. 1-17-1907 Clyde E. Buckles b. 4-15-1884, Clyde, KS. A son.

(1) Clyde[6] Nelson Buckles b. 12-7-1921, Independence, KS.

f. James[5] G. Henderson b. 7-11-1884.

g. Ollie[5] May Henderson b. 1-8-1888 m. C. A. Noel, Novinger, MO.

h. Louise[5] Henderson b. 2-8-1894 m. J. E. Husbands.

i. Fannie[5] Pauline Henderson b. 1-16-1897 m. Ernest A. Shultheiss, Yarron, MO.

5. Jane[3] Rex, b. Jefferson, PA 3-25-1815 d. 1-9-1879, Carmichaels,

PA. m. John Haver 3-8-1832. He b. 10-12-1802 in Greene Co., PA, son of George Haver, Jr. and Priscilla Villars (*History of Greene Co.* p. 738). John Haver d. 4-17-1894 in Jefferson, PA. 11 children.

A. †George[4] Rex Haver b. 5-10-1833 in Jefferson, PA and d. 8-3-1914 in Centerville, IA. Was a farmer. m. 1-1-1856 Anna Sarah Neil b. 2-21-1839 in Jefferson, PA d. 7-31-1913 in Appanoose Co., IA. (George Rex Haver, 86th Iowa Vol. Inf. Gen. Dooke Reg. Co. E. Capt. Vermillion Rg.) 7 children.

  a. George[5] William Neil Haver b. 1-18-1857 Jefferson, PA and d. about 12-30-1943 in Centerville, IA. Burried Iconium Cem., Appanoose Co., IA. Worked as farmer. m. 12-24-1883 in Centerville, IA to Emma Adalaide Lemaster born 8-21-1863, Monroe Co., IA and d. 9-22-1943 in Centerville, IA. She was daughter of Willaim A. Lemaster and Clara.

  b. Jane[5] Rex Haver b. 3-10-1859 in IA. m. 10-24-1880 in Appanoose Co., IA to Frank A. Brown who was b. 10-10-1856 in OH and d. 7-29-1926. 1 son.

    (1) George[6] E. Brown b. 1-17-1882 m. 1-1-1907 Leida Newcomb b. 7-20-1887. 2 daughters.

      +Marjorie[7] Eloise Brown b. 3-25-1912, Centerville, IA.

      +Marion[7] Elaine Brown b. 2-29-1915.

  c. Martha[5] June Haver b. 6-1-1861 in Plano, IA and d. 5-17-1880 in Iconium, IA. Burried in Iconium Cemetery, IA. m. 4-3-1879 in Appanoose Co., IA to Alexander Jackson Argo who was b. 11-20-1853 in Pickaway Co., OH and d. 10-25-1932 in Monroe Co., IA. He son of William and Sarah Argo. 3 children.

    (1) Nellie[6] Maud Argo b. 9-29-1880 and d. 6-1963. m. 6-26-1920 John L. Haines b. 12-14-1877.

    (2) Fred[6] Neal Argo b. 8-13-1886 in Appanoose Co., IA and d. 12-12-1963 in Bloomfield, IA. Burried in Iconium Cemetery, IA. m. 9-21-1918 Allie Hawk b. 12-2-1885 and d. 1970 in Albia, IA. She the daughter of James Hawk and Loucinda Hamlin.

    (3) John[6] Roscoe Argo b. 3-20-1894 in Monroe Co., IA m. 6-26-1915 Stella Sytsma b. 5-3-1896.

  d. George[5] Bainet Jake Haver b. 4-23-1863 in IA and d. 12-29-1930 in OK. Burried in Lincoln Co., OK. m. 12-8-1888 in Appanoose Co., IA to Hannah Winnorah Winnie Youngker b. 9-13-1868 in IA and d. 1942. Bur Lincoln Co., OK. She daughter of Benjamin Franklin Youngker and Susan

Funkhouser. 3 children.

(1) Hazel[6] Haver b. 5-18-1889 Springview, NE. d. 10-23-1964 Stillwater, OK. Bur. Stillwater, OK. In a letter from Robert Lyle Williams, "Hazel recalled coming to OK with her parents in a covered wagon between 1892 and 1896. She recalled her brother, Lloyd, asking , 'When will we get there:' during the first mile of the trip. They are believed to have come from Appanoose Co., IA. m. in OK 5-29-1907 to Ledru Barnes b. 11-3-1877 MO and d. 8-28-1943 in Lincoln Co., OK. He son of Richard Franklin Barnes and Mary Jane Hereford. Ledru was a rural mail carrier in the Logan and Lincoln Co. area of OK. He used his salary and local knowledge to acquire a number of farms which later provided a living for his two sons, and mineral rights for the whole family. He was killed while riding a horse alone. The horse, Smokey, was owned by his son Lyle, who was so distraught that he could not attend the funeral. 5 children.

+Frances[7] Maxine Barnes b. 1914 d. 1914.

+Eula[7] May Barnes b. 5-28-1916 Merrick, OK d. 1-17-1994 Bartlesville, OK. m. 3-5-1939 in Stillwater, OK to †Clifford Lyle Williams b. 10-13-1915 in Nowata, OK and d. 2-13-1974 Nowata, OK. He son of George Edward Williams and Maggie May Whittaker. He was an accomplished trombone player in High School. He joined the military and was sationed at the 'Bomber Plant' (now the McDonnell Douglas/American Airlines facilities) in Tulsa, OK from 1943 to 1945. He then ran a lumberyard until his death in 1974. 2 children.

^Robert[8] Lyle Williams b. 6-22-1942 Nowata, OK OK State U. 1964 BS Economics, Baylor 1965 MBA. Officer USN. Employed financial management at Ford then Treasurer Agrico Chemical, Tulsa, OK, then VP/CFO Texas City Refining, Houston, then Private consulting, then joined FBI. m. 6-12-1965 in Nowata, OK to Lorene Linnet Dillahunty b. 7-8-1943 Barnsdall, OK. She daughter of Fred Dillahunty and Ruby Amelia Broam. She received BS in Bocational Home Economics from OK State U in 1965. She taught in High School but became accomplished water colorist. 1 daughter.

~Eleanor[9] Lynn Williams b. 10-17-1969 Dearborn, MI.

Received graduate level certificate in arts administration from NY City U.

^George[8]Lee Williams b. 8-14-1947 Bartlesville, OK. Grad NE OK Junior College. Lives San Diego, CA. m. 11-16-1979 San Diego, CA to Rachel b. about 1947.

+Elmo[7] George Barnes b. 2-13-1919 Merrick, OK. m. 8-26-1942 Inez Christy Hinde b. about 1919.

+Elaine[7] Francis Barnes b. 7-13-1921 Logan Co., OK d. 4-4-1962 CT. m. 8-26-1938 in Stillwater, OK to Lawrince Alvin Crable b. about 1921

+Eugene[7] Lyle Barnes b. 4-24-1924 Logan Co., OK. m. 1st Betty Ruth Demaree b. about 1924. m. 2nd 12-13-1946 Ella Nadine Hesser b. about 1924.

(2) George[6] Lloyd Barnes Haver b. 1892 m. 1911 Mattie Graham b. 1893. 2 children.

+Forrest[7] Lloyd Haver b. 1912. m. Luena b. about 1912.

+Roland[7] Haver b. 1917.

(3) Richard[6] P. Haver b. 1896 m. 1916 Grace Cooper b. 1897. 2 children.

+Kathryn[7] Haver b. 1919.

+Eldred[7] Haver b. 1927.

e. John[5] Chauncy Haver b. 12-29-1868 in Greene Co., PA and d 1947. Burried in Lincoln Co., OK. m. 1st 1-13-1897 Ola Newby b. 9-19-1872. d. 5-13-1908. m. 2nd Stella Johnson Smith b. 1-29-1882. 3 children by first wife.

(1) Stella[6] Margaret Haver b. 7-8-1898 m. 2-11-1916 J. F. Cassidy b. 6-4-1892. 4 children.

+Baby girl[7] Cassidy b. and d. 11-16-1916.

+Clifford[7] Cassidy b. 2-6-1918.

+Clyde[7] Cassidy b. 9-17-1920.

+Mary[7] Maxine Cassidy b. 10-12-1923.

(2) John[6] Rex Haver b. 2-28-1902 Merrick, OK Territory and d. 7-20-1983 in Centerville, IA. Burried in Moravia, IA. m. 3-28-1923 Leta Faye Cicle b. 3-21-1905 in Chandler, OK and d. 10-8-1989 in Centerville, IA. She was daughter of William Levi Cicle and Lillie Riggs. 2 children.

+Ola[7] Faye Haver b. 10-19-1924 in OK and d. 1930.

+Edward[7] Rex Haver b. 12-20-1925 in Fallis, OK and d. 3-3-1990 in Centerville, IA. m. 6-22-1955 in Moravia, IA to Betty Kathryn Wakefield b. 12-27-1929 in Mystic, IA. She was daughter of Glen Arthur Wakefield and Louise Shulski. 1 daughter.

^Julie[8] Kay Haver b. 12-28-1957 in Centerville, IA. m. 3-13-1976 in Unionville, MO to Timothy Michaels Seals b. 8-3-1959. 4 children.

~Shannon[9] Renee Seals b. 10-4-1976 in Centerville, IA.

~Michael[9] Ryan Seals b. 2-8-1979 in Ottumwa, IA

~Ashley[9] Jo Seals b. 3-1-1984 in Centerville, IA.

~Kriston[9] Kay Seals b. 10-6-1989 in Centerville, IA.

+Phyllis[7] Colene Haver b. 9-20-1933 in Moravia, IA. m. 11-25-1950 to John Hiner b. about 1933. 2 children.

^Johnette[8] Colene Hiner b. 6-20-1951 in Centerville, IA. m. 9-14-1974 to Terry Rodriquez b. about 1951. 3 children.

~Jolene[9] Rodriquez b. about 1976.

~Gina[9] Rodriquez b. about 1978.

~Nicholas[9] Rodriquez b. about 1978.

^Gregory[8] Alan Hiner b. 6-13-1955 in Davenport, IA. m. 7-6-1974 to Denise b. about 1955. 3 children.

~Anthony[9] Hiner b. about 1976.

~Brett[9] Hiner b. about 1978.

~Cara[9] Hiner b. about 1980.

^Joseph[8] Paul Hiner b. 2-23-1959 in Davenport, IA. m. to Dawn b. about 1959.

(3) Mildred[6] Edna Haver b. 6-9-1905 in Merrick, OK and d. 4-4-1982 in Centerville, IA. Buried in Dale Cemetery, Appanoose Co., IA. m. 6-8-1933 in Centerville, IA to Golda Deahl b. about 1905.

f. Eldred[5] Glover Haver b. 5-1-1872 in IA. Lived in Merrick, OK. m. 10-29-1893 in Appanoose Co., IA to Suda Younker, she b. 1873.

g. Sarah[5] Anna Haver b. 7-1879 in IA d. 8-1881 in Appanoose Co., IA. Bur. Salem Cem. Appanoose Co., IA.

B. Sarah[4] Jane Haver b. 9-25-1835 in Greene Co., PA and d. 5-25-1870 m. 2-21-1856 in Greene Co., PA to John Davis b. 4-15-1834 and d.-12-22-1919. He son of William Davis and Harriet. 4 children.

a. George[5] Christopher Davis 4-5-1860 near Jefferson, PA. Educated Monongahela College and Southwestern PA State Normal. 21 years a teacher, principal Greensboro, PA Schools, etc. m. Carrie Throckmorton (daughter Mary and James T.) 9-20-1887. In real estate business Birmingham, AL since 1906. 3 children.

   (1) Mary[6] Sarah Davis b. 6-19-1888 Jefferson, PA m. 6-30-1909, Birmingham, AL Alfred Hickman Wiltshire, d. 1-1-1917. 1 son.

   +George[7] Cullett Wiltshire b. 7-24-1911, d. 1-1-1915.

   (2) Katie[6] May Davis b. Greensboro, PA 8-31-1890 m. Robert Llewellyn Hawkins 9-20-1911, Birmingham, AL. Electrician R. R. Shops Meridian, Miss. 4 sons all b. Birmingham, AL.

   +James[7] Llewellyn Hawkins b. 8-21-1912.

   +William[7] Harvey Hawkins b. 11-23-1914.

   +Donald[7] Andrew Hawkins b. 9-30-1917.

   +Robert[7] Davis Hawkins b. 12-9-1919.

   (3) Anna[6] Throckmorton Davis b. 1-20-1896 Carmichaels, PA. m. Charles Bondurant Bernard 9-14-1916 Birmingham, AL. 2 children

   +Eleanor[7] Bernard b. 8-5-1917.

   +Charles[7] B. Bernard, Jr. b. 9-30-1919.

 b. William[5] Randolph Davis b. 6-8-1862 m. Annie McNeely b. about 1862. 7 children.

   (1) Wayne[6] Davis b. about 1887.

   (2) Pearl[6] Davis b. about 1889.

   (3) Eva[6] Davis b. about 1891.

   (4) Charles[6] Davis b. about 1893.

   (5) George[6] Davis b. about 1895.

   (6) Mary[6] E. V. Davis b. about 1897.

   (7) William[6] Davis b. about 1899.

 c. Charles[5] Gibson Davis b. 10-3-1864 and d. 1933. Burried in Greene Co., PA m. Laura B. Smith d. 1919. 2 children.

   (1) John[6] H. Davis b. 6-5-1897 Jefferson, PA and d. 1960. Burried in Greene Co., PA. Was farmer and never m.

   (2) Mary[6] H. Davis b. 12-23-1899 Jefferson, PA and d. 9-19-1996 in Waynesburg, PA. Bur. Greene Co., PA.

 d. Ida[5] E. Davis b. 3-14-1867, d. single.

C. John[4] Haver, Jr. b. 10-18-1837 in Jefferson, Greene Co., PA. disappeared. Was stock dealer.

D. Priscilla[4] Haver b. 1-26-1840 Greene Co., PA. d. 2-21-1913 in Jefferson, PA.

E. Mary[4] Elizabeth Haver b. 2-10-1842 Jefferson, PA. d. 12-24-

1924 Jefferson, PA. Never m. Bur. Cumberland Pres. Church Cem. Jefferson, PA.

F. †Hiram[4] Haver b. 3-20-1844 Greene Co., PA. d. 6-4-1912 Omaha, NE. Burried in Bonesteel Pilot Cm., Gregory Co., SD. On 3-7-1867 m. Hannah Rush who was b. 3-29-1846 d. 3-3-1923. She was daughter of Jacob Strawn Rush and Charlotte Kelley. He enlisted Union Army 11-11-1861 joining 85th Reg. Co. D Penna. Vol. Served 3 yrs, 3 mos. Moved to Iconium, IA about 1869 then lived Fairfax, S. D. and worked as a farmer. 7 children.

a. Charlotte[5] Jane Haver b. 6-10-1867 in PA, and d. 12-2-1940 in SD. Bur. Bonesteel, SD. m. Edward B. Tarr. He b. 4-27-1868 in IL. and d. 6-2-1946 in Bonesteel, SD. He was son of John Tarr and Regina Weinberg. 9 children.

(1) Horace[6] B. Tarr b. 11-2-1889 in IA m. Dora Fruits. She b. 6-21-1892. 4 children.

+ †Verne[7] V. Tarr b. 4-14-1915. Served in USN during WW II. m. Eileen London b. 9-24-1921. 8 children.

^ †Robert[8] Vern Tarr b. 12-25-1942. 1st US Army. m. Muriel L. Benson. She b. 12-31-1946. 1 son.

~Robert[9] Joseph Tarr b. 8-6-1965.

^Patricia[8] Lynn Tarr b. 3-24-1945. 1 daughter.

~Camille[9] Lynn Tarr b. 8-3-1965.

^Susan[8] Kaye Tarr b. 6-19-1947. m. Roy Tyndall b. 1-13-1945. 1 son.

~Mark[9] Christopher Tyndall b. 7-31-1966.

^Michael[8] Horace Tarr b. 6-4-1949.

^Douglas[8] Eugene Tarr b. 12-2-1950.

^Charles[8] Ray Tarr b. 2-22-1952.

^Timothy[8] Jon Tarr b. 3-5-1954.

^Shelly[8] Ann Tarr b. 12-22-1955.

^Steven[8] Joseph Tarr b. 10-28-1960.

+Murle[7] Aileen Tarr b. 4-10-1916 m. Orlin Siedenburg b. 8-28-2925. 2 daughters.

^Lana[8] Murle Siedenburg b. 3-14-1943. m. Dennis Johnson b. 3-5-1943.

^Mary[8] Jill Siedenburg b. 1-5-1948.

+Charlotte[7] L. Tarr b. 5-26-1919 m. Vernon Smith b. 8-26-1914. 3 children.

^Diane[8] Jeanne Smith b. 2-17-1943. m. Gerald Orlin Rabe b. about 1943.

^Vernon[8] Ray Smith b. 1-16-1948

^Cynthia[8] Lou Smith b. 8-26-1953.

+ †Tim[7] Edward Tarr b. 1-2-1928. In US Navy Lived McLean, VA. m. Nancy Brown b. 12-20-1936

+Samuel[7] Burton Tarr b. 7-2-1935 in US Navy lived Warrenton, VA. m. Elizabeth Goff b. 7-29-1934. 2 children.

^Samuel[8] Burton Tarr, Jr. b. 9-6-1961.

^Donna[8] Elizabeth Tarr b. 9-24-1963.

(2) Floyd[6] H. Tarr b. 12-23-1891 in NE and d. 7-14-1941 in Bonesteel, SD. Bur. Bonesteel, SD.

(3) Lois[6] Marle Tarr b. 3-25-1894 in SD and d. 9-10-1920 Bonsteel, SD. m. Erwin Martin Schultz b. 11-20-1892 and d. 1-11-1964. 3 children.

+Eunice[7] Lois Schultz b. 5-30- 1914 m. Lawrence Frank Huelle b. 7-20-1915. 3 children.

^Robert[8] Laurence Huelle b. 1-11-1941. m. Kathleen Gieschen b. 7-22-1941. 2 daughters.

~Kim[9] Renee Huelle b. 1-1-1961.

~Kari[9] Lynn Huelle b. 10-26-1962.

^Keith[8] Dennis Huelle b. 4-3-1944 m. Jo Ann Rogers b. 10-16-1944. 2 children.

~Carma[9] Huelle b. 1-29-1965.

~Russel[9] James Huelle b. 4-25-1966.

^Jerald[8] Erwin Huelle b. 1-15-1948.

+Dale[7] Erwin Schultz b. 11-10-1915 m. Ruth Neoma Ballantyne b. 12-16-1917. 5 children.

^Neoma[8] Ruth Schultz b.9-6-1941. m. Ronald Dean Higman b. 9-29-1939. 4 children.

~Tamara[9] Lyn Higman b. 9-28-1960.

~Richelle[9] Jean Higman b.5-13-1962.

~Stacia[9] Carol Higman b.5-6-1964.

~Kimberly[9] Deane Higman b. 5-23-1966.

^Carol[8] May Schultz b. 5-3-1943.

^David[8] Dale Schultz b. 11-25-1945.

^Margaret[8] Eunice Schultz b.7-12-1949.

^Nancy[8] Gail Schultz b. 9-20-1953.

+Harlen[7] Lee Schultz b. 9-5-1920. m. 1st Eyvonne Finger b. about 1920 lived in Colbert, WA. 3 children.

^Gerald[8] Lee Schultz b. 6-5-1945.

^James[8] Roland Schultz b. 8-19-1948.

^Lois[8] Jane Schultz b. 3-30-1951.

m. 2nd Roberta[8] Jeanne Eddy b. about 1920. 2 children.

^Debra[8] Lynn Schultz b. 8-4-1955.

^Ellen[8] Schultz b. 6-20-1961.

(4) Goldie[6] Regina Tarr b. 6-6-1896 in SD and m. Frank Vosacek b. 6-4-1885 and d. 11-13-1949. Lived Soux Falls, SD. 2 children.

+ †Richard[7] Tarr Vosacek b. 6-6-1929. In Regular Army lived in San Antonio, TX. m. Lois Burrell b. 7-23-1928. 3 Children.

^Cheryl[8] Vosacek b. 2-23-1950.

^Richard[8] Frank Vosacek b. 4-14-1952.

^Debra[8] Renee Vosacek b. 9-25-1955.

+ †Robert[7] Haver Vosacek b. 7-25-1930. Served Korean Conflict. Lives Longmont, CO. m. Jo Ann Robb b. 7-11-1934. 3 children.

^Jamie[8] Lee Vosacek b. 8-22-1955.

^Denese[8] Jo Vosacek b. 4-20-1958.

^Mark[8] Haver Vosacek b. 9-9-1960.

+Ronald[7] Frank Vosacek b. 5-20-1933. m. Marie Paige b. about 1933.

+Lois[7] Beth Vosacek b. 5-20-1933. m. August McGuffin b. 12-4-1926. 3 children

^Thomas[8] Frank McGuffin b. 7-31-1954.

^Wendy[8] Jill McGuffin b. 10-6-1956.

^Bruce[8] Fred McGuffin b. 2-9-1959.

(5) Helen[6] Eva Tarr b. 4-26-1899 in SD. m. Frank Nebola b. 4-14-1898 and d. 9-11-1937. 4 children.

+Shirley[7] Lorene Nebola b. 11-30-1921. m. 1st Russell Bower b. about 1921. 2 children.

^Dorothy[8] Jane Bower b. 2-7-1940. m. Larry Ray Donohoe b. about 1940 Live in St Maries, ID. 3 children.

~Steward[9] Ray Donohoe b. 5-28-1958.

~Mitchell[9] W. Donohoe b. 12-3-1960.

~Shirlene[9] Kay Donohoe b.9-8-1962.

^Russell[8] Edward Bower b. 7-26-1942. m. Sharon b. about 1942.

Shirley[7] Lorene Nebola m. 2nd Edward N. Briggs b. 8-7-1911. 3 children.

^Terry[8] Lee Briggs b. 4-29-1947.

^James[8] Edward Briggs b. 8-23-1950.

^Sandra[8] Shirlene Briggs b. 3-25-1955.

+Dorothy[7] Helen Nebola b. 1924 d. 1932.

+Frances[7] Jane Nebola b. 11-14-1927. m. Frank E. Hall b. 8-26-1925. 4 children.

  ^Greg[8] Allen Hall b. 3-25-1950.

  ^Gary[8] Ray Hall b. 2-28-1952.

  ^Colleen[8] Kay Hall b. 6-11-1954.

  ^Debra[8] Ann Hall b. 6-4-1955.

+Edward[7] Frank Nebola b. 1-10-1934. m. 1st Marlene Shippy b. 7-26-1935. Live in Yankton, SD. 3 children.

  ^Dorinda[8] Lou Nebola b. 3-23-1955.

  ^Kenneth[8] Frank Nebola b. 3-21-1957.

  ^Melinda[8] Sue Nebola b. 4-11-1962.

  Edward[7] Frank Nebola m. 2nd Albert Moles b. about 1899 no children.

(6) Harry[6] Edward Tarr b. 8-9-1903 and d. 7-16-1960 Bonesteel, SD. Never married and no children.

(7) Lottie[6] Jane Tarr b. 3-12-1906 and d. 5-29-1961 bur. in Bonesteel, SD. m. George Fauser b. 10-28-1904. 3 children.

  +Floyd[7] Louis Fauser b. 11-18-1938 m. Carol Lambert b. 10-1-1948 and live Buena Vista CO. 1 son.

    ^ Danny[8] Louis Fauser b. 3-13-1967.

  +Daniel[7] George Fauser b. 6-3-1943 and d. 1-18-1953.

  +Burt[7] Fauser b. 5-20-1947.

(8) Twins: Mattie[6] May Tarr b. 5-2-1907 and d. 1993 in CT. m. George Kalhurst b. 7-28-1909. 3 children.

  +George[7] Tarr Kalhurst b. 1-17-1939.

  +Lois[7] Jane Kalhurst b. 5-7-1942. m. Richard Emery Bernier b. about 1942. 3 children.

    ^Richard[8] Bernier b. 2-24-1962.

    ^Guy[8] Christopher Bernier b. 12-15-1963.

    ^Christopher[8] Guy Bernier b. 5-13-1965.

  +Helen[7] Jennings Kalhurst. m. to Andrew L. Reinke b. about 1945 .

(9) Mayme[6] M. Tarr b. 5-2-1907. Never married no children.

b. Emma[5] Louise Haver b. 4-5-1869 in IA and d. 9-1951. m. 1st on 12-25-1883 Sherman Burns in Appanoose Co., IA. He b. 1862. 1 child.

(1) Frank[6] Burns b. 8-1884. m. Florence Hoyt b. about 1884. 4

children.
+Burrell[7] Burns b. about 1909.
+Cleo[7] Burns b. about 1911.
+Rex[7] Burns b. about 1913.
+Estelle[7] Burns b. about 1915.
Emma[5] Louise Haver m. 2nd Joseph Garringer, 3 children.
(2) Lester[6] Garringer b. 1891.
(3) †Roy[6] D. Garringer b. 1894 SD, killed in France. 1919, Co. E. 125th Inf. Bur Bonesteel, SD
(4) Lola[6] L. Garringer b. 5-11-1897 SD and d. 7-26-1959. m. Everett Ferguson b. about 1895. 3 children.
+Lorraine[7] D. Ferguson b. 1921.
+Marjorie[7] Ferguson b. 1923.
+Lola[7] Jean Ferguson b. 1925.
c. Anna[5] Belle Haver b. 10-30-1871 in IA and d. 5-15-1948, bur. in Bonsteel, SD. m. Lewis Randolph Tarr in IA. He b. 9-6-1869. 8 children.
(1) †Otis[6] Leo Tarr b. 1-21-1893 and d. 5-25-1961. Veteran of WW I. m. Hazel Irena Christenson Haugham b. 3-16-1898. Lived in Norris, SD. 4 children.
+Lucille[7] Ida Christenson Tarr b. 10-22-1916. m. Clarence Cecil Russell b. 4-11-1906. 4 children.
^Irena[8] Mae Russell b. 1-23-1938.
^Jackie[8] Lee Russell b. 7-16-1939.
^Donald[8] Clarence Russell b. 7-28-1943.
^Frederick[8] David Russell b, 3-12-1946.
+Leonard David Christenson Tarr b. 5-31-1918. m. Wilmena Anna Koellmann b. 3-31-1923. 3 children.
^Harvey[8] Arthur Tarr b. 1-8-1942.
^Richard[8] Allen Tarr b. 1-10-1943 and d. 8-5-1946.
^Franklin[8] Leonard Tarr b.2-26-1944.
+Otis[7] Leo Tarr, Jr. b. 8-18-1926 and d. 11-10-1927.
+Janet[7] Belle Tarr b. 11-29-1928. m. Leonard Hicks b. 8-4-1927. Lived in Norris, SD. 5 children.
^Carol[8] Ann Hicks b.5-6-1950.
^Cheryl[8] Jean Hicks b. 6-28-1954.
^Darlene[8] Rose Hicks b. 11-12-1955.
^Jo Ann[8] Hicks b. 7-12-1959.
^Jerry[8] Andrew Hicks b. 11-26-1967
+Twins: Leo[7] Otis Tarr b. 10-8-1930 and d. 5-15-1950.

+ †Lyle[7] Otis Tarr b. 10-8-1930. Served US Army 1955-1957. m. Gerilyn Wooden Knife b. 3-9-1929. 4 children.

    ^Rita[8] Yvonne Tarr b. 7-28-1953.

    ^Cheryl[8] Jean Tarr b. 7-6-1954 and d. same day.

    ^Leo[8] Richard Tarr b. 1-2-1957.

    ^Larry[8] Evan Tarr. b. 10-31-1958.

+Peggy[7] Ann Tarr b. 3-13-1938. m. Louis Howard Moran b. 9-2-1937. 4 children.

    ^Alneen[8] Rose Moran b. 11-23-1957.

    ^Louis[8] Otis Moran b. 5-21-1959.

    ^Clifford[8] Allen Moran b. 12-10-1960.

    ^Lyle[8] Lee Moran b. 8-29-1962.

+Rose[7] Etta Tarr b. 6-21-1939. m. Virgil Milton Huber b. 3-3-1934. 3 children.

    ^Leon[8] Virgil Huber b. 11-13-1958.

    ^Lyndon[8] Dale Huber b. 11-17-1960.

    ^Anita[8] Peggy Huber b. 12-10-1965.

(2) Isa[6] Verl Tarr b. 12-25-1894 m. Albert Hermsen b. 11-30-1893. 4 children.

+ †Donald[7] Hermsen b. 12-3-1917. WW II veteran. m. Jenny McKay b.5-18-1927. 1 daughter.

    ^Kathy[8] Ann Hermsen b. 8-4-1958.

+Delmar[7] Vere Hermsen b. 6-14-1924. m. Jewel Pitchford b. 8-19-1922. 2 children.

    ^Keith[8] D. Hermsen b. 2-10-1943. m. Marjory Frash b. 7-19-1944. 1 son.

        ~Rodney[9] Neal Hermsen b. 2-21-1963.

    ^Judel[8] Ann Hermsen b. 11-3-1947. m. Lee Weidner b. about 1947. 2 children.

        ~Beth[9] Ann Weidner b. 4-5-1966.

        ~Steven[9] Lee Weidner b. 4-21-1967.

+Albert[7] Hermsen, Jr. b. 1-31-1926. m. Joyce Rehberg b. 7-26-1926. 2 children.

    ^Gayle[8] Elizabeth Hermsen b. 5-29-1952.

    ^Gregg[8] Richard Hermsen b. 4-15-1952.

+Wayne[7] Rex Hermsen b. 4-17-1934. m. Marcella Vroman b. 2-27-1934. 5 children.

    ^Robin[8] Lee Hermsen b. 6-20-1952.

    ^Darcy[8] Ann Hermsen b. 12-4-1955.

    ^Darla[8] Rae Hermsen b. 4-26-1958.

^Rory^8 Wayne Hermsen b.12-24-1960
^Darcella^8 Rae Hermsen b.5-24-1963.
(3) John^6 Hiram Tarr b. 8-21-1897 m. Martha Bendig b. 2-21-1905. 5 children.
  +Bertha^7 Tarr b. 12-9-1921. m. Harold Metcalf b. 7-5-1915. 3 children.
    ^Rene^8 E. Metcalf b. 9-16-1942. m. Neva Siddall b. 1-24-1946. 1 son,
    ~Michael^9 M. Metcalf b. 12-2-1964.
    ^Gary^8 O. Metcalf b. 12-13-1943. m. Barbara Otto b. 6-17-1947. 1 son.
    ~Edward^9 L. Metcalf b. 4-10-1966.
    ^Martha^8 F. Metcalf b. 1-7-1949. m. George E. Skinner b. 12-25-1947.
  +Billie^7 Gerald Tarr b. 10-18-1926. m. VaLaura Crawford b. 1-7-1932. 3 children.
    ^Diana^8 Lou Tarr b. 8-23-1951.
    ^John^8 Edmond Tarr b. 5-15-1953.
    ^Gerald^8 LaWayne Tarr b. 12-2-1955.
  +Jack^7 Louis Tarr b. 2-4-1929. m. Maureen Webber b. 7-4-1929. 5 children.
    ^Dale^8 Louis Tarr b. 6-19-1952.
    ^Jack^8 Louis Tarr, Jr. b. 2-4-1955.
    ^Cindy^8 Marie Tarr b. 1-11-1957.
    ^Kevin^8 Bernard Tarr b.5-2-1960.
    ^Kyle^8 John Tarr b. 2-2-1965.
  +Twila^7 Tarr b. 7-6-1931. m. Delbert Wade b. 2-4-1920. 3 children.
    ^Catherine^8 Wade b. 5-10-1957.
    ^Delbert^8 Wade, Jr. b. 6-12-1958.
    ^Raymond^8 Wade b. 6-9-1959.
  +Anna^7 Belle Tarr b. 4-14-1933. m. Clayton Leo Muller b. 8-10-1928. 3 children.
    ^Phyllis^8 June Muller b. 1-19-1952.
    ^Susan^8 Kay Muller b. 10-6-1953.
    ^John^8 Leo Muller b. 8-6-1956.
(4) Edna^6 Mae Tarr b. 4-28-1899 m. Pat A. Johnson b. 5-18-1892. and d. 2-18-1935. 5 children.
  +Betty^7 Jean Johnson b. 9-1-1924. m. Raymond Nagel b. 9-17-1921 and d. 12-9-1958. 1 son.

^Dennis[8] Dean Nagel b. 12-10-1949.
+Velda[7] Mae Johnson b. 5-16-1926. m. Stanley Vosika b. 4-20-1925. 2 children.
   ^Sandra[8] Kay Vosika b. 5-10-1945. m. Weary Young b. 6-16-1945. 2 children.
      ~Brent[9] Leroy Young b. 6-20-1967.
      ~Brenda[9] Leann Young b. 5-25-1967.
   ^Craig Stanley Vosika b. 6-29-1960
+Kenneth[7] Ward Johnson b. 8-20-1929. m. Patricia Ann Abel b. 3-3-1931. 5 children.
   ^Kenneth[8] Ward Johnson, Jr. b. 5-30-1953.
   ^Carol[8] Ann Johnson b. 1-3-1955.
   ^Connie[8] Johnson b. 3-18-1956.
   ^Ronnie[8] Johnson b. 3-18-1956.
   ^Scott[8] Patrick Johnson b. 11-1-1965
+Dwight[7] Leroy Johnson b. 5-1-1931. m. Ruth Stores b. 9-1-1932. 2 daughters.
   ^Debra[8] Lee Johnson b. 8-20 1954.
   ^Danna[8] Lynn Johnson b. 10-17-1955.
+Patricia[7] Ann Johnson b. 2-23-1935. m. Walter Jame Whiting b. 6-2-1928. 3 children.
   ^Ricky[8] James Whiting b. 7-2-1957.
   ^Cheryl[8] Ann Whiting b. 4-5-1959.
   ^Tammy[8] Jo Whiting b. 11-26-1966.
(5) Harold[6] Arthur Tarr b. 2-19-1902 m. Inda F. Blitzkie b. 9-23-1900. 3 children.
   +Loreen[7] Mae Tarr b. 11-20-1925. m. Alfred W. Schultz, Sr. b. 9-15-1921. Lived in Bonesteel, SD. 4 children.
      ^Alfred[8] W. Schultz, Jr. b. 9-24-1948.
      ^Eugene[8] Schultz b. 5-6-1951.
      ^Bonnie[8] Schultz b. 10-3-1952.
      ^Myron[8] Schultz b. 11-26-1956.
   +Geraldine[7] Joyce Tarr b. 10-22-1927 and d. 1-15-1959. m. Robert L. Stahlecker b. 11-26-1927. 4 children.
      ^Rodney[8] James Stahlecker b. 7-25-1947.
      ^Roberta[8] Stahlecker b. 12-31-1948.
      ^Randy[8] Stahlecker b. 3-17-1950.
      ^Roger[8] Stahlecker b. 2-6-1957.
   +Coreen Jean Tarr b. 8-23-1936. m. Harold Dobbin b. 6-15-1927. 5 children.

^Beverly[8] Dobbin b. 7-4-1953.

^David[8] Dobbin b. 1-7-1955.

^Lorin[8] Dobbin b. 9-25-1957.

^Dorinda[8] Dobbin b. 3-28-1959.

^Ellen[8] Dobbin b. 11-7-1961.

(6) Lawrence[6] Lewis Tarr b. 1-14-1904.

(7) Doris[6] June Tarr b. 6-6-1906 and d. 11-6-1913..

(8) Ruth[6] Bernita Tarr b. 4-30-1910. m. Ted Klein b. 12-24-1904. 1 son

+Max[7] Lee Klein b. 2-2-1947.

(9) Thelma[6] Marie Tarr b. 6-14-1916 and d. 4-18-1965. m. Irwin Schlacht b. 3-14-1915 and d. 1-5-1964. 1 daughter.

+Jacqueline[7] Marie Schlacht b. 7-18-1947. m. Myron Runzeloff b. about 1947. 1 son.

^Dale[8] Allen Runzeloff b. 9-8-1965.

d. Mary[5] Elizabeth Haver b. 10-31-1873 in Icomiun, IA. and d. 4-1-1960 in Burke, SD. Bur.in Bonesteel, SD. m. 12-26-1894 in SD James Henry Preston Williams b. 4-22-1869 and d. 6-22-1933 in Bonesteel, SD. He was son of Stephen Henry Dixie Williams b. 8-10-1843 Smith Co., VA and d. 12-8-1913 Gregory Co., SD, bur. Burke, SD and Rachel Matilda Cassel b. 12-10-1846 in Withville, VA and d. 8-3-1926 bur. Lucas, SD. He worked as a Farmer, ran a creamery, and was rural mail carrier in Bonesteel, SD. 8 children.

(1) Frank[6] Ray Williams b. 11-14-1895 in Bonesteel, SD and d. 7-29-1974 in Bonesteel, SD. m. 3-8-1919 Mabel Beck b. 4-9-1897 and d. 10-17-1967 in Burke, SD. 4 children.

+Beverly Ben[7] Williams b. 7-3-1920 in Bonesteel, SD and d. 4-30-1940 in Bonesteel, SD.

+Neva[7] Ruth Williams b. 4-13-1922 Bonesteel, SD and d. 6-30-1980. m. 4-10-1948 in CA Norbert Andrew Schuman b. 3-14-1920 in MN. 2 children.

^Dean[8] Jacob Schuman b. 8-22-1951 in Inglewood, CA. 2 children

~Michelle[9] Jean Schuman b. 1971.

~Michael[9] Dean Schuman b. 1975.

^Debra[8] Ann Schuman b. 2-14-1954 in Inglewood, CA. m. Gary Tortorella b. about 1954. 2 children.

~Jenny[9] Tortorella b. about 1979.

~Paul[9] Tortorella b. about 1981.

+Dennis[7] Robert Williams b. 12-8-1929 in Bonesteel, SD. m. Geraldine Shaffer b. 2-3-1932. She daughter of Sanford Lloyd Shaffer and Margaret Springer. 3 children.

^Connie[8] Williams.

^Marty[8] Williams.

^Lisa[8] Williams.

+Glenn[7] Harlen Williams b. 1-13-1932 in Bonesteel, SD.

(2) Verna[6] Leota Williams b. 7-29-1897 in Bonesteel, SD and d. 9-25-1991 Sioux Falls, SD m. 6-4-1925 in Bonesteel, SD Rudolph Oliver Nelson b. 6-27-1891 in Brandon, SD and d. 8-9-1982 Sioux Falls, SD. He son of Ole Nelson and Olivia Anderson. 4 children.

+Jean[7] Anne Nelson b. 10-13-1926 Gregory, SD. m. 3-8-1952 Archie Robert Wells b. 1-28-1923 in Lindsay, SD and d. 12-3-1963 in Sheridan, CO. 6 children.

^Wayne[8] Anthony Wells b. 3-28-1952 Sioux Falls, SD. m. 4-5-1980 in Denver, CO Tamyra Jean Burt b. 9-24-1946 Bonne Terre, MO. 1 daughter.

~Shannon[9] Erin Wells b. 2-19-1986 Denver, CO.

^Patricia[8] Jean Wells b. 10-1-1953 Valley Springs, SD. m. 5-16-1970 in Denver, CO to Larry A. Sitter b. about 1954. 3 children.

~June[9] Starr Sitter b. 12-3-1970 in ND.

~Tela[9] Rene Sitter b. 12-14-1975 in ND.

~Curtis[9] Jay Sitter b. 6-9-1982.

^Alice[8] Marie Wells b. 1-21-1957 in Denver, CO. m. 1st to Jim Roberts in Delhart, TX. 2 sons.

~Brian[9] Starbuck Roberts b. 7-16-1972 in Denver, CO. m. Charmaine b. about 3-3-1972. 1 son.

#Wesley[10] Roberts b. 10-28-1993 Ft. Knox, KY.

~Benjamin[9] Santana Roberts b. 10-6-1973 in San Diego, CA. m. on 3-9-1994 in CA to Tricia b. about 1973. 1 child.

#Kaitlin[10] Lakota Roberts b. 4-12-1994 in San Diego,CA.

Alice[8] Marie Wells m. 2nd Steve Calac b. about 1956

Alice[8] Marie Wells m. 3rd May 1992 Billy Joe Bowens b. about 1956.

^Wilda[8] Kay Wells b. 7-14-1958 in Denver, CO. Father of first child Nathan Garcia. Mother and he were never married.

~Monetta[9] Ann Wells b. 11-23-1973 Denver, CO.m.
Michael Armond Gutierrez b. about 1956. 2 children.

~Michael[9] Armond Gutierrez, Jr. b. 12-11-1975 Denver,
CO.

~Olivia[9] Jean Gutierrez b. 1-15-1977 Lompoc, CA.

^Joanne[8] Verna Wells b. 10-10-1959 in Denver, CO. m.
Yousef Alakan Abdulla b. about 6-2-1960 Dubai, UAE.
5 children.

~Jacob[9] Yousef Abdulla b. 10-10-1977 Denver, CO.

~Isaac[9] Yousef Abdulla b. 6-21-1982 Denver, CO.

~Abraham[9] Yousef Abdulla b. 6-19-1984 Dubai, UAE.

~Rachel[9] Abdulla b. 6-20-1986 Dubai, UAE.

~Nassar[9] Yousef Abdulla b. 10-17-1987 Dubai, UAE.

^Samuel[8] John Wells b. 11-29-1962 in Denver, CO.

+Bethel[7] Marie Nelson b. 9-7-1928 Brandon, SD. m. 6-12-
1948 Norbert Herb Goehring b. 1-27-1928. He was son of
Albert Goehring and Christina Lindeman. 2 children.

^Miles[8] Kent Goehring b. 11-2-1949 Parkston, SD. m.
6-2-1967 Parkston, SD Betty Jo Brunken b. 1-11-1950.
She daughter of Donald Henry Brunken and Martha
Freier. 2 children.

~Dawn[9] Michele Goehring b. 12-25-1967 Parkston, SD.
m. 1st unknown. 1 child.

Christopher[10] Goehring b. 7-26-1984 CA.

Dawn[9] Michele Goehring m. 2nd Paul Anderson b. about
1965. 1 child.

#Jessica[10] Anderson b. 2-28-1991 MN.

~Chad[9] Michael Goehring b. 9-26-1969 Parkston, SD.

^Meribeth[8] Lynn Goehring b. 10-10-1953 Parkston, SD. m.
5-20-1972 Larry Emil Fink. He son of Alvin Fink and
Rose Wegehaupt. 2 children.

~Michelle[9] Lynn Fink b. 1-23-1977 Parkston, SD.

~Lori[9] Ann Fink b. 5-31-1979 Mitchell, SD.

+Robert[7] Dee Nelson b. 6-28-1931 Brandon, SD. m. 9-4-
1954 in Alexandra, VA Kathryn Louise Long b.11-4-1934
Akron, OH. She daughter of Carl William Long and Nora
Fay Dougherty. 3 children.

^Karen[8] Jo Nelson b. 9-2-1955 Brookings, SD. m. 1st and
divorced Charles Richard Palmer, Jr. b. 7-18-1954 in

Cleveland, OH. He son of Charles Richard Bud Palmer and Carol Burnett. 4 children.

~Brian[9] Richard Palmer b. 12-21-1978 Berea, OH.

~Adam[9] Carl Palmer b. 3-3-1980 Berea, OH.

~Melissa[9] Faye Palmer b. 3-9-1982 Berea, OH.

~Robert[9] Edward Palmer b. 7-13-1984 in Miami, FL.

Karen[8] Jo Nelson m. 2nd on 8-5-1993 Jeffrey Franklin Dalton b. 1-7-1957 Miami, FL. 2 children.

~Timothy[9] Franklin Dalton b. 11-17-1993 Miami, FL.

~Katelyn[9] Lucille Dalton b. 4-26-1995.

^Nancy[8] Louise Nelson b. 2-10-1960 in Akron, OH and d. 5-5-1991 in Naples, FL. m. 10-22-1988 Douglas Fay Bush b. 10-22-1958. Divorced.

^David[8] Carl Nelson b. 2-16-1963 in Akron, OH. m. on 7-10-1993 in Miami, FL Isabel Cristina Salcedo b. 5-28-1966 Miami, FL. 1 daughter.

~Amanda[9] Olivia Nelson b. 7-21-1995.

+Mary[7] Jane Nelson b. 4-6-1933 in Sioux Falls, SD. m. 4-5-1952 in Worthington, MN to Donald Wahl b. 7-22-1927 in Larchwood, IA. Live in Larchwood, IA. 4 children.

^Rebecca[8] Lynn Wahl b. 11-10-1952 in Sioux Falls, SD. m. on 5-26-1984 to Merlyn Grave b. 2-24-1954 in Sioux Falls, SD. He son of Mike Grave and Norleen. 2 sons.

~Michael[9] Dean Grave b. 4-20-1986 in Sioux Falls, SD.

~Matthew[9] William Grave b. 7-5-1991 in Sioux Falls, SD.

^Thomas[8] Iver Wahl b. 6-18-1954 in Valley Springs, SD. m. on 2-14-1977 to Bridget Bonnstetter b. about 1954. 2 daughters.

~Michelle[9] Wahl b. 7-13-1979 in Rock Rapids, IA.

~Erin[9] Lynn Wahl b. 11-5-1981 in Rock Rapids, IA.

^Jeffrey[8] Dean Wahl b. 8-30-1955 in Valley Springs, SD. m. on 10-6-1973 to Starr Darlene Page b. about 1955. 3 daughters.

~Nicole[9] Marie Wahl b. 3-18-1974 in Dell Rapids, SD. m. in 4-1974 in Sioux Falls, SD to Kirby Muilenburg b. about 1974. 1 daughter.

#Lakin[10] Samanth Muilenburg b. 10-7-1993 in Sioux Falls, SD.

~Brandi[9] Rene Wahl b. 12-14-1976 in Madison, SD.

~Emily[9] Robin Wahl b. 5-30-1984 in Chamberlain, SD.

^Gerald[8] Stuart Wahl b. 1-5-1960 in Rock Rapids, IA. m. on 7-7-1978 to Susan Morrison b. about 1952. 2 children.

 ~Jeffrey[9] Thomas Wahl b. 10-17-1979 in Colorado Springs, CO.

 ~Rebecca[9] Elaine Wahl b. 1-17-1981 in Colorado Springs, Co.

(3) Cecile[6] Eva Williams b. 6-6-1899 m. on 3-10-1925 to Ernest Victor Larsen b. 11-4-1897 and d. 11-8-1959. 1 son.

+Larry[7] Larsen b. 7-24-1934. m. on 12-22-1956 to Beverly Jean Stetter b. 1-12-1934. He owned a consulting business. 2 children.

 ^Larry[8] Victor Larsen b. 11-8-1959. m. on 9-1-1984 to Sheila Toner b. about 1959. He Graduate of Montana State 1982.

 ^Lori[8] Lee Larsen b. 8-20-1963. Graduate of Montana State 1988.

(4) Jessie[6] M. Williams b. 8-5-1902 and d. 12-2-1975. Bur. Omaha, NE. m. Wait Pugh b. 3-4-1884 and d. 4-18-1956. 2 sons.

+Gene[7] Richard Pugh b. 1-3-1932. m. on 1-5-1955 to Verta Lou Martens b. 9-16 1932. 3 children.

 ^Joni[8] Anne Pugh b. 3-26-1956. m. on 3-29-1985 to Martin David Wolf b. 11-25-1958. He President of Computerland division of Marisel Corp. 2 children.

 ~Abigail[9] Rave Wolf b. 9-28 1988.

 ~Jessica[9] Jordon Wolf b. 8-25-1990.

 ^Martin[8] John Pugh b. 12-28-1959. m. 1st on 7-21-1990 to Patty Kollar b. about 1959. m 2nd to Rena Minor b. about 1959.

 ^Charles[8] Patrick Pugh b. 11-9-1962. m. on 10-10-1987 to Anita Brandt b. about 1962. 2 sons.

 ~Nathan[9] Alexander Simon Pugh b. 3-5-1989.

 ~Samuel[9] Patrick Pugh b. 11-7-1992.

+James[7] William Bill Pugh b. 1-2-1934. m. on 1-24-1959 to Beverly Jean Erickson. 2 daughters.

 ^Terri[8] Jolene Pugh b. 1-25-1961.

 ^Lynda[8] Jean Pugh b. 1-7-1964.

(5) Hannah[6] Matilda Williams b. 1-16-1904 in SD and d. 12-12-1983. m. on 6-13-1928 to George N. Burdick b. 4-28-

1892 and d. 5-8-1973. Bur Sturgis, SD. 3 children.

+Mary[7] Margaret Burdick b. 10-21-1929. m. 8-29-1948 to
†Melvin Symonds b. 7-7-1923. He served in Korean
Conflict. 2 daughters.

    ^Ruth[8] Arlene Symonds b. 6-24-1949. m. on 11-8-1968 to
    Jeff Billingsley b. about 1949. 1 son.

        ~Ryder[9] Dane Billingsley b. 1-6-1969. m. on 2-14-1990
        to Gwen Lobato b. about 1969. 2 children.

           #Marc[10] Anthony Billingsley b. 10-22-1990.

           #Aubrey[10] Danielle Billingsley b. 4-23-1992.

    ^Lynette[8] Ilene Symonds b. 6-12-1951. m. 1st on 10-8-1969
    to Bernabe Sandoval b. about 1951. 2 sons.

        ~Bernabe[9] Trey Sandoval III b. 11-4-1973. m. 6-17-1995
        to Becky Blackwood b. about 1973.

        ~Wayne[9] Sandoval b. 8-14-1975.

    m. 2nd on 8-11-1978 to Howard Miller b. about 1951.

    m. 3rd 7-5-1991 to Jonathon Carroll.

+Billings[7] George Burdick b. 7-29-1934. m. on 10-28-1953
to Marie Pollard b. 10-28-1930. 1 son.

    ^Larry[8] Dean Burdick b. 5-1-1955. m. on 6-21-1976 to
    Mary Lorraine Owen b. about 1955. 1 daughter.

        ~Kathleen[9] Marie Burdick b. 12-12-1983

+Geraldine[7] Ann Burdick b. 4-8-1940. Works as medical
technologist in Wagner, SD. m. on 6-21-1959 to Arthur G.
Todriff b. about 1939. 6 children. First 3 by father's 1st
marriage. Mother not known.

    ^Jean[8] Anne Todriff b. 12-8-1956.

    ^Arthur[8] G. Todriff b. 6-21-1958.

    ^Linda[8] Todriff b. 2-17-1959.

    ^Randal[8] George Todriff b. 11-17-1963. m. about 6-10-
    1989 Amy b. about 1963. 1 child. b 1-2-1991.

    ^Noelle[8] Renee Todriff b. 12-18-1968. m. on 4-30-1988 to
    Kevin Mervar b. about 1968.

    ^Todd[8] William Todriff b. 11-17-1971.

(6) Myrtle[6] Marie Williams b. 4-19-1906 and d. 2-13-1986.
Worked as school teacher, Sears & Roebuck clerk, and bank
teller. Never married. Bur. Bonesteel, SD.

(7) James[6] Henry Preston Williams, Jr. b. 9-11-1911 and d.
5-14-1986. Lived in Pierre, SD. m. on 12-30-1933 to Elaine
Gordon Newman b. 1-20-1911 and d. 10-2-1979. Bur. Pierre,

SD. 5 children.

+James[7] Herbert Williams b. 3-16-1935 and d. 6-17-1970. m. 1st on 5-26-1956 to Judith Ann Rhodes. Div. 1 daughter.

  ^Vicky[8] Lynn Williams b. 5-5-1957. m. 1st on 11-22-1972 to Fred Gloc b. about 1955. Divorced. 2 daughters.

    ~Jennifer[9] Lee Gloc b. 6-20-1973. 1 son.

      #Frederick[10] James Gloc b. 4-6-1995.

    ~Elizabeth Faye Gloc b. 7-5-1975.

  Vicky[8] Lynn Williams m. 2nd on 11-25-1987 to Albert Joe Hatturn b. 7-21-1959. Farmer.

+Carolyn[7] Elaine Williams. b. 8-8-1936. m. on 8-22-1957 to Charles DeWayne Sterling b. 3-31-1935. 2 children.

  ^John Charles[8] Sterling b. 8-25-1958. m. on 10-3-1979 Patricia Ann Smith b. 5-25-1952. He works as lunch hauler in Pierre, SD. She works in child day care. 4 sons.

    ~Eric[9] Patrick Sterling b. 12-29-1971

    ~John[9] Henry Sterling b. 1-4-1983.

    ~Buddy[9] James Sterling b. 11-27-1984.

    ~Beau[9] DeWayne Sterling b. 10-3-1986.

  ^Karen[8] Elaine Sterling b. 11-19-1961. m. on 8-7-1982 to Thomas Neil Luther b. 1-16-1959. He maintenance worker, Pierre public schools. 3 children.

    ~Kristy[9] Marie Luther b. 8-30-1980.

    ~Kay[9] Elaine Luther b. 8-31-1983.

    ~Neil[9] Thomas Luther b. 12-20-1984.

+Robert[7] Newman Williams b. 6-7-1938. m. on 2-5-1967 to Karen Kay Smith b. 1-16-1947. 1 son.

  ^David[8] Matthew Williams b. 11-1-1974. Adopted.

+Gwendolyn[7] Jean Williams b. 1-20-1940. m. on 11-22-1961 to Daniel Fredrick Hoffer b. 1-12-1936. 3 sons.

  ^Michael[8] Daniel Hoffer b. 1-10-1963. m. on 2-21-1981 to Joyce Buum b. 12-29-1964. 4 children.

    ~Tyler[9] Hoffer b. 2-26-1981.

    ~Michael[9] Hoffer b. 2-18-1982.

    ~Christena[9] Hoffer b. 1-14-1983.

    ~Bren[9] Hoffer b. 8-9-1988.

  ^Bryan[8] Lee Hoffer b. 2-13-1966 m. on 8-12-1989 to Liesa Marie Monson b. about 12-13-1966. He works as ranch hand in Relience, NE. She works as second grade teacher in Relience, NE. 2 children.

~Bry[9] Anna Marie Hoffer b. 12-18-1990.

~Baxter[9] Dane Hoffer b. 8-7-1992.

^Colin[8] Hoffer b. 4-10-1969. Works as farmer and ranch hand.

+Joan[7] Rae Williams b. 10-2-1941. m. on 3-1-1963 to Stanley Allen Sterling b. 10-22-1940. Lived in Pier, SD. Divorced. 2 children.

^Raelene[8] Sterling b. 10-3-1965. Graduated Souix Falls College in 1988. Works in police work in Scotland, SD. m. on 9-1-1990 to Clint Andrew Layne b. 4-9-1957. 1 son.

~Clint[9] Andrew Layne b. 4-26-1991. Has Hurler's syndrome and is terminal.

^William[8] Eugene Sterling b. 10-25-1968. m. on 1-2-1993 to Teresa Mercer b. 9-18-1957.

(8) Mary[6] Irene Williams b. 4-11-1914 in Bonesteel, SD. m. on 5-13-1931 to Chester George Carsten b. 4-26-1914 in Bonesteel, SD and d. 11-18-1951 in Lynch, NE. Bur. Botd Co., NE. He was farmer. 3 children.

+Alyce[7] Marie Carsten b. 8-13-1931 in Bonesteel, SD. m. on 10-6-1950 to Eldon Leroy Mills b. 3-19-1929 Lynch, NE. He was son of Lloyd Mills and Frances Sidlacheck. He was farmer lived in Riverton, WY. 7 children.

^Brian[8] Lynn Mills b. 8-11-1951 in Lynch, NE. Works on oil rigs. m. on 3-18-1972 to Nancy Marie Pfeiffer b. 11-17-1952. 2 daughters.

~Kerrie[9] Ann Mills (adopted) b. 7-28-1971 in Salt Lake City, UT. m. on 1-4-1992 in Riverton, WY to Raphael Freeman Metcalf b. about 1971. He is Oilfield worker. 1 child.

#Jessie Raphael Metcalf b. 8-11-1992 Riverton, WY.

~Kelly[9] Lynn Mills b. 7-26-1980 Riverton, WY.

^Timothy[8] Lyle Mills b. 8-11-1951 in Lynch, NE. Works on oil rigs. m. 1st 7-22-1972 to Alfreda Diane Balders b. 2-14-1956 in Riverton, WY. 4 children

~Nicole[9] Dawn Mills b. 6-27-1973 in Riverton, WY. m. 10-23-1992 Riverton, WY to Lance David Bolte b. 4-16-1969 in Riverton, WY. Works as truck driver for Pepsi Cola.

~Timothy[9] Lee Mills b. 4-22-1974 in Riverton, WY. m.

on 4-29-1992 in Elko NV to Jonnel Jo Hintz b. 2-6-1974 in Rock Springs, WY. She is daughter of John Franklin Hintz and Debra Potter. 2 children.

#Ashley[10] Denae Mills b. 7-7-1992 in Jackson, WY.

#Shad[10] Allen Mills b. 4-13-1994 in Jackson, WY.

~Jay[9] Manuel Mills b. 11-28-1975 in Grants NM.

~Phillip[9] Lyle Mills b. 4-16-1977 in Riverton WY.

Timothy[8] Lyle Mills m. 2nd on 2-18-1994 in Riverton, WY to Cheri Marten Gotich b. 3-23-1948.

^Jennifer[8] June Mills b. 4-24-1953 in Lynch, NE. m. 6-15-1974 to Gary Merrill Rees b. 2-20-1949 in Salt Lake City, UT. Both self employed as water trucks to oil wells. 3 children.

~Tami[9] Marie Rees b. 11-2-1976 in Jackson, WY.

~Michelle[9] Ann Rees b. 11-28-1979 Jackson, WY.

~Jeffrey[9] Scott Rees b. 6-30-1981 in Jackson, WY.

^Samuel[8] Ray Mills b. 3 16 1955 in Lynch NE. m. 1st on 12-18-1976 in DuBois, WY to Rhonda Rae Erdmann b about 1956 in IL. 1 son.

~Nathan[9] Lawrence Mills b. 11-16-1974 in Moline, IL

Samuel[8] Ray Mills m. 2nd on 6-11-1994 in Collbran, CO to Francine Florence Hammond b. 7-1-1950. Works as cook. 1 son.

~Samuel[9] Ray Mills II b. 4-23-1983 in Albequerque, NM.

^Arthur[8] Floyd Mills b. 5-8-1956 in Lynch, NE. Worked as carpenter. Lived Americus, GA. m. on 7-11-1982 in Riverton, WY to Kathleen Annette Wagner b. 7-11-1961 in GA. 4 children.

~Jeremy[9] Leon Mills b. 6-3-1984 in Americus, GA.

~Alicia[9] Marie Mills b. 1-24-1987 in Americus, GA.

~Amy[9] Elizabeth Mills b. 11-10-1988 in Americus, GA.

~Daniel[9] Patrick Mills b. 12-6-1992 in Americus, GA.

^Sheila[8] Fae Mills b. 12-2-1963 in Riverton, WY. m. on 8-3-1985 to Bertram Roy Hankins, II b. 7-28-1964 in Riverton, WY. He son of Bertram Roy Hankins and Ella Mae McCary. He works as heavy equipment mechanic. 2 children.

~Clayton[9] Reed Hankins b. 4-7-1987Riverton, WY.

~Randie[9] Lynn Hankins b. 1-23-1989 Riverton, WY.

^Rodney[8] Lee Mills b. 8-5-1967 Riverton, WY. m. to Jennifer Brownlee. 3 sons.

~Robert[9] Brownlee b. 6-8-1990.

~Dylan[9] Brownlee b. 10-11-1992.

~Caleb[9] Brownlee b. 2-2-1995.

+Gerald[7] William Carsten b. 6-21-1936 in Carnes, NE. m. 10-25-1958 Bonesteel, SD to Laura Louise Counts b. 7-8-1938 in Gregory, SD and d. 2-5-1996 Cherokee, IA. Bur. Aurelia, IA. 2 children.

^Sharon[8] Louise Carsten b. 11-7-1960 in Lynch NE. m. on 4-7-1990 in Sioux Falls, SD to Tim Plucker. He son of Harley Plucker and Valeria Friedrich. 2 children.

~Madelyn[9] Bridget Plucker b. 2-13-1992 in Sioux Falls, SD.

~John[9] Wessel Plucker b. 2-12-1994 in Sioux Falls, SD.

^Joyce Irene Carsten b. 4-28-1962. m. on 11-3-1990 in Sioux Falls, SD to James William Loudenslager b. 5-28-1964 Sioux Falls, SD. He son of William Loudenslager and Bonnie Adams. Works as computer programmer. 1 son.

~Aaron[9] William Loudenslager b. 4-20-1993 in Sioux Falls, SD.

+Robert[7] Lee Carsten b. 5-24-1938 Page, NE. Worked for the Metropolitan Utilities District in Omaha, NE. m. on 7-22-1960 to Peggie Lou Kuhney b. 8-28-1937. Social worker at Missouri Valley Hospital. 3 children.

^Julie[8] Ann Carsten b. 3-15-1961 in Omaha, NE. Employed as secretary. m. on 3-28-1981 to Doug Eugene Anderson b. about 1961. 2 children.

~Stephanie[9] Ann Anderson b. 5-3-1982 in Omaha, NE.

~Bryan[9] Eugene Anderson b. 1-9-1985 in Omaha, NE.

^Chester[8] Alan Carsten b. 4-17-1962. m. on 11-25-1982 to Dorothy Fionken b about 1962. He employed in industry as laborer and she employed as office worker. 3 children.

~Bridget[9] Elisbeth Carsten b. 3-31-1983.

~Troy[9] Michael Carsten b. 10-31-1984.

~Trevor[9] Alan Carsten b. 11-4-1986.

^Valerie[8] Kay Carsten b. 11-29-1966. Employed as cook and waitress. m. on 6-3-1985 to Jay Delong b. about 1985. 3 children.

~John[9] Emery Delong b. 6-27-1987.

~Erin[9] Leigh Delong b. 8-2-1988.

~Dolton[9] James Delong b. 6-28-1995.

m. 2nd on 11-5-1963 Walter Joseph Sondgeroth b. 12-9-1908 and d. 5-8-1979 in Rawlins, WY. Bur. Pinedale, WY.

e. Georgia[5] Florence Haver b. 3-7-1876 in Iowa d. 1-6-1953. Bur. Bonesteel, SD. m. on 4-29-1894 to Clyde Pepper b. 8-13-1870 in Iowa and d. 10-23-1955. Bur. in Bonesteel, SD. 6 children.

(1) Gladys[6] Mayme Pepper b. 1-1-1895 in SD. Lived in Petaluma, CA. m. on 8-31-1922 Louis McMichael b. about 1895. 2 adopted children.

+Glenn[7] McMichael b. about 1920.

+Mary[7] McMichael b. about 1922.

(2) Grace[6] Marie Pepper 1-13-1897 in SD. Lived in Bonesteel, SD. m. 1st on 6-12-1923 George Haidle b. 6-29-1896 and d. 12-22-1948. 2 daughters.

+Pauline[7] Mae Haidle b. 5-17-1925. m. Philip Bancroft b. 8-26-1924. 2 children.

^Linda Jo Bancroft b. 11-22-1947.

^Danny Pepper Bancroft b. 1-27-1951.

+Phyllis[7] Gay Haidle b. 7-28-1931. m. Sanford Dewey Owen b. 9-16-1929. 3 children.

^Gary[8] Sanford Owen b. 8-8-1952.

^Phillip[8] Owen b. 6-28-1954.

^Judy[8] Lynn Owen b. 8-26-1955

Grace[6] Marie Pepper m. 2nd Carroll McCoy b. about 1897.

(3) Glenn[6] Haver Pepper b. 8-22-1899 in SD. m. Eloine Claire Atkinson b.8-10-1901. 1 son.

+Byron[7] Glenn Pepper b. 4-11-1934. m. Peggy Joyce Boggs b. 1-4-1937. 2 sons.

^Melvin[8] Byron Pepper b. 4-5-1960.

^Brett[8] Bruce Pepper b. 10-15-1964.

(4) Archibald[6] Alexander Pepper b. 7-9-1902in SD. m. on 5-22-1926 to Muriel Virginia Doane Arnold b. 8-24-1902. 4 sons.

+Duane[7] Arnold Pepper b. 2-25-1927. m. Cleone Ila Herman b. 7-21-1926. 2 children.

^Carol[8] Jean Pepper b. 11-13-1949.

^Dwight[8] Keith Pepper b. 9-30-1951.

+Dennis[7] Leroy Pepper b. 4-8-1931. m. Naomi Irene
Jansen b. 11-30-1933. 5 children.

^Karen[8] Kay Pepper b. 9-27-1951.

^Debra[8] Lynn Pepper b. 1-12-1953.

^Dennis[8] Lee Pepper b. 9-19-1954.

^Michael[8] Alexander Pepper b. 3-26-1956.

^Donald[8] Allen Pepper b. 10-28-1959.

+Gerald[7] Elbert Pepper b. 9-4-1933. Lives in Bonesteel, SD.
m. Goldean Faye Knobbie b. 8-5-1936. 3 sons.

^Darrell[8] Bruce Pepper b. 6-4-1956.

^Elbert[8] Allen Pepper b. 5-28-1958.

^Timothy[8] Dean Pepper b. 1-2-1963.

+Roland[7] Gene Pepper b. 4-4-1946.

(5) Hazel[6] Edith Pepper b. 6-5-1904 in SD. m. 1st on 5-24-1921
Clarence Eugene Budd b. 6-2-1903. 2 daughters.

+Bonnie[7] June Budd b. 8-28-1926. m. 1st Luther Prentice b.
about 1926. 1 child.

^Lona[8] Cheryl Prentice b. 12-10-1947. m. John Mark
Wylie b. about 1947.

m. 2nd Charles Henry Gaut b. 4-4-1927. 4 children

^Janice[8] June Gaut b. 7-25-1951.

^Carrie[8] Hazel Gaut b. 10-30-1952.

^Dwight[8] Henry Gaut b. 1-4-1956.

^Eugene[8] Budd Gaut b. 10-2-1959.

+Donna[7] Marie Budd b. 8-21-1928. m. Al Hall b. 3-30-1939.
5 children.

^Charlene[8] Ann Hall b. 12-11-1948.

^Karen[8] Marie Hall b. 8-19-1953.

^Steven[8] Harry Hall b. 10-7-1954.

^Loren[8] Ray Hall b. 1-28-1957.

^Loreen[8] Kay Hall b. 1-28-1957.

(6) Dale[6] Randolph Pepper b. 6-6-1907 in SD. m. on 3-20-1930
Estelle Lucille McWhirter b. 9-16-1909. 3 children.

+Velma[7] Mae Pepper b. 8-15-1931. m. Leo Max Uecker b.
3-6-1929. 5 children.

^Brenda[8] Jean Uecker b. 9-24-1950.

^Lori[8] Ann Uecker b. 7-6-1954.

^Richard[8] Leo Uecker b, 11-27-1955.

^Lynn Estelle[8] Uecker b. about 9-28-1957.

^Robert[8] Allen Uecker b. 9-27-1964.

+Vernon[7] Dale Pepper b. 12-6-1933. m. Georgene Ann Baun
b. 12-14-1936. 4 daughters.
  ^Pamela[8] Jo Pepper b. 9-18-1954.
  ^Anita[8] Rae Pepper b. 2-10-1956.
  ^Kelly[8] Lynne Pepper b. 3-13-1957.
  ^Srlene[8] Marie Pepper b. 2-27-1963.
+Georgia[7] Louise Pepper b. 7-16-1936. m. Gerald Dean
Smith b. 1-21-1934. 5 children.
  ^Roddy[8] Dean Smith b. 5-7-1955.
  ^Robyn[8] June Smith b. 4-22-1957.
  ^Brian[8] Scott Smith.
  ^Barbara[8] Lee Smith b. 6-19-1961.
  ^Penny[8] Sue Smith b. 9-20-1963.
f. Della[5] Elma Haver b. 3-23-1879 in IA and d. 5-28-1960. Bur. in
Bonesteel, SD. Lived in Retirement, SD. m. in SD to Joseph H.
Lewis b. 8-6-1875 in NE and d. 11-4-1947. 3 children.
(1) Ethel[6] Mae Lewis b. 3-22-1904 in SD. m. Wallace Peppel b.
12-10-1901 and d. 5-14-1966. 3 children.
  +Joan[7] A. Peppel b. 7-24-1926. m. Leon H Krueger b.
11-26-1923. 5 children.
    ^Connie[8] Carol Krueger b. 11-15-1945. m. Eugene Pistulka
b. 9-10-1945. 2 daughters.
      ~Angela[9] Pistulka b. 8-19-1965.
      ~Christina[9] Pistulka b. 2-16-1967.
    ^Betty[8] Krueger b. 2-19-1948. m. Jim Hoar b. about 1948.
1 daughter.
      ~Linda[9] Lea Hoar b. 11-3-1966.
    ^James[8] Krueger b. 10-25-1950.
    ^Daniel[8] Lynn Krueger b. 5-31-1955.
    ^Judy[8] Marie Krueger b. 1-2-1962.
  +Robert[7] L. Peppel b. 4-26-1934. m. Francis Lorraine
Higgins b. 5-4-1938. 3 children.
    ^Timothy[8] Robert Peppel b. 5-4-1960.
    ^Debra[8] Kay Peppel b. 5-20-1961.
    ^Kevin[8] John Peppel b. 3-25-1966.
  +Carol[7] Mae Peppel b. 2-3-1938. m. on 6-11-1956 to Robert
L. Gray b. 12-5-1936.3 children.
    ^Ronald[8] Robert Gray b. 12-31-1957.
    ^Randall[8] Edward Gray b. 12-27-1960.
    ^Lisa[8] Marie Gray b. 6-4-1965.

(2) Everett[6] Lewis b. 5-29-1907 in SD m. 1st Elizabeth Knobell
b. about 1906. 1 child.
  +Mary[7] Lou Lewis b. 1930.
m. 2nd Mildred Wright b. 7-28-1912.
(3) Belva[6] Helen Lewis b. 9-19-1914 in SD. m. John Thompson
Haisch b. 4-10-1915. 4 children.
  +Johnadee[7] Helen Haisch b. 10-29-1935. m. James Stuart
White b. 9-30-1930. 3 sons.
    ^James[8] Samuel White b. 5-20-1955.
    ^John[8] Robert White b. 3-22-1958.
    ^Stuart[8] Travis White b. 12-30-1963.
  +Evelyn[7] Jo Haisch b. 4-16-1938. m. Lyle Larry Bauer b.
9-24-1932. 4 children.
    ^Lyle[8] Jo Bauer b. 9-22-1957.
    ^Susan[8] Kay Bauer b. 12-1-1959.
    ^Larry[8] John Bauer b. 3-13-1963.
    ^Gina[8] Marie Bauer b. 5-15-1964.
  +Michael[7] John Haisch b. 7-17-1950.
  +Avel[7] Rae Haisch b. 12-31-1960 and d. same day.
g. Martha[5] Lillian Haver b. 1-18-1882 in IA. m. in SD to George
H. Cross b. 8-1-1879 in NE. 6 children.
  (1) Genevieve[6] Marie Cross b. 7-13-1903 SD. m. Mosley Hoblit
b. 2-25-1905. 2 children.
    +Wayne[7] Cross Hoblit b. 9-23-1923 in SD. m. Virginia M.
Swenson b. abt. 1923. 2 children.
      ^Beverly[8] Jean Hoblit b. 10-27-1946. m. Jerry Myers b. abt
1923.
      ^David[8] Wayne Hoblit b. 4-11-1950.
    +Clare[7] Elmer Hoblit b. 2-7-1926. m. Marilyn Stukenberg b.
about 1926.
    (2) Haver[6] William Cross b. 7-4-1905 in SD. m. Thalia
Eldora Anderson b. 8-14-1910, 5 children.
  +Thomas[7] Haver Cross b. 10-13-1929. m. Mary Ellen Baker
b. 10-18-1932. 3 children.
    ^Bradley[8] Thomas Cross b. 1-4-1956.
    ^Ellen[8] Jean Cross b. 8-20-1959.
    ^William[8] Murray Cross b. 12-9-1961.
  +Jerald[7] Clair Cross b. 1-29-1931. m. Dorothy Joan West b.
8-24-1930. 4 daughters.
    ^Karen[8] Kay Cross b. 5-9-1952.

^Kathleen[8] Ann Cross b. 4-13-1954.

^Nancy[8] Joan Cross b. 4-26-1958.

^Janice[8] Jeri Cross b. 7-27-1965.

+Rita[7] Ann Cross b. 12-26-1938. m. Gene Frank b. 9-2-1939.
4 children.

^Rita[8] Marie Frank b. 10-31-1960.

^Pamela[8] Gene Frank b. 8-30-1962.

^Brenda[8] Joan Frank b. 8-15-1963.

^Bruce[8] Allen Frank b. 12-19-1965.

+Alan[7] Lee Cross b. 2-20-1945. m. Viki Wipf b. 7-16-1946.

+Donald[7] Morley Cross b. 8-19-1948.

(3) Cecil[6] Clare Cross b. 1-3-1909 in SD m. 1st on 3-29-1930
Marguerite V. Schar b. about 1908. m. 2nd Doris Virginia
Shepherd b. 12-13-1916. 3 children.

+Virginia[7] Ann Cross b. 8-26-1947. m. Dennis Norman
Stricker b. about 1947. 1 daughter.

^Sandra Esther Stricker b. 9-26-1966 adopted.

+Richard[7] Wayne Cross (adopted) b. 1-14-1952.

+Ronald[7] Clair Cross b. 10-24-1952.

(4) Mildred[6] L. Cross b. 10-9-1911 in SD. m. Robert Moore
Kiser b. 1-5-1903. 3 children.

+Marjorie[7] Joan Kiser b. 8-31-1933. m. James Wesley
Wheeler b. 10-13-1930. 2 daughters.

^Jacquelin[8] Eliabeth Wheeler b. 10-23-1958.

^Jamie[8] Joan Wheeler b. 11-6-1959.

+Barbara[7] Jean Kiser b. 6-24-1942. m. George Edwin Dyer b.
10-23-1941. 2 daughters.

^Eleanor[8] Jean Dyer b. 2-11-1963.

^Sheryl[8] Ann Dyer b. 9-26-1966.

+George[7] Robert Kiser b. 2-13-1945. m. Sharon Lorraine
Porter b. 9-5-1948.

(5) Marjorie[6] Cleva Cross b. 3-16-1915 in SD. m. Vernon Dale
Brown b. 7-3-1906. 5 children.

+LaVerne[7] Kay Brown b. 1-20-1940. m. James Lee
Whitehead b. 7-26-1940. 3 children.

^Cameron[8] Jay Whitehead b. 12-22-1959.

^Kevin[8] Scott Whitehead b. 8-31-1961.

^Steven[8] Jon Whitehead b. 3-4-1963.

+Karen[7] Mattie Brown b. 11-2-1942.

+Robert[7] Dale Brown b. 6-2-1946.

+Joseph[7] Porter Brown b. 10-30-1949.

+Margean[7] Ann Brown b. 8-30-1953.

(6) Lylah[7] Georgean Cross b. 3-25-1921 and d. 4-4-1921.

G. Jacob[4] Haver b. 9-13-1846 in Jefferson Twp., Greene Co., PA and d. 8-15-1905 in Greene Co., PA. m. 1-30-1871 Martha Annetta Cotterel b. 1-17-1847 d. 3-27-1910 in Greene Co., PA. She daughter of John Cotterel and Permelia Milliken. 6 children.

a. John[5] Cotterel Haver b. 10-2-1871 in Green Co., PA and d. 10-3-1949 in Jefferspn, Green Co., PA. Bur. Cumberland Pres. Church Cem, Jefferson, PA. m. 2-4-1896 in Jefferson, PA. to Laura Virginia Keigley b. 8-17-1869 in Sycamore, Green Co., PA and d. 9-29-1961 Somerset, PA. 5 children.

(1) George[6] Milton Haver b. 1-20-1897 in Mather, PA and d. 11-25-1967 Somersett, PA. m. on 9-21-1920 in Elwood City, PA to Fannie Leona Thompson b. 2-12-1898 in Carmichaels, PA and d. 2-27-1968 in Somerset, PA. She daughter of Minor Thompson and Amanda Stone. 3 children.

+Paul[7] Minor Haver b. 7-11-1921 Rices Landing, PA. Lives in Sewickley, PA. Physician (MD). m. on 3-25-1948 in Carnegie, PA to Alice Finley Campbell b. 7-10-1923. 5 children.

^David[8] Campbell Haver b. 4-4-1949 in Pittsburgh, PA and d. 10-30-1973 in Hartford, CT. m. on 8-8-1972 in New Wilmington, PA to Joyce Roberta Rockhill b. 5-3-1949 in Greenville, PA She daughter of Victor Rockhill and Helen..

^Donald[8] Scott Haver b. 3-31-1951 in Pittsburgh, PA. m. on 6-16-1979 in San Jose, CA to Susan Ann Epes b. 12-22-1955 in Manila, Philippines. 4 children.

~Kyle[9] David Haver b. 9-30-1981 in San Jose, CA

~Sean[9] Benjamin Haver b. 3-2-1983 in San Jose, CA.

~Taryn[9] Ashley Haver b. 9-17-1986 in Voorhees, NJ.

~Ryan[9] William Haver b. 5-30-1989 in Voorhees, NJ

^Richard[8] Alan Haver b. 12-4-1952 in Pittsburgh, PA. m. on 10-7-1978 in Waynesburgh, PA to Susan Jane Heberling b. 2-18-1952 in Pittsburgh, PA. She daughter of A. Lyle Heberling and Jane.

^Douglas[8] Paul Haver b. 7-18-1957 in Sewickley, PA. m. 10-22-1983 in Greenland, NH to Linda Jean Gilker b. 4-15-1956. She daughter of William K. Gilker and Ruth.

2 children.

~Dustin[9] Paul Haver b. 8-4-1985 in North Conway, NH.

~Amy[9] Elizabeth Haver b. 11-16-1988 in North Conway, NJ.

^Charles[8] Mark Haver b. 4-11-1959 in Sewickley, PA.

+Robert[7] Lewis Haver b. 6-10-1925 in Rices Landing, PA. m. about 8-6-1946 to Shirley Young b. about 1925. 3 children.

^Bonnie[8] Lynn Haver b. 4-5-1948 and d. 8-20-1985.

^Robert[8] Terry Haver b. 12-10-1949. Lives in Hamilton Square, NJ. m. on 6-23-1973 to Linda Sue Bullock b. about 1949. 3 children.

~Christopher[9] Haver b. 9-27-1976.

~Nicole[9] Haver b. 3-5-1979.

~Matthew[9] Haver b. 1982

^Susan[8] Melissa Haver b. 7-13-1955.

+Doris[7] Audrey Haver b. 5-15-1928 in Rices Landing, PA and d. 9-4-1991 in Silver Springs, MD. m. 12-2-1950 in Somerset, PA to James Albert Cunningham b. about 1926. 3 children.

^Michael[8] Cunningham b. 10-10-1953.

^Diane[8] Cunningham b. 5-25-1956. m. Anil Mukherjee b. about 1956. 2 sons.

~Sean[9] Mukherjee b. 10-16-1986.

~Ryan[9] Mukherjee b. 10-28-1988.

^Cathi[8] Cunningham b. 10-27-1962. m. Joseph Triplett b. about 1962. 1 daughter.

~Dorie[9] Triplett b. 1994.

(2) Jacob Rex[6] Haver b. 8-30-1898 in Mather, PA and d. 8-1-1982 in Lock Haven, PA. m. 7-24-1929 in Brookville, PA to Rebecca Jane Jennie McKinley b. 10-3-1907 Jefferson Co., PA and d. after 1982. 1 daughter.

+Edith[7] Virginia Haver b. 4-30-1932 in Lock Haven, PA. m. on 7-24-1954 in Lock Haven, PA to John Ronald Beck b. 8-11-1932 in Lock Haven, PA. 1 daughter.

^Jennifer[8] Beck b. 3-12-1954 in Carlisle, PA. m. 5-4-1991 in St Louis, MO to Stephen William Vogel b. 3-4-1954 in St. Louis, MO.

~Jonathan[9] Forest Vogel b. 10-22-1994 in St. Louis, MO.

(3) William[6] Cotterel Haver b. 5-16-1905 Mather, PA and d.

2-16-1993 Washington, PA. m. 7-9-1931 in Rices Landing, PA to Wanda Moniger b. 6-10-1910 in Green Co., PA and d. 5-13-1989 Washington, PA. Bur. Mather, PA. She Daughter of Edison Moniger and Pearl Moore. 2 sons.

+Wilber[7] Allan Haver b. 2-29-1932 Jefferson, PA. Lived in Dillwyn, VA. m. 9-1-1956 in Norfolk, VA to Mary Anne Seay b. 12-15- 1938 in Andersonville, VA. She daughter of Rice Lawrence Seay and Mary Lovelace. 4 children.

^Sharon[8] Anne Haver b. 10-21-1957 in Martin, KY. m. on 3-6-1982 in Richmond, VA to Francis James Barcalow, Jr. b. about 1957. 2 daughters.

~Mary[9] Katherine Barcalow b. 10-26-1986.

~Sarah[9] Elizabeth Barcalow b. 8-18-1989.

^Donna[8] Kaye Haver b. 12-20-1958 in Martin, KY. m. on 5-19-1990 in Richmond, VA to Joseph Ronald Bullard b. about 1958. He son of Asher Bullard and Venia. 1 daughter.

~Carrie[9] Anne Bullard b. 5-1-1995 in Richmond, VA.

^Nathan[8] Allan Haver b. 9-19-1960 in Martin, KY. m. on 8-20-1985 in Andersonville, VA to Sue Ellen Fish b. about 1960. She daughter of Theodore Fish and Janette.

^William[8] Rice Haver b. 6-12-1970 Mt Lebanon, PA. m. 2-3-1996 in Andersonville, VA to Stephanie Brown May b. about 1970.

+William[7] Dale Haver b. 6-23-1934 Jefferson, PA. m. 1-28-1961 in Tulsa, OK to Barbara Anne Offutt b. 2-27-1936. She daughter of Earl Offut and Ruby. 2 children.

^Ronald[8] Andrew Haver b. 9-22-1966 Tulsa, OK

^Alice[8] Ann Haver b. 3-5-1969 in Tulsa, OK. m. 6-7-1991 in Bartlesville, OK to Michael Anthony Shiflet, b. about 1969

(4) Homer[6] Lawrence Haver b. 5-17-1907 Jefferson, PA and d. 1-3-1990 in Waynesburg, PA. Bur. Mather, PA. m. 11-15-1930 in Cumberland, MD to Anna Leora McCann b. 2-12-1912 in Carmichaels, PA d. 5-17-1978 Waynesburg, PA. Bur. Mather, PA. She daughter of William Henry McCann and Alice Phillips. 1 daughter.

+Dorothy[7] Lois Haver b. 3-1-1933 Carmichaels, PA. m. 12-5-1952 in Carmichaels, PA to William Henry Cole b. 2-3-1930 in Nemacolin, PA. 2 sons.

^William[8] David Cole b. 6-8-1954 in Waynesburg, PA. m. 5-25-1985 in Waynesburg, PA to Janet Louise Chamberlain b. 2-6-1947 in Greene Co., PA. 1 son.

~Karl[9] David Cole b. 6-26-1987 in Morgantown, WV.

^Robyn[8] Lee Cole b. 4-21-1957 in Waynesburg, PA. m. 7-10-1992 in Rices Landing, PA to Angela Dawn Kelly b. 2-4-1968 in Morgantown, WV. 2 sons.

~Casey[9] Lee Cole b. 6-5-1996.

~William[9] Tyler Cole b. 6-27-1996.

(5) John[6] Wesley Haver b. 10-16-1909 and d. 5-7-1950 in Greene Co., PA. m. 5-11-1947 Irene D. Johns b. about 1909.

b. Jane[5] Rex Haver b. 2-15-1876 in Jefferson, PA and d. 12-9-1980 in Washington, PA. m. on 2-25-1903 to Albert Reynolds b. 9-2-1860 in Jefferson, PA and d. 8-28-1953 in Waynesburg, PA. 2 sons.

(1) John[6] Haver Reynolds b. 9-23-1906 in Jefferson, PA and d. 8-22-1983 Washington, PA. m. 1st Alice Gower b. about 1906. m. 2nd Elizabeth Moore Brownlee b. 2-27-1910 in Washington, PA. No children.

(2) William[6] Albert Reynolds b. 3-21-1909 in Cumberland, PA and d. 5-4-1988 in Point Marion, PA. Was employed by Cumberland Twp. School District. m, 3-31-1937 to Cleola Price b. 9-21-1919 in Zanesville, NC and d. 6-21-1991 in Fredericktown, PA. 5 children.

+William[7] Albert Reynolds, Jr. b. about 1939.

+Richard[7] F. Reynolds b. about 1941. Lives in Omaha, NE.

+Gary[7] A. Reynolds b. about 1943. Lived in Marion, PA.

+Leanna[7] Jane Reynolds b. about 1945. Lived in Fredericktown, PA m. Albert Chapman b. about 1945.

+Donna[7] D. Reynolds b. about 1947. Lives in Carmichaels, PA. m. 1st Tragarden b. about 1947. m. 2nd Payton. Lives in Ocean City, MD.

c. Laura[5] Belle Haver b. 3-2-1878 in Greene Co., PA and d. 12-14-1958 in Greene Co., PA., single.

d. Joseph[5] Bell Haver b. 6-24-1881 in Greene, Co., PA and d. 9-27-1951 in Pittsburgh, PA. m. 9-5-1905 in Greene Co., PA to Veronica McVay. 6 children.

(1) Francis Bradley[6] Haver b. 6-7-1906 in Marianna, PA and d. 1-1-1964 in Duquesne, PA. in. about 1-1932 in Fredericktown, PA to Ann Guaiski b. 4-27-1915. 4 children.

+Joseph[7] Bradley Haver b. 6-9-1933 in Fredericktown, PA. m. 8-3-1955 in Brownsville, PA to Janet Lunden b. about 1933.

+Samuel[7] R. Haver b. 6-28-1934 in Fredericktown, PA. m. 2-25-1956 in Brownsville, PA to Gay Lunden b. about 1934.

+Robert[7] W. Haver b. 1-29-1938 in Fredericktown, PA. Lives in Malvern, PA.

+John[7] D. Haver b. 6-16-1941 in Fredericktown, PA. m. 10-13-1962 in Fredericktown, PA to Helen Romladora b. about 1941.

(2) Joseph[6] Wallace Haver b. 1-6-1908 in Marianna, PA and d. 11-7-1975 in Washington, PA. m. in Pittsburgh, PA to Marie b. about 1908 and d, 7-1984. 3 children.

+Judy[7] Haver b. 1939. m. Genst b. about 1939.

+Mary Frances Haver b. 9-26-1941 in Pittsburgh, PA. m. 1-9-1965 in Allegheny Co., PA George Edward Milliken, Jr. b. 6-6-1940 in Pittsburgh, PA. He son of George Edward Milliken, Sr. and Dorothy Ballantyne. 4 children.

^Douglas[8] Edward Milliken b. 1-8-1966 in Pittsburgh, PA. m. 5-29-1993 in Indiana, Pa to Christine Louise Hickey b. 11-14-1967.

^Beth[8] Lynn Milliken b. 5-22-1967 in Pittsburgh, PA. m. 8-21-1989 in Anderson IN to Jeffery Lynn Bates b. about 1967. 1 child.

~Kyle[9] Barrett Bates b. 1-14-1993 Anderson, IN.

^Susan[8] Anne Milliken b. 6-30-1969 in Pittsburgh, PA.

^Mark[8] Joseph Milliken b. 12-19-1971 in Pittsburgh, PA.

+Richard[7] Haver b. 7-28-1954.

(3) Annetta[6] Virginia Haver b.8-21-1909 in Marianna, PA and d. 7-18-1986 in Brownsville, PA. m. 2-8-1942 to Harry Christy b. about 1909 and d. 11-25-1953 in Fredericktown, PA. 2 sons.

+William[7] A. Christy b. 9-9-1942 in Brownsville, PA. m. 1st 2-8-1964 in Fredericktown, PA to Patricia George. m. 2nd 12-3-1994 to Lorene Ring.

+Henry[7] Wallace McVay Christy b. 10-21-1943 in Brownsville, PA. m. 1st in Berea, OH Ann now divorced.

(4) Robert[6] Regis Haver b. 12-10-1912 in Marianna, PA and d. 3-23-1985 in McKeesport, PA. m. 9-15-1940 in Duquesne, PA to Sue Snyder b. 3-14-1912 in Duquesne, PA. 2 sons.

+Joseph[7] Regis Haver b. 7-1-1956 in McKeesport, PA. m. 8-3-1968 to Cathy Bendos b. about 1956.

+Edward[7] J. Haver b. 11-27-1958 in McKeesport, PA

(5) Mary[6] Genevive Haver b. 3-22-1914 in Marianna, PA. Lives in Fredericktown, PA.

(6) William[6] Cotterel Haver b. 11-11-1919 in Pittsburgh, PA. m. 9-21-1946 to Esther Bauer b. 12-9-1919 in Pittsburgh, PA. 1 daughter.

+Linda[7] Haver b. 7-3-1947 in Brownsville, PA. m. 1st Huff b. about 1947 and 2nd to Ron Todd b. about 1947.

e. William[5] Haver b. 6-24-1881 in Jefferson, PA and d. about 6-27-1881 in Jefferson, PA.

f. Elizabeth[5] Haver b. 6-4-1884 in Jefferson, PA and d. 9-28-1967 in Greene Co., PA. Taught piano. Never married.

H. Charles[4] Henry Haver b. 1-22-1849 in Jefferson, PA and d. 1-4-1929 in Jefferson, PA. m. 1-22-1880 Isabella McClure b. 9-21-1851 in Greene Co., PA and d. 10-5-1903 in Jefferson, PA. She daughter of James M. McClure and Susan Brown. 3 children.

a. James[5] Clyde Haver b. 9-28-1881 in Greene, Co., PA and d. 6-1-1970 in Anniston, AL. m. 12-7-1904 in Jefferson, PA to Anna May Campbell b. 2-15-1882 in Perulack, PA and d. 7-24-1961 in Piedmont, AL. She daughter of John Campbell and Nancy Jane Love. 6 children.

(1) Charles[6] William Haver b. 12-14-1905 in Jefferson, PA and d. 3-19-1991 in Akron, OH. m. 12-24-1934 in Akron, OH to Florence J. Maloney b. 1-24-1911. 3 children.

+Robert[7] William Haver b. 12-3-1935. m. 3-9-1957 to Shirley Thomas b. 6-13-1939. 5 children.

^Kenneth[8] William Haver b. 9-30-1958.

^Lora[8] Jean Haver b. 12-1-1959 in SC. 1 daughter.

~Amber[9] b. 11-30-1981 in Akron, OH.

^Dennis[8] William Haver b. 2-13-1961.

^Lisa[8] Ann Haver b. 4-22-1965.

^Charles[8] William Haver b. 10-30-1975.

+Eleanor[7] Marie Haver b. 2-3-1938. Lives in VT. m. 9-15-1962 to Theodore Eisenman b. 2-5-1939. 2 children.

^Cynthia[8] Ann Eisenman b. 8-21-1963. m. 10-2-1993 in NY, NY to Alan Eisenman Rousso b. 10-25-1962 in Queens, NY.

^Dwight[8] Howard Eisenman b. 11-23-1969

+Phyllis[7] Ann Haver b. 11-10-1945. m. 1st 8-11-1961 to George Bissell b. 3-27-1937 and d. 4-25-1989 in Cuyahoga Falls, OH. 3 children.

^David[8] Watson Bissell b. 4-4-1963.

^Steven[8] William Bissell b. 3-13-1965.

^Susan[8] Marie Bissell b. 7-24-1968. m. 3-19-1994 in Akron, OH to Michael Robert Zager b. 6-16-1969.

m. 2nd 5-16-1993 to Walter Salyer b. 3-4-1932.

(2) Harry[6] Campbell Haver b. 12-9-1907 in Jefferson, PA. m. 10-15-1933 in Calhoun Co., AL to Lenox Olivia Propes b. 11-25-1909 in Calhoun Co., AL. 3 children.

+William[7] Martone Tony Haver b. 8-24-1938 in Duke, AL. m. 5-7-1961 to Juanita Humphries b. 3-28-1939 in Weaver, AL. 2 daughters.

^Lanita[8] Gay Haver b. 5-4-1962 in Anniston, AL.

^Karen[8] Anne Haver b. 5-4-1964 in Anniston, AL. m. about 1965 Ronald Rigney.

+Lawrence[7] Haver b. 9-9-1940 in Calhoun Co., AL and is deceased. m. 1st June Massey b. about 8-24-1940. 2 children.

^Gerald[8] Wayne Haver b. 1-28-1962. m. 11-27-1986 to Karen Renee Blakeley b. about 1962. 2 children.

~Jordan[9] Nicole Haver b. 2-2-1995 in Eagle River, AK.

~Justin[9] Campbell Haver b. 1996 in Eagle River, AK.

^Debra[8] Haver b. 9-18-1968.

m. 2nd Carrie b. about 1940.

+Connie[7] Haver b. 5-16-1947 in Calhoun Co., AL. m. Gary Sanford b. about 1947. 2 daughters.

^Lisa[8] Sanford b. 4-28-1975.

^Jill[8] Sanford b. 7-5-1978.

(3) Clifford[6] Lawrence Haver b. 4-18-1909 in Jefferson, PA and d. 11-10-1971 in Jefferson, Pa. m. 8-23-1936 in Jefferson, PA to Nelle Vankirk Thistlethwaite b. 10-26-1910 in Jefferson Co., PA. She was daughter of David Dunham Thistlethwaite and Emma Bell Vankirk. 2 daughters.

+Suzanne[7] Haver b. 4-27-1943 in Waynesburg, PA. m. 4-6-1962 in Jefferson, PA to Fred Keefe Palone b. 10-22-1944. He son of Fred Palone and Kathryn McMasters. 2 daughters.

^Susan[8] Dawn Palone b.11-23-1962 in Waynesburg, PA.

^Tracy[8] Lynn Palone b. 10-13-1965 in Fairview Park, OH.

m. 5-4-1985 to Edward Allen Laroe b. 1-25-1964. in Ann
Arbor, MI. 2 children.

~Edward[9] Clifford Laroe b. 12-21-1985 in Ann Arbor,
MI.

~Nicole[9] Lynn Laroe b. 2-4-1988 in Ann Arbor, MI.
+Janice[7] Lee Haver b. 3-1-1947 in Waynesburg, PA. Lives in
Jefferson, PA. m. 2-9-1969 to Barry Joe Tekavec b. 3-8-
1945 in Greene Co., PA. He son of Joseph A. Tekavec and
Genevieve Marie Sharpnack. 1 son.

^Adam[8] Brooke Tekavec b. 10-31-1971 i Waynesburg, PA.
(4) Edwin[6] Reuben Haver b. 10-27-1911 in Jefferson, PA and d.
9-11-1981 in Birmingham, AL. m. 9-20-1936 in Etowah Co.,
AL to Johnnie Pentecost b. 11-16-1916 in Wellington, AL. 3
children.

+James[7] Edwin Haver b. 2-24-1938 in Centre, AL. m. 6-17-
1961 to Trudell Franklin b. 6-2-1940 in Athens, AL. 2
daughters.

^Moira[8] Anne Haver b. 7-7-1963 in Dugway, UT. m.
6-9-1990 in Decatur, AL to Danny Clark Cameron. 1 son.

~Joshua[9] Tyler Cameron b. 11-4-1994 in Huntsville, AL.

^Cassandra[8] Trudell Haver b. 1-11-1969. m. 1-21-1994 in
Nashville, TN to Thomas Fite Cone, Jr. b. 2-14-1969
+William[7] Franklin Haver b. 3-4-1942 in Ohatchee, AL. m.
6-1-1963 in Decatur, AL to Doris Lee Wardlow b. 11-28-
1941. 2 children.

^Jennifer[8] Leigh Haver b. 11-2-1966 in Tuscaloosa, AL. m.
4-19-1995 in Birmingham, AL to Scott Richard Russell b.
11-16-1966.

^William[8] Franklin Haver, Jr. b. 6-24-1975 in Birmingham,
AL.
+Peggy[7] Diane Haver b. 12-5-1945 in Glencoe, AL. m.
1-27-1967 to Joseph Charles McCorquodale III b. 8-8-1945.
2 children.

^Elizabeth[8] Haver McCorquodale b. 9-9-1967. m. 2-17-
1990 to Robert Kerry Beard b. 2-14-1966. 1 son.

~Robert[9] Tyler Beard b. 10-17-1993.

^Joseph[8] Charles McCorquodale IV b. 8-15-1973 now in
law school.
(5) Alfred[6] Clyde Haver b. 4-14-1914 in Jefferson, PA. m. 1st
12-15-1944 in Alexandria, AL to Vivian Geneva Birmingham

b. 9-20-1915 and d. 5-26-1988 in Birmingham, AL. 2 children.
+Marie[7] Elaine Haver b. 1-10-1947 in Anniston, AL. m.
Danny Royce Bryant in Wellington, AL and now divorced.
+Alfred[7] Dale Butch Haver b. 1-10-1950 in Anniston, AL.
m 2nd 6-21-1990 in Wellington, AL to Lola Mae Nelson b.
4-14-1924 in Glenco, AL.
(6) William[6] Owen Haver b. 4-25-1921 in Ohatchee, AL. m.
7-4-1947 in Ohatchee, AL to Dorothy Virginia Polle b. 4-11-
1926 in Ohatchee, AL. She daughter of Leo Polle and Rilla
Martin. 2 children and 1 adopted son.
+Alvin[7] Clyde Haver b. 3-26-1949 in Anniston, AL. m.
Christy Murdock b. about 1949. 2 sons.
^Michael[8] Elijah Haver b. 6-13-1976.
^Joshua[8] Aaron Haver b. 11-18-1977.
+Janet[7] Freida Haver b. 4-17-1952 in Anniston, AL. m. Paul
Henry b. about 1952 and now deceased. 1 son.
^Micah Michael Henry b. 12-23-1980.
b. William[5] Owen Haver b. 3-27-1884 in Jefferson, Pa and d.
9-25-1939 in Hannibal, MO. Worked in vaudeville and rode a
motorcycle in carnivals. m. 2-19-1918 to Olive Hager b. about
1884. Divorced.
c. Suda[5] Maria Haver b. 9-29-1893 in Jefferson, PA and d.
8-6-1969 in Washington, PA. m. 10-9-1918 in Greene Co., PA to
Paul Feitt b. 10-21-1890 in Blairsville, PA and d. 4-9-1971 in
Jefferson, PA. He son of Christian J. Feitt and Ellen Amelia
Curtis. 1 daughter.
(1) Mary[6] Elizabeth Feitt b. 9-7-1919 in Jefferson, PA. m.
12-9-1944 in Washington, D.C. to Herbert Carlton Smith b.
2-4-1918 in Bloomsburg, PA. 3 children.
+Paul[7] Ashton Smith b. 5-22-1946 in Washington, DC. m. 1st
1-24-1970 in College park, MD to Virginia Mae Luke b.
5-22-1946 in Washington, DC. She daughter of Carl Luke
and Gladys. 3 children.
^Michael[8] Philip Smith b. 5-23-1972 in Takoma Park, MD.
^Sara[8] Linnea Smith b. 12-31-1974 in Jacksonville, FL.
^Carl[8] Ashton Smith b. 2-15-1977 in Olney, MD.
m 2nd 4-5-1985 in Wilmington, DE to Ruth Louise Sherrill b.
10-6-1949. She daughter of Horace Cleveland Sherrill, Jr. b.
10-21-1921 and Mary Louise Wilson b. 7-2-1922.
+Robert[7] Carlton Smith b. 11-12-1949 in Washington, DC.

m. 12-29-1973 in University Park, MD to Joanne Carol
Shepherd b. 7-1-1952 in Washington, DC. She daughter of
Julius Canoy Shepherd b. 8-17-1922 and Ruth Naomi
Cromie b. 5-23-1925. 1 son.

^Robert[8] Edward Feitt Smith b. 10-18-1981 in Baltimore,
MD.

+Virginia[7] Sue Smith b. 8-8-1952 in Washington, DC. m.
11-17-1973 in Hyattsville, MD to Lawrence Gaither
Silvestro b. 8-31-1948 in Washington, DC. 6 children.

^Lauren[8] Rebecca Silvestro b. 12-23-1978 in Silver Spring,
MD.

^Julia[8] Sue Silvestro b. 5-29-1980 in Silver Spring, MD.

^Kristin[8] Elizabeth Silvestro b. 8-8-1982 in Silver Spring,
MD.

^Tessa[8] Nicole Silvestro b. 7-29-1985 in Silver Spring,
MD.

^Carlton[8] Gaither Silvestro b. 7-12-1987 in Silver Spring,
MD.

^Bradley[8] Jacob Silvestro b. 12-7-1989 in Silver Spring,
MD.

I. Hannah[4] Margaret Haver b. 4-12-1851 in Greene Co., PA and d.
9-2-1880. m. 7-1-1874 David A. Cosgray b. 6-14-1851. 1 daughter.

a. Daisy[5] Haver Cosgray b. 10-16-1876 m. 2-26-1927 Chauncey
M. White.

J. Emma[4] Haver b. 10-23-1853 in Greene Co., PA and d. 5-23-1860.

K. James[4] Harper Haver b. 3-11-1856 in Greene Co., PA and d.
7-26-1935 in Fullerton, CA. m. 8-14-1879 in Masontown, PA
Elizabeth (Lizzie) Capitola L. Vernon b. 6-1856 in Greene Co., PA
and d. 6-6-1923 in Fullerton, CA. James Harper and Elizabeth
Haver, his wife, both attended Washington and Jefferson College,
Washington, PA. where they were born and raised. m. at
Masontown, PA. Moved to Highland and Hiawatha, KS. 5
children.

a. Clark[5] Jamison Haver b. 7-2-1880 d. 5-20-1915, Hiawatha, KS.
m. 6-28-1905 Maude M. Truitt b. 7-15-1883 KS d. 1-1963. Both
attended Hiawatha Academy, members Christian Church.
Grocery business. 1 son.

(1) Harland[6] Haver b. 10-17-1910 d. 10-12-1923.

b. John[5] Leslie Haver b. Highland, KS. 12-18-1881. Grocer,
moved to CA. m. Ethel M. Babbitt 10-20-1906. 2 children.

(1) Dorothy[6] Jean Haver b. Fullerton, CA 8-16-1914. H. S. Grad.

(2) Forrest[6] Elden Haver b. Fullerton, CA 8-7-1917. H. S. Grad.

c. Theodosia[5] Rebecca Haver b. Highland, KS 8-22-1883. m. 6-17-1911 Rollyn R. Meisenheimer b. about 1883 and d. 8-17-1924. 2 children.

(1) Wiles[6] Kenlian Meisenheimer b. 10-11-1913. H. S. Grad. Fullerton, CA.

(2) Shiral[6] Adron Meisenheimer b. 6-21-1918.

d. Clifford[5] Vernon Haver b. 7-26-1888 and d. 11-1968. m. 8-1913 Hazel Cahill in Kansas City, KS.

e. Mary[5] Lenore Haver b. 11-4-1891 Grad. Hiawatha, KS. Academy 1911 m. 11-14-1928 Paul H. Youngquist.

6. George[3] Rex 3rd (Figure 41) (6th child of Jane and George[2], George[1]) b. 4-6-1816 in Westmoreland, PA. d. 9-23-1863 Palmyra, MO. Is said he closely resembled his Uncle Benjamin Rex. He was a very religious man, and the rearing of his children and the manner of living was strictly Puritanic. There could be no noise on the Sabbath and all food possible was prepared Saturday for the next day, tea being the only part of the meal served warm on Sunday. Church buildings were not so numerous then and his home was often the place where religious services were held.

Figure 41. George Rex III.

This training must have been productive for a grand-daughter, Carrie Howell Martin, says her Uncle George Franklin Rex was the best Christian man she ever knew. In the last illness of George 3rd, his daughter Mary J. and her husband, John Howell, were sent for and took with them their 11 month old baby Thos. Franklin who also passed away during their stay and was buried in Palmyra with his grandfather. George Rex 3rd was married three times, **first** to Louisa Townsend 3-1840 who was b. 10-6-1817 d. 10-22-1843. To them two children were born.

A. Mary[4] Jane Rex b. 6-29-1841 m. at Ashton, Mo. John Wesley Howell, who was b. 12-9-1843, d. 4-29-1923. 8 children.

a. Thomas[5] Franklin Howell b. 11-5-1862 d. 10-1-1863.

b. Sarah[5] Harper Howell b. 11-26-1864, Ashton, m. 7-1881 John

Martin Smith of Luray, Mo. 2 children by 1st husband. m. 2nd A. J. Grube, 1929, Los. Angeles, CA.

(1) James^6 Wesley Smith.

(2) Elvia^6 Smith m. 1st John Hummel 1898. 2nd George Lenhart.

c. Carrie^5 E. Howell (twin) b. Ashton, 8-31-1867 m. Jacob W. Martin, Memphis, MO. 6 children.

(1) Carl^6 Waldo Martin b. 7-8-1891 m. at Kahoka, MO 2-6-1909 Verne F. Meryhue. 2 children.

+Virginia^7 Meryhue b. 1-14-1910.

+Kirk^7 Bernard Meryhue b. 6-14-1912.

(2) Leo^6 Howell Martin b. 3-12-1893 m. Maybel Robinson 8-1915, Oakhill, KS. 3 children.

+Marjorie^7 Maxine Martin b. 8-16-1917.

+Geneva^7 Carolyn Martin b. 3-5-1919.

+Robert^7 Leo Martin b. 7-6-1929.

(3) Nettie^6 Irene Martin (teacher) b. 3-12-1896 m. Wayne Hockett. 1 son.

+Wayne^7 Hockett, Jr. b. 8-30-1918, Harve, MT.

(4) Mary^6 Louise Martin (teacher) b. 4-23-1900 m. Elman Francis Sherman 6-20-1920, Ashton, MO. 1 son.

+Donald^7 E. Sherman b. and d. 1-1923.

(5) Lynn^6 Phillip Martin b. 1-26-1907 m. 11-28-1929 Ruth Davis, Ft. Madison, IA.

d. Nettie^5 V. Howell b. 8-31-1867 (twin) m. Elmer E. Yolton, Memphis, MO. 1 son.

(1) Eugene^6 Howell Yolton b. 11-15-1896 m. Mildred Walters.

e. William^5 H. Howell b. 3-31-1870 m. Sidney L. Yolton, Ashton, MO. 4 children.

(1) †Marvin^6 Lee Howell b. 1892 m. Nettie Hendricks, Keokuk, IA. Served in World War. I. 1 child.

+Doris^7 Alta Howell b. 11-11-1920.

(2) Esther^6 Marie Howell b. 1896 m. Paul Foster, Granger, MO. 4 children, 1st one died in infancy.

+Billie^7 Grant Foster b. 1-1919.

+Peggie^7 Marie Foster b. 2-1925.

+Donald^7 Stewart Foster b. 1929.

(3) †William^6 Rex Howell b. 1899 m. Edna Bucket, Mendota, IL. In Navy 6 yrs. 1 son.

+William^7 Stanley Howell b. 1-1925.

(4) Frank^6 Stewart Howell b. 1907, single. Diamond Ranch,

Chugwater, WY.

f. John[5] Linley Howell b. 11-29-1873 m. Bertha May Drollinger. 3 children.

  (1) Herbert[6] Monroe Howell b. 1895 d. 1897.

  (2) Daisy[6] Irene Howell b. 10-1899 d. 1901.

  (3) Helen[6] Luell Howell b. 6-1897 m. Joseph Hall 1914. 3 children.

   +Joseph[7] Mae Hall b. 1916 d. same day.

   +Clara[7] Mae Hall b. 1920.

   +Billie Hall b. 1923.

g. George[5] Etsel Howell b. 11-27-1878 d. 1-29-1888 (heart failure, fell dead while at play).

h. Zac[5] Townsend Howell b. 5-8-1884 m. Ethel Burns, Omaha, NE. 5 children.

  (1) Zac[6] Townsend Howell, Jr.

  (2) Herbert[6] Howell.

  (3) Elizabeth[6] Howell.

  (4) Paul[6] Howell.

  (5) Billie[6] Howell.

B. †George[4] Franklin Rex (Figure 42) b. 10-14-1843 d. Kahoka, Mo. 11-24-1922. m. Carrie L. Bartlett 10-29-1871, Clark City, Mo. Ceremony by Rev. Guy Hamilton. She b. 2-27-1844 d. Kahoka 6-3-1896. George F. R. enlisted Union Army 12-1861 Kahoka, MO Co. A. 2nd Regiment, Mo. Vol. His father George R. 3rd was also serving in the war as hospital steward. Elizabeth Emery Rex, 3rd wife of George 3rd, was serving too as matron in the hospital from 6-1861 to 6-1863. George 3rd d. Palmyra, MO 9-23-1863, then the son of G. F. R. took his place as steward and served until

Figure 42. George Franklin Rex.

the end of the war. George F. R. was building contractor and a devout Methodist. 6 children, all born in Clark Co., MO.

a. Louise[5] Bartlett Rex b. 9-5-1872 m. Frank Taylor Beckett at Kahoka 12-4-1902 who was born Frankfort, KA. 10-2-1870. She was a teacher grad. Mo. State Normal Class 1896, is a P. E. O. and Methodist. 6 children.

  (1) Mary[6] Frances Beckett b. 10-30-1903, San Marcial, NM. m.

Ray W. Gierhart 12-27-1926, El Reno, OK. She is grad. Stevens; Kappa Delta Phi also grad. OK U. Chi Omega. 1 son.

+Billie[7] Ray Gierhart b. 10-24-1928.

(2) Barbara[6] Bell Beckett b. 8-14-1912 Tucumcari, NM. Won State Vocal Contest, Okla. City 1930, Stevens College.

(3) Frank[6] Taylor Beckett b. 10-12-1914 El Reno, OK.

(4) Robert[6] Beckett, d. infant.

(5) Jennie[6] Louise Beckett, d. infant.

b. Mary[5] Celest Rex b. 10-7-1873. m. Frank M. Clough at Woodward, Okla. 4-9-1907. He d. 6-10-30 El Paso, TX where he was Supt. of Bridge and Building for El Paso and S. W. She was a P. E. O., Eastern Star and Presbyterian. 3 children all b. in Tucumcari, NM.

(1) Sara[6] Carlyn Clough b. 11-24-1909. m. Claude C. Mencus, Santa Rota, NM. 6-29-1926. Episcopalians. 1 son.

+Cloud[7] Clough Mencus b. 8-4-1926, El Paso, TX.

(2) Mildred[6] Gertrude Clough b. 1-1911.

(3) Frankie[6] Rex Clough b. 2-1921.

c. George[5] Everett Rex (Figure 43) b. 9-8-1876 m. 1st Eva O. Hoober at Watseka, IL 6-18-1902. She d. 12-8-1909. 2 children b. to them. V. Pres. Natl. Lumber and Creosoting Co. K. C. MO. Educated at Kahoka, MO. and on an honor scholarship attended Iowa Weslyn Methodist. Member American Soc. for Testing Materials, American Soc. Civil Engineers, American Railway Engineers Assn., American Wood Preservers Assn. m. 2nd Florence Matlick at Kohoka, MO. 2 children.

Figure 43. George Everett Rex.

(1) George[6] Everett Rex, Jr. (Figure 44) b. 12-1-1903, Topeka, KS. m. 1921 and has two children. Was in same business as father with headquarters Texarkana, TX.

(2) Helen[6] Rex b. 11-1905 Argentine, KS d. Marceline, MO 1906.

d. Flora[5] Belle Rex b. 12-24-1878 Grad. Kahoka College, Presbyterian and Eastern Star. m. Robert L. Woodfuff at San Marcial, N. M. 6-1903. 1 daughter.

Figure 44. George Everett Rex, Jr.

(1) Margaret[6] Louise Woodfuff b. 11-14-1905 S. M. N. M. Grad. Hardin Jr. College, Phi Theta Kappa, Grad. N. E. MO State Teacher's College, Kappa Delta, Eastern Star, Teacher Kahoka H. S.

e. Laura[5] Grace Rex b. 11-24-1880 m. Alvine E. Overhulser at Kahoka 11-5-1902. 3 children.

(1) Marjorie[6] Wynonia Overhulser b. 12-31-1903, Kahoka, MO.

(2) William[6] Franklin Overhulser b. 7-18-1908, Marceline, MO. Grad. Park College 6-1930, then entered N. Y. Biblical Seminary.

(3) Mary[6] Alice Overhulser b. 6-25-1913, Marceline, MO.

f. †Clarence[5] Bartlett Rex b. 6-2-1884, Gen. Auditor St. L. S. F. R. R. 32° Mason, Methodist and in World War. m. Dixie Bell McCleary at Topeka, KS 9-11-1907. d. 11-28-1934 at St. Louis, MO. 1 son.

(1) Clarence[6] Bartlett Rex, Jr. b. 12-19-1910, Topeka, KS.

6. †George[.3] Rex III (George[2], George[1]) m. 2nd Elizabeth Kennedy 8-18-1844. She d. 7-18-1848 in Boone Co., KY. (daughter of Samuel and Clemintine Emery-Kennedy, Emery Genealogy by Rev. Rufus Emery). 2 children.

C. †William[4] H. Rex b. Aurora, IN 3-7-1845 m. Mary E. Ivie who was b. 11-3-1857. Farmer and Stockraiser. Private in Co. F. 21st Mo. Inf. Discharged for disability Nov. 1862. Reenlisted as Private Co. D. 3rd Mo. Cav. 2 4-1864, mustered out at New Orleans, LA 7-27-1865. 5 children.

a. Violet[5] Rex b. 5-14-1880 m. Robert V. Reynolds 8-12-1909.

b. Essie[5] Rex b. 4-14-1882.

c. Louise[5] Rex b. 1-7-1884 d. 9-4-1906, single.

d. William[5] H. Rex b. 9-28-1885 m. Myrtle Orstein 9-6-1908 who was b. 2-25-1890. 1 daughter.

(1) Louise[6] Mary Rex b. 7-2-1913.

e. James[5] Rex b. 4-28-1887 m. 9-12-1913 Elsie Shuster who was b. 4-16-1889.

D. Louisa[4] Rex b. 11-7-1847 d. 3-8-1862, single. George[3] Rex m. 3rd Elizabeth Emery (first cousin of his 2nd wife - see Emery Genealogy, Rev. Rufus Emery) b. N. Market, O. 3-17-1821 daughter of Samuel (Ambrose, James, Johnathon, John) and Sarah Anderson Emery. Were married 12-30-1848, she d. in Denver, CO. 6-17-1904. 6 children.

E. Sarah[4] Samantha Rex (Figure 45) b. 8-25-1850 Versailles, Ind. m. David Henry Wood (Figure 46) 1-27-1879 at Castle Rock, CO. He b. 11-7-1845 Dubuque, IA. She d. 6-10-1939 in Denver, CO. He d. 5-11-1918 in Denver CO. 2 children.

Figure 45. Sarah Samantha Rex.

Figure 46. David Henry Wood.

  a. Lelah[5] Alice Wood (Figure 47) b. 11-9-1879 m. James Strugnell, Denver. She d. 1-18-1941. He d. 6-27-1921. 1 daughter.

    (1) Muriel Strugnell (Figure 47) b. 9-29-1911. d. 11-24-1980. m. †Tom Jack Mullins, retired as 1st Sgt. US Army. 2 children.

Figure 47. Left to right: James Strugnell, Muriel Strugnell, and Lelah Alice Wood Strugnell.

      +Robert Rankin Mullins b. 4-19-1931 Adams CO. d. 6-4-1986 Pittaburg, TX. m. Francia Elizabeth Sherrill 6-17-1955 Athena TX. She b. 2-25-1931 Malakoff, TX. 4 Children.

        ^Roberta Elizabeth Mullins, Jr. b. 9-26-1956.

        ^Robert Rankin Mullins, b. 6-28-1958.

        ^Charles Evan Mullins, b. 10-24-1965.

        ^William Padric Mullins, b. 10-14-1965.

      +Thomas Edward Mullins (Figure 48) b. 12-16-1932 Adams, CO. m. 1st Caroline Eloise Baker. She b. 12-1-1932 Rochester, NY. 3 children.

Figure 48. T. E. Mullins and wife, Margery

        ^Steven Kent Mullins, b. 5-13-1958.

        ^Melissa Keye Mullins, b. 1-15-1961.

        ^Kathleen Ann Mullins, b. 3-15-1966.

      m. 2nd 12-28-1995 in Denver, CO Margery Cheever b. 7-3-1944.

  b. Grace[5] Anna Wood (Figure 49) b. 9-26-1885 m. David W. Thomas (Figure 50), Denver 10-5-1910. She d. 1-8-1960 Denver. He d. 12-10-1938 Ft. Collins CO. 2 boys.

    (1) †Robert[6] Rex Thomas (Figure 51) b. 9-5-1911, m. Bonita

Garland England 1-1-1932.
He d. 2-14-1978. In US Navy
during WW II. 4 children.
　+Mayanne[7] Thomas 9-16-
　1932.
　+Nancy[7] Thomas 2-20-1936.
　+Donald[7] Thomas 10-28-
　1942.
　+Douglas[7] Thomas 10-28-
　1942.

Figure 49. Grace
Wood Thomas.

Figure 50. David
W. Thomas.

Figure 51. (L to R) Mayanne Thomas Clatt, Nancy Thomas, Bonnie Thomas, Robert
Rex Thomas, Doug Thomas, Donald Thomas. Photo taken 1976.

(2) †David[6] Benjamin Thomas (Figure 52) b.
2-20-1917 m. Vivian Alice Dutton 1-24-
1942. She d. 5-27-1987. He was 1st
Lieutenant, Army Air Corps WW II, d.
10-15-1992. 4 children.
　+William[7] David Thomas (Figure 53) b.
　9-4-1945 in Bronx, NY. Technical writer
　for Pentax Corp. Co-Editor/Author of
　Second Edition *Rex Genealogy*. m. 1st
　Yvonne Odett Clifton 3-19-1966 in
　Denver, CO. She b. 10-6-1946 in
　Boulder, CO. 2 children.

Figure 52. Vivian Al-
ice Dutton and David
Benjamin Thomas.

　　^Cynthia[8] Louise Thomas (Figure 54) b. 3-5-1968 in
　　Aurora, CO. m. Russell William Taylor 7-6-1988 in
　　Littleton, CO. 4 children.
　　　~Kathleen[9] Taylor b 7-17-1989 in Rexburg, ID.
　　　~William[9] Russell Taylor b. 6-4-1991 Provo, UT.
　　　~Stephen[9] Andrew Taylor b 9-19-1993 Burley ID.

Figure 53. Jane Diane Bruland Thomas and William David Thomas.

Figure 54. The Taylors: 1. Cynthia, 2. Will, 3. Russ, 4. Katie, 5. Stephen, 6. Derek.

Figure 55. Jason Eugene Thomas, Benjamin R. Thomas.

~Derek[9] James Taylor b. 9-14-1995 Burley, ID.

^ †Jason[8] Eugene Thomas (Figure 55) b. 8-22-1970 in Englewood, CO. m. Amelia Christiana Wakeham 11-2-1991 in Arvada, CO. 1 son.

  ~Benjamin[9] Reed Thomas (Figure 55) b. 3-20-1993 in Beaufort, SC

m. 2nd Jane Diane Bruland 11-20-1974. She b. 10-6-1946.

+Adrianne[7] Ruth Thomas b. 11-3-1946. Denver, CO. d. 6-13-1950. Sonoma, CA.

+Carol[7] Louise Thomas. (Figure 56) b. 4-12-1952 San Jose, CA. m. Anthony Michael Carleo 8-27-1977 Denver, CO. He b. 12-3-1952 Pueblo, CA. 4 children.

  ^Lea[8] Marie Carleo b. 5-24-1982 in Dallas TX.

Figure 56. The Carleo Family: 1. Michael. 2. Elizabeth. 3. Carol. 4. Andonia. 5. Anthony 6. Lea.

  ^Andonia[8] Jeanine Carleo b. 6-15-1984 in Irving TX.

  ^Elizabeth[8] Ann Carleo b. 1-14-1987 in Irving TX.

  ^Michael[8] Anthony Carleo b. 10-7-1989 Irving TX.

+James[7] Benjamin Thomas (Figure 57) b. 2-4-1955 Denver, CO.

F. Rebecca[4] Olive Rex b. 9-25-1852 Rexville, IN. m. Julius A. Hooker 10-25-1884 Denver. She d. 1-1-1889. 1 son.

Figure 57. James B. Thomas

a. Oliver^5 Walcott Hooker b. 12-24-1888.

G. Samuel^4 Watson Rex b. Versailles, IN 10-16-1864 d. 3-8-1862.

H. John^4 Emery Rex b. Ashton, Mo. 12-7-1856 m. Bessie Mills of Louisville, KY. Is interested in this genealogy and has assisted in the work. No issue. Many years Eng. Dept. Northern Pac. R. R., Denver.

I. Nancy^4 Isabelle (Belle) Rex b. Ashton, MO 1-22-1859 m. 7-2-1878 Mark Sawyer Ward who was b. Maquoketa, IA 3-13-1854 d. 1929 Denver. 3 children.

  a. Ralph^5 Sargent Ward b. 5-20-1879 m. Myrtle McKenzie of Howard, NE.

  b. Nellie^5 Hortense Ward b. 8-29-1885 m. Alex W. Allyn 12 5-1904. He d. 2-14-1932. (Auto on wrong side of Mountain road struck his motorcycle and he was instantly killed.)

  c. Mildred^5 Wanda Ward b. 10-29-1897.

J. James^4 Isadore Rex b. Clark City, MO 10-4-1861 d. 8-1908, Denver. m. at Centerville, IA Caroline M. Kreuger of Kankakee, IL 9-4-1885. She b. Germany 11-26-1866. Had 1 child.

  a. Ida^5 Clara Rex b. 6-17-1886, Denver.

7. Sarah^3 Rex (7th child of Jane and George^2, George^1) (Figure 58) b. Jefferson, PA 3-25-1817 d. 11-13-1883. (In Oak Grove Cemetery, Uniontown, Pa. with husband and son, J. Morgan Messmore) m. John Messmore 5-25-1837 who was b. 2-18-1808 d. 5-7-1879. Owned flour mill at Messmore, PA. Parents of 6 children. (Figure 58)

Figure 58. Sarah Rex and husband, John Messmore, and family.

A. J.^{4} Morgan Messmore (called Morg) m. Molissa (called Lissa) d. 9-28-1880. A son.

  a. George^5 D. Young.

B. Albert[4] Messmore d. 12-2-1902 m. Rebecca Knight who d. 12-1-1924. 2 daughters.
  a. Florence[5] Messmore b. 7-28-1870, deceased.
  b. Lyda[5] Messmore b. 9-14-1877 m. McCune Penna St. Uniontown, PA.
C. William[4] Messmore, went west.
D. George[4] Rex Messmore b. 3-9-1840 d. 1-1906 m. Emma Floyd b. 1-1855 d. 8-19-1910. 8 children.
  a. John[5] Thomas Messmore b. 10-16-1874 d. 1904.
  b. Anna[5] Messmore d. in infancy.
  c. Baily[5] Dawson Messmore m. Margaret Miller, Wheeling, WV. 3 children.
    (1) Sarah[6] Adeline Messmore.
    (2) Dorothy[6] Margaret Messmore.
    (3) John[6] Rex Messmore.
  d. Pearl[5] Weaver Messmore.
  e. Sara[5] Adeline Messmore.
  f. Francis[5] Daniel Messmore b. 1-29-1886 d. 4-5-1923.
  g. George[5] Rex Messmore, Jr.
  h. Blanche[5] Playford Messmore. deceased.
E. Elizabeth[4] Messmore, m. Mosley.
F. Jane[4] Messmore m. Jamison, is dead but family in Kans. From a statement by Charles Rex, a younger brother, in a letter addressed to C. S. Rex, dated Jan. 9, 1923, we quote "My father's Bible, Prayer Book, silverspoon, silver plate and looking glass that belonged to grandfather George Rex 1st, at my father's request, came into my hands. I being single at the time, left them in the care of my sister, Sarah Messmore. At her death, I suppose some of the children took charge of them."

8. Henry[3] Benjamin Rex (8th child of Jane and George[2], George[1]) b. 1-5-1819 d. 10-15-1836.

9. Hannah[3] Rex (9th child of Jane and George[2], George[1]) b. Jefferson, PA 8-20-1821 d. 1-18-1852 m. Archibald Kerr 11-15-1838 who d. 11-1893.

10. †Harper[3] Rex (10th child of Jane and George[2], George[1]) b. Jefferson, PA 8-29-1825 m. Nancy Crago 12-12-1844. He was called a lefthanded fiddler by his nephew Jacob Haver. Was a private in Co.

A 18th Pa. Cav. His grave in new Cemetery Jefferson, PA. marked by a G.A.R. marker which reads "Died Sept. 26, 1896, Aged 73 yrs. 6 mo. 26 days." Lived near Rice's Landing, PA. 6 sons of which one was Charles.

11. †Charles[3] Hughes Rex (ll[th] child of Jane and George[2], George[1]) b. Jefferson, PA. 3-11-1830 d. 4-15-1903. After the death of his father, 1856, he left Pa. and went to Unionville, MO. On 12-27-1867 he m. Sarah Stearns who was b. 1-10-1841 d. 12-12-1919. They lived on a farm 8 miles southeast of Unionville. He joined the Union Army was; in Co. D. 18th Reg. MO Inf. Enlisted 12-1861 and served until the end of the war. 16 children as follows:

A. Elizabeth[4] Ann Rex b. 10-20-1858 d. 10-20-1913. m. Louis Hill 1-25-1880.
B. George[4] William Rex b. 3-2-1860 d. 12-11-1860.
C. John[4] Liberty Rex b. 9-26-1861 d. 6-12-1920. m. Mary Ann Lawson 9-27-1880. She b. 1863 d.1910 9 children.
   a. Jesse[5] A. Rex b. 5-1881.
   b. William[5] Calvin Rex b. 8-1883.
   c. Charles[5] W. (Charley) Rex b. 2-1886.
   d. Lewis[5] W. (Lennie) Rex b. 7-1888.
   e. Martha[5] J. Rex b. 7-1892.
   f. Arestie[5] Rex b. 2-1898 (Twin.)
   g. Maretta[5] (Retta) Rex b. 2-1898 (Twin.)
   h. Mae[5] Rex b. about 1900.
   i. Silas[5] Rex b. about 1902.
D. Nancy[4] Evaline Rex (Figure 59) b. 9-17-1865 d. 7-22-1944 m. Jonathan Allen Valentine 3-12-1886. He b. 7-28-1861 d. 11-6-1943. 6 children.
   a. Albert[5] Valentine b. 12-26-1885 Wynochie, WA. d. 2-4-1964 m. Nancy Ruthie Jane Rose 2-22-1907.

Figure 59. Left to right: Bessie Lora Valentine, Jonathan Allen Valentine, Albert Valentine, Roxie Valentine, Nancy Eveline Rex Valentine, Flossie Valentine, Phoeba Lola Albert Valentine.

She b. 1-25-1885 d. 4-28-1938. 9 children.

(1) Samuel[6] Rex Valentine b. 11-24-1907 d. 2-14-1908.

(2) Flossie[6] Lee Valentine b. 5-28-1909 d. 4-1986. m. Thomas Herbert Jenni 8-4-1927. He b. 1-20-1909 d. 9-1987. 2 chidren.

+Tommy[7] Joan Jenni b. 12-21-1928 in Tulsa Oklahoma. m. Carroll Truett Sanders 12-19-1947 in Tulsa, OK. She b. 4-9-1923 Tulsa, OK. 3 children.

^Kathryn[8] Joan Sanders b. 11-1-1949 Tulsa, OK. m. Michael David Rusk 5-11-1973 in Tulsa OK. He b. 9-18-1949 in Baton Rouge, LA.

^Michael[8] Mark Sanders b. 9-14-1952 in Tulsa, OK. m. Gloria Beth Holliday 12-29-1979 in Tulsa, OK. she b. 7-10-1952 in Ft. Worth, TX. 2 daughters.

~Molly[9] Marie Sanders b. 2-9-1981 in Marion, VA.

~Ashley[9] Elizabeth Sanders b. 3-14-1983 in Marion, VA.

^Jennifer[8] Dawn Sanders b. 8-25-1956 in Tulsa, OK. m. 1st David Dale Mullinnix 10-22-1977 in Tulsa, OK. 1 son.

~Aaron[9] David Mullennix b. 10-5-1984 in Charlotte, NC.

m. 2nd Benjamin Franklin Copeland 10-8-1992. He b. 12-14-1958 in Charlotte, NC. 1 daughter.

~Kate[9] Sanders Copeland b. 6-20-1994 in Charlotte, NC.

+Herbert[7] Lee Jenni b. 9-23-1931 in Tulsa, OK d. 10-15-1984 in Shreveport, LA. m. Jane Langwell 6-14-1953 in Bartlesville, OK. 2 children.

^John[8] Christian Jenni b. 9-22-1954 in Louisville, KY. d. 9-23-1982 in Houston TX.

^Carol[8] Ann Jenni b. 8-18-1956 in Louisville, KY.

(3) Clara[6] Ruby Valentine b. 1-24-1913 d. 3-25-1913.

(4) Adeline[6] Hayden Valentine b. 1-1-1914 in Tulsa, OK. d. 9-26-1991 in Tulsa, OK. m. 1st George Virgil Thompson 12-25-1929 in Tulsa, OK. He b. 12-10-1907 in Decater, IL. d. 1-25-1932 in Tulsa, OK.. 1 son.

+Virgil[7] Ivan Thompson b. 1-7-1932 in Tulsa, OK. d. 6-26-1992 Tulsa, OK. m. Thelma Lucille Dufner 9-4-1954 in Springfield, IL She b. 1-7-1932 in Tulsa, OK. d. 6-26-1992 in Tulsa, OK. 3 children.

^Mark[8] Allen Thompson b. 8-13-1956 in Tulsa, OK. m. Jeannie Marie Spinner 9-26-1987 in Denver, CO. She b.

1-1-1953 in FL.

^Valerie[8] Lynne Thompson b. 6-5-1958 in Tulsa, OK. m. Timothy Joel Williams 8-5-1978 in Tulsa, OK. He b. 10-6-1956 in Denver, CO. 2 children.

~Christopher[9] Joel Williams b. 10-20-1979 in Shawnee, OK.

~Emily[9] Suzanne Williams b. 12-29-1981 in denver, CO.

^Dwayne[8] Lee Thompson b. 10-2-1963 in Tulsa, OK. m. Deann Sheryl Park 5-11-1985 in Tulsa, OK. She b. 7-5-1964 in Tulsa, OK. 3 daughters.

~Alyssa[9] Rene Thompson b. 5-28-1990 in Shawnee, OK.

~Brandi[9] Nicole Thompson b. 5-28-1990 in Shawnee, OK.

~Christin[9] Ann Thompson b. 4-5-1992 in Shawnee, OK. m. 2nd James Theodore Allen 5-4-1933. He b. 1-8-1903 d. 5-4-1983. 1 son.

+Jimmie[7] Ray Allen b. 6-18-1935 Tulsa, OK. m. Mary Linda Blackwood Maisano 6-18-1954. McAlester, OK. She b.2-17-1937 McAlester, OK. 3 children.

^Larry[8] Michael Allen b. 11-18-1955 in Tulsa, OK. m. 1st Teresa Stanart 8-15-1976 in Tulsa, OK. She b. 8-3-1959 in Casper, WY. 1 son.

~Justin[9] Scott Allen b. 6-7-1980 in Tulsa, OK m. 2nd Billie Jean (Thomas) Moore.

^Linda[8] Dianne Allen b. 10-13-1957 in Tulsa, OK. m. Jimmy Dale Horn 10-7-1978 in Claremore, OK. He b. 6-26-1955 in Sapulpa, OK. 2 sons.

~James[9] Russell Horn b. 10-16-1980, Tulsa, OK.

~Daniel[9] Lance Horn b. 11-13-1984 in Tulsa, OK.

^Karen[8] Lea Allen b. 3-24-1961 in Tulsa, OK. m. 1st Raymichael Gagne 1-29-1982 in Tulsa, OK. He b. 10-17-1962 in Ft. Worth, TX. 1 daughter.

~Cherise[9] Nicole Gagne b 7-28-1984 in Abeline, TX. m. 2nd Harold Gene Bruton 9-8-1990.

(5) John[6] Sanford (Leo) Valentine b. 9-17-1916 in Tulsa, OK. d. 6-21-1944. Albuquerque, NM m. Verden Young 3-1-1936 Tulsa, OK. 2 daughters.

+Sarah[7] Ruth Valentine. m. Jim Murry. 2 sons.

^Kyle[8] Murry.

^Jeffery[8] Murry.

+Nancy[7] Valentine b. Tulsa, OK. m. Tom Stevens. He b. Tulsa, OK. 1 daughter.

^Robin[8] Stevens b. Tulsa, OK.

(6) Mary[6] Evelyn Valentine b. b. 9-14-1918 Tulsa, OK. d. 11-16-1933 in Tulsa, OK. m. Elbert Douglas Mayfield 6-9-1933 Tulsa, OK. He b. 7-20-1912 in Webb City MO and d. 11-12-1962 in Tulsa, OK. 2 sons.

+Ronald[7] Bruce Mayfield b. 10-21-1939 in Tulsa, OK. m. Angela Sexton 8-312-1957 in Tulsa, OK. She b. 1939. 3 children.

^Michael[8] (Mickey) Mayfield b. Tulsa, OK d. 5-22-? Tulsa,OK.

^Mathew[8] Bruce Mayfield b. Tulsa, OK. m. Lisa Gail Luke.

^Lori[8] Anne Mayfield b. Tulsa, OK. m. Brian James Hart. 2 children.

~Taylor[9] Hart.

~Spencer[9] Hart.

+Steven[7] Elbert Mayfield b.1-15-1947 in Tulsa, OK. m. Deborah Hayes 4-3-1971 in Tulsa, OK. 2 children.

^Justin[8] Mayfield b. Tulsa, OK.

^Loren[8] Mayfield b. Tulsa, OK.

(7) Lucille[6] Rose Valentine b. 3-5-1923 Tulsa, OK. m. Denver McCoy 2-21-1946 Tulsa, OK. 8 children.

+Timothy[7] Dee McCoy b. 1-12-1947 in Tulsa, OK.

+John[7] Randal (Randy) McCoy b. 12-5-1949 in Panama City, FL.

+Patrick[7] Lee McCoy b. 8-17-1953 in San Antonio, TX.

+Nancy[7] Marie McCoy b.7-16-1952 in Denver, CO.

+Brett[7] McCoy b. 10-1-1956 in Tulsa, OK.

+Laura[7] Ann McCoy b. 9-6-1958 in Riverside, CA.

+Joseph[7] Clay McCoy b. 3-27-1960 in Riverside, CA.

+Michael[7] Dale McCoy b. 2-1-1963 in Smyrna, TN.

(8) William[6] Lewis Valentine b. 3-7-1925 in Tulsa, OK. m. Hazel Cagle 12-27-1950. She b. 2-12-1927 in Tulsa, OK. 2 daughters.

+Gretchen[7] Valentine b. 10-24-1960 in Tulsa, OK.

+Rachel[7] Valentine b. 12-28-1962 in Tulsa, OK.

(9) Albert[6] Liburn Valentine b. 6-15-1928 Tulsa, OK. m. Sarah Frances (Sally) Griffith 11-18-1957 in Tulsa, OK. She b.

4-6-1935 in Memphis, TN. 4 children.

+Albert[7] Russell Valentine b. 4-16-1960 in San Pedro, CA.

+Steven[7] Patrick Valentine b. 3-19-1962 in Rock Springs, WY.

+Brian[7] William Valentine b. 10-21-1965 in Rock Springs, WY.

+Emily[7] Kay Valentine b. 11-22-1966 in Rock Springs, WY.

b. Baby Girl[5] Valentine b. 3-27-1887 d. 3-27-1887.

c. Phoebe[5] Lola Valentine b. 2-1-1889 Artic, WA d. 12-27-1976 Groom, TX. m. John Benjamin Shockley 11-5-1907 Tucumcari, NM. He b. 4-27-1884 in Hebo, GA. d. 5-11-1962 Groom, TX. 4 children.

(1) Bernice[6] Opal Shockley b. 10-15-1908 Tucumcari, NM. m. Armon Coyn Stamps 8-23-1925 in Panhandle, TX. He b. 2-23-1900 and d. 10-18-1977 in LaHabra, CA. 9 children.

+Billy[7] Joe Stamps b. 1-21-1926 in Reed OK. d. 4-10-1931 in Colorado City, TX.

+Dorothy[7] Lee Stamps b. 3-27-1927 in Groom, TX.

+Bobby[7] Eugene Stamps b. 4-23-1928 in Groom, TX. d. 8-26-1928 in Reed, OK.

+Raymond[7] Leon Stamps b. 5-19-1929 in Groom, TX.

+Kenneth[7] Lueville Stamps b. 8-12-1930 in Colorado, TX.

+Armon[7] Coyn Stamps, Jr. b. 5-28-1932 in Colorado, TX.

+Nora[7] Winnona Stamps b. 11-11-1935 in Hermleigh, TX.

+Beulah[7] Fawn Stamps b. 5-21-1938 in Pharr, TX.

+Jerry[7] Darline Stamps b. 12-2-1940.

(2) Clora[6] B. Shockley b. 4-9-1910 Tucumcari, NM. d. 6-24-1933 Amarillo, TX. m. Lawrence Edward Black 5-16-1927 in Clarendon, TX. He d. 9-8-1980 in Amarillo, TX. 2 children.

+Bonnie[7] Nell Black b. 1-18-1929 in Groom, TX.

+Lawrence[7] Edward Black, Jr. b. 4-23-1931 in Groom, TX. m. Lillian Smith 5-6-? in Panhandle, TX.

(3) William[6] Allen Shockley b. 9-22-1912 Tucumcari, NM. m. Frances Nelson 4-8-1939 in Shamrock, TX. She b. 4-5-1919. 2 daughters.

+Sue[7] Ellen Shockley b. 8-21-1942 in Groom, TX.

+Carol[7] Ann Shockley b. 4-3-1945 in Groom, TX.

(4) Beulah[6] Avis Shockley b. 9-21-1915 Groom, TX.

d. Bessie[5] Lora Valentine b. 9-3-1891 Unionville, MO. m. L. Z. Lester 12-24-1910 Tucumcari, NM.

e. Flossie[5] Valentine b. 1-5-1893 Unionville, MO. d. 12-22-1910 Tucumcari, NM.
f. Roxie[5] Valentine b. 7-5-1895 Boylermill, MO. d. 11-3-1973 Porterville, CA. m. Walter Adair McAnally 6-18-1914 Tucumcari, NM. He b, 3-22-1893 Decatur, AR. d. 12-10-1926 Porterville, CA. 4 children.
   (1) Charles[6] Wesley McAnally b. 6-8-1913 Tucumcari, NM d. 3-17-1982 Austin, TX. m. Virginia Frances Stewart.
   (2) Lawrence[6] Cellie McAnally b. 9-6-1916 Tucumcari, NM. d. 1945. m. Alice.
   (3) Nancy[6] Lillie McAnally b. 11-13-1923 Tucumcari, NM. m. Quentin Theodore Olson 9-16-1946.
   (4) Walter[6] Adair McAnally b 2-6-1926 Ft. Sumner, NM. m. Betsy 6-13-1949.
E. Sarah[4] Rex (twin) b. 3-10-1867 MO. m. August Anderson 10-13-1887. In MT.
F. Mary[4] A. Rex (twin) b. 3-10-1867 m. R. E. Hill 9-26-1885 Jefferson Co., MT.
G. Margaret[4] Arizona (Maggie) Rex b. 1-18-1869 MO m. William Hill 2-27-1886 Alexander, NE.
H. Viola[4] Rex b. 8-1871 d. 11-2-1872.
I. James[4] David Rex b. 4-9-1873 MO. m. Maud Brooks 10-6-1897 Olex, Oregon.
J. Laura[4] Rex (twin) b. 6-5-1875 m. Leroy Livezey 4-28-1895 Pittsburg, KS.
K. Flora[4] Rex (twin) b. 6-5-1875 Missouri m. Lin E. West 10-19-1886, Putnam Co., MO.
L. Charles[4] William Rex b. 6-17-1877 Missouri. m. Roxie Smith 10-27-1900, Seattle, WA.
M. Rebecca[4] Jane Rex 6-6-1879 MO. d. 12-12-1913 m. Albert Brooks 2-27-1907.
N. Ida[4] May Rex b. 1-18-1882 m. Zora H. Smith 7-8-1900 Putnam Co., MO. 1 daughter.
   a. Hazel[5] I. Smith Sanford b. Newton, MO who has a daughter.
O. Rose[6] Rex b. 3-11-1884 d. 8-13-1884.
P. Dana[4] E. Rex b. 7-27-1888 d. 3-12-1889.

From a letter to Mrs. Sarah J. Beggs from Charles H. Rex he says: "Port Chewalla, Tenn. Apr. 6, 1863. I have been in the army over twenty months and have seen some sport but the hardships overbalance the sport so you see I don't love soldiering very much, especially when it comes to fighting. It will be one year tomorrow morning since we were pushed into the battle of Shiloh. Desperate was the scene that I witnessed on that bloody field. I was in the battle before Corinth, Iuka and the battle of Corinth of the 3rd and 4th of October. Address Co. D 18th Regiment Mo. Vol. Corinth, Miss. Signed: Charles Rex. Written on Easter Day."

12. Elizabeth[3] Rex (12th child of Jane and George[2], George[1]) b. Jefferson, 1-8-1832. PA. m. Smith Crago 3-18-1848. Lived Carmichaels, PA.

Chapter 6

Martha[2] Rex (4th child of Margaret Kepler and George[1] Rex) b. in Mifflin Co., PA 1-15-1780 d. 1-31-1853. m. William Winters b. in Lancaster Co., PA in 1777 and d. 9-19-1849 in 73rd year of age. He came to Jefferson Co., OH in 1802. 7 children.

1. Elizabeth[3] Winters (Figure 60) b. 9-2-1798 d. 8-13-1880 m. 1-21-1819 to David Gladden b. 11-8-1796 d. 3-25-1859. He was a native of Washington Co., PA. His parents moved to Jefferson Co., OH 1880. He lived at Two Ridges and had 4 daughters.

A. Mary[4] Gladden m. John Dinsmore, 1 daughter.

a. Ella[5] Dinsmore,

B. Elizabeth[4] Gladden m. Jacob Huffman, several children.

C. Martha[4] Gladden d. 9-3-1821 (1 yr. 7 mo. old).

Figure 60. Elizabeth Winters (Mrs. David Gladden).

D. Hannah[4] Gladden m. Alex S. Welday and they had 3 children.

  a. David[5] Welday m. Pamelia Johnson. 1 son.

    (1) Harry[6] Welday m. Blanche Winters. They had 2 children.

      +David[7] Welday m. Mary Brown.

      +Dorothy[7] Welday.

  b. William[5] Welday m. Mary Wyant. 1 son.

    (1) Curtis[6] Welday m. Carrie Rhinehart. 1 son.

      + William[7] Welday m. Frances Hulse.

  c. Martha[5] Welday m. John B. Mays. 3 children.

    (1) Harry[6] Mays m. Bess Lamb. 4 children.

      +Burton[7] Mays.

      +Helen[7] Mays.

      +Ruth[7] Mays.

      +Janet[7] Mays.

    (2) Ray[6] Mays m. Frances Collins.

    (3) Omah[6] Mays m. James Shirley. 4 children.

      +Dean[7] Shirley.

      +Roy[7] Shirley.

      +Isabelle[7] Shirley.

+John[7] Herbert Shirley.

2. Martin[3] Winters (son of Martha[2] and William Winter, George[1]) b.
1813 d.____ m. 1st Rachael she b. 11-3-1818 d. 1837. m. 2nd Susan
Myers b. 1820. M. W. was a trader. Moved to Ohio, then Indiana,
then Iowa in 1853. 4 children.
  A. Rachael[4] Winters b. 1840, OH.
  B. David[4] R. Winters b. 1843, OH.
  C. Charles[4] M. Winters b. 1848, IN.
  D. Lewis[4] J. Winters b. 1850, IN.

3. Ross[3] Winters (child of Martha[2] and William Winters, George[1])
9-22-1814 d. 9-1-1884. m. 8-29-1839 Elizabeth Welday, she b.
8-30-1822 d. 1-22-1894. R. W. b. on farm where he resided in 1880,
was his father's old place. 1 daughter.
  A. Martha[4] Winters m. William L. Rhinehart. 5 children.
    a. Elizabeth[5] Rhinehart m. Rev. H. H. McQuilkin. 4 children.
      (1) James[6] McQuilkin m. Marion, 2 children.
        +Robert[7] McQuilkin.
        +Baxter[7] McQuilkin.
      (2) Frances[6] McQuilkin m. Dr. Albert Hulett, 1 son
        +Richard[7] Hulett.
      (3) William[6] McQuilkin.
      (4) Walter[6] McQuilkin.
    b. Ross[5] Rhinehart m. Florence Reed. 2 children.
      (1) Elizabeth[6] Rhinehart m. David Sedgwick. 1 daughter.
        +Jane[7] Sedgwick.
      (2) George[6] Rhinehart m. Katherine Campbell. 3 children.
        +George[7] Rhinehart.
        +William[7] Rhinehart.
        +Stanley[7] Rhinehart.
    c. Carrie[5] Rinehart m. Curtis A. Welday. 1 son.
      (1) William[6] Welday m. Francis Hulse.
    d. Baxter[5] Rhinehart m. Maud E. Lloyd.
    e. Stanley[5] Rhinehart m. Lucille Leibolt.

4. William[3] Winters m. Sarah. Their 4 children,
  A. John[4] Winters.
  B. Nora[4] Winters.
  C. Cora[4] Winters.

D. Lon[4] Winters.

5. Rhoda[3] Winters m. Dr. Riddle.

6. Hannah[3] Winters m. Charles Elliott.

7. John[3] Winters m. Maria Duval. 3 children.
   A. Adeline[4] Winters d.
   B. Keppler[4] Winters d.
   C. Byanthia[4] Winters m. Frank C. Porter and had 5 children.
      (1) Gertrude[5] Porter.
      (2) Jessie[5] Porter.
      (3) Harvey[5] Porter.
      (4) Stella[5] Porter.
      (5) May[5] Porter.

Chapter 7

Edward[2] Rex, called Ned (5th child of Margaret Keppler and George[1] Rex), was b. 11-24-1782 in Mifflin Co., PA. He located near Zanesville, OH in 1817 and m. Hettie Huffdale 11-22-1821. He d. in Boliver, OH 2-28-1845. Hettie Huffdale Rex was b. 10-20-1796. Sometime before 1893, the family moved to Cherokee, KS. They were the parents of 9 children, all born at Zanesville, OH. After the death of Edward Rex, his widow married the husband of her deceased sister Jane, Abraham Milliken, who was a brother of Mrs. Jonas Rex.

1. Emily[3] Rex b. 9-23-1822. d. 8-19-1832.
2. Sarah[3] Rex b. 12-26-1824 d. 4-23-1842.
3. Jane[3] Rex b. 1-5-1827 d. 1905, Cherokee, KS. m. George Wiles and had 3 children.
   A. Thomas[4] Wiles d. 1930.
   B. Lucy[4] Wiles m. J. McCants d. 1930.
   C. Eleanor[4] Wiles m. T. J. Lisenbee.
4. Edward[3] Rex 2nd b. 12-9-1828, d. same day.
5. Jacob[3] Huffdale Rex (5th child of Hetty Huffdale and Edward[2] Rex, George.[1]) b. 11-13-1829 at Zanesville, OH. Said to have been a tall man. m. Julia Bell 10-29-1867. She b. 3-14-1838, Zanesville, OH. They moved to Muscatine, IA where they remained until the children were b. and then moved to Cherokee, KS where he d. 4-17-1900. She d. there 5-29-1914. 6 children.
   A. Addie[4] J. Rex b. 8-20-1868. m. James E. Ausemus 12-28-1887, Cherokee, KS and had 4 children.
      a. Carl[5] Frederick Ausemus b. at Cherokee 1-17-1889. m. Emma Armstrong 9-4-1910, and they are the parents of 8 children.
         (1) Bertha[6] Irene Ausemus b. 9-3-1913, Cherokee, KS.
         (2) Helen[6] Ausemus b. 1-13-1913, Cherokee, KS.
         (3) James[6] Alphus Ausemus b. 7-13-1914, Hiattville, KS.
         (4) Earl[6] Ausemus b. 9-26-1916, Hiattville, KS.
         (5) Kenneth[6] Howard Ausemus b. 4-15-1918, Hiattville, KS.
         (6) Chester[6] Ausemus b. 6-26-1920, Hiattville, KS.
         (7) Addie[6] Favon Ausemus b. 11-23-1921, Hiattville, KS.
         (8) Elsie[6] Eileen Ausemus b. 9-4-1924.
      b. Ada[5] Hettie Ausemus b. Cherokee, KS 10-19-1891 m. Arthur Armstrong at Topeka, KS 4-28-1916. 3 children.
         (1) Rex[6] Armstrong b. 3-4-1916, Farlington, KS.

(2) Ray[6] Armstrong b. 2-18-1918, Farlington, KS.

(3) Aline[6] Adeline Armstrong b. 7-12-1920, Pittsburg, KS.

  c. Elmer[5] Rex Ausemus b. 1-22-1894, Cherokee. m. Wincel Crocker, 9-3-1899.

  d. Lloyd[5] Andrews Ausemus b. 6-6-1904, Cherokee.

B. Howard[4] Bell Rex b. 3-2-1870 d. 4-22-1930, Topeka, KS. A Mason. m. Minnie Watt 8-20-1896 at Cherokee, KS. 2 children.

  a. Howard[5] Earl Rex b. 8-12-1898, Cherokee. Lives in Lawrence, KS. 3 children.

    (1) Maxine[6] Rex.

    (2) Robert[6] Earl Rex.

    (3) Charles[6] Raymond Rex.

  b. Ruth[5] Marie Rex b. 2-21-1901, Cherokee lived in Henryetta, OK. m. Harry Holman.

C. Charles[4] W. Rex b. 1-20-1874 d. 8-23-1874.

D. Carrie[4] Rex b. 8-13-1880 d. 8-24-1880.

E. Clarinda[4] Effie Rex b. 1-14-1882. m. Thomas Leeper 7-11-1905, Cherokee, KS. 2 children.

  a. Helen[5] Irene Leeper b. 12-19-1908, Cherokee, KS.

  b. Harold[5] Leeper b. 1-5-1916, d. same day.

6. Clarinda[3] Rex (Figure 61) b. 10-11-1833 d. 3-13-1911, single.

7. Bennoni[3] Rex b. 11-29-1836 d. 4-1-1840.

8. Isabella[3] Rex b. 5-7-1839 d. 1-2-1840.

9. George[3] Rex (Figure 62) (9th child of Hetty and Edward[2] Rex, George[1]) b. 3-10-1842 near Zanesville, OH. d. 4-1-1906 at El Rito, NM. He was a tall man. m. Margaret G. Ness who was b. in Richie Co., WV 11-2-1868. (Her father, Joshua W. Ness, d. at Durango, CO 2-10-1928, aged 100 yrs. 1 mo. 6 days). She d. 5-16-1926. They were m. at Cherokee, KS 12-10-1889 where they lived until 1905 when

Figure 61. Clarinda Rex.

they moved to El Rito, NM and thence to Durango, CO. 8 children, all but the youngest child b. at Cherokee, KS.

A. Mary[4] Pauline Rex b. 5-24-1891 m. John Clark Bonds 11-29-1913 at Durango. 5 children.

  a. Margaret[5] Ellen Bonds b. 9-10-1915 d. 9-18-1915, Farmington, NM.

  b. William[5] Rex Bonds b. 9-19-1917 at Durango, CO.

c. John[5] Clark Bonds 2nd b. 7-25-1919 d. 3-28-1920, Durango, CO.

d. Bernace[5] Bonds b. 12-2-1921 d. 12-2-1921, Durango, CO.

e. Carrley[5] Ann Bonds b. 3-30-1926 d. 2-15-1929 (scarlet fever).

B. Hettie[4] Blanch Rex b. 4-6-1893 m. 1st Walter Hamilton 10-7-1912 at Durango, CO. He d. 11-2-1918 at Ignacio, CO. 4 children.

Figure 62. George Rex.

a. Gertrude[5] Louise Hamilton b. 7-30-1913 d. 8-20-1923.

b. Howard[5] Vance Hamilton b. 7-4-1916, Ignaco, CO.

c. Wilma[5] Blanch Hamilton b. 2-22-1917 d. 11-12-1920.

d. Guy[5] Robert Hamilton b. 6-4-1919 d. 11-9-1920.

m. 2nd Lloyd J. Greer 3-10-1928. 2 sons.

Note: Credit for the little information we have on this line is due to Hettie B. Rex-Hamilton-Greer.

e. Douglas[5] Greer b. 1-22-1929, Kline, CO.

f. Charles[5] Lloyd Greer b. 6-28-1930 d_____.

C. †Charles[4] Edward Rex b. 3-29-1895. Was in the WW I in France one year.

D. Leslie[4] Wakefield Rex b. 11-6-1897 m. Ellen Rea 2-18-1922 at Durango, CO. He is employed in the Smelters at Durango. 2 children.

a. Norinne[5] Fay Rex b. 5-16-1924, Durango, CO.

b. George[5] Wakefield Rex b. 11-1928, d. Dec. (scarlet fever).

E. Margaret[4] Mildred Rex b. 10-30-1899 d. 12-1-1899.

F. George[4] Raby Rex b. 3-16-1901. Ranchman at Arboles, CO.

G. Margery[4] Ernestine Rex b. 2-3-1904. m. Ralph Rea 9-16-1922 at Durango, CO. 3 children.

a. Ralph[5] E. Rea b. 10-14-1926.

b. Earl[5] Rea b. 7-16-1928.

c. Ruth[5] Elarine Rea b. 6-21-1930.

H. Kathleen[4] Gertrude Rex b. 10-21-1906 at El Rito, NM. m. George W. Greer 1st, Kline, CO 4-7-1927. 2 children.

a. Gertrude[5] Ramona Greer b. 4-16-1928.

b. George[5] Winfield Greer, 2nd, b. 5-11-1929.

Chapter 8

Jonas[2] Rex (6th child of Margaret Keppler and George[1] Rex) was b. 2-4-1785 in Mifflin Co., PA. d. Richmond, Jefferson Co., Ohio 12-6-1841, where he had lived for 30 years. J. Rex and Rhoda Milliken (Figure 63) were m. at the home of his sister Martha (Mrs. William Winter) 2-16-1808. She was b. 12-8-1788, d. 3-22-1870, age 81 yrs. 3 mo. 14

Figure 63. Rhoda Milliken Rex

Figure 64. Gravestone of Rhoda Rex.

ds. Buried at Two Ridge (Figure 64). 10 children. The first 2 children were b. in PA. In 1811, the family moved to Jefferson County, OH and in 1815 they bought a farm, as a homestead, from Isaac Winter, where seven of the Rex children were born (Figure 65). In 1842, after Jonas Rex d. in 12-1841, the estate was partitioned and the farm went to William and John Stiles. William deeded his interest to John S. and the farm remained in his name until the year 1900. (See Figure 67, Bible and pictures of this Line).

Figure 65. Gravestone of Jonas Rex.

1. George[3] W. Rex was b. in Greene Co., PA 5-18-1809. He d. 4-7-1871 in his 62nd year. He m. Rachel Coe in Jefferson Co., OH 4-3-1838. She b. about 1809 and d. 6-7-1884 in her 73rd year, or so say the stones in Bacon Ridge Cemetery, OH. They had 6 children.

  A. Dr. George[4] Rex - disappeared in the West.

  B. Jonas[4] Rex at 50 m. Etta Cochran. Both d. at Bolling Green, OH. No children.

  C. Permelia[4] Rex d. 3-26-1844.

  E. †William[4] Rex d. in Andersonville Prison, SC 7-9-1864. 2nd O.V.I. Co. K. (See

Figure 66. Jonas Rex home, Jefferson County, Ohio.

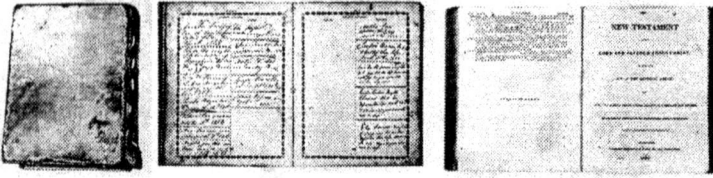

Figure 67. Jonas Rex Bible given to him by his father George Rex 1st

Roster, Vol. 2 p. 58).

F. Rhoda[4] Rex was drowned.

G. †Benjamin[4] C. Rex b. 1839, d. 10-8-1863, buried at Bacon Ridge, OH. G. A. R. marker on grave 1861-1865. (See Roster Vol. 4, p. 664).

2. Permelia[3] Rex (2nd child of Jonas and Rhoda M. Rex, George[1]) b. in Greene Co., PA 2-14-1811 m. Rasillas Castner (called "Sill") in Jefferson Co., OH 1-20-1834. She d. 3-26-1844. 4 children.

A. †Michael[4] Castner, b. 10-15-1835 and d. 5-23-1914 in Jefferson Co., OH. He was a member of Company E, 157th Reg., Ohio National Guards. Enlisted 5-2-1864 for 100 days at Winterville, OH, by Capt. Thomas Ramble. Mustered in 5-5-1864 at Camp Chase by Capt. Douglass. MCC at Camp Chase Sept. 2, 1864. (See Ohio Roster, Vol. 9, p. 250). At the close of the war, he returned to Jefferson Co., OH. m. Sarah Samantha Ross and they had 5 children. He is buried in Two Ridge Cemetery.

    a. Sarah[5] Permelia Castner b. 6-14-1865.

    b. Mary[5] Jennie Castner b. 1868. m. Scott. 1 child.

      (1) Frank[6] Scott.

    c. Anna[5] Emma Castner b. 8-20-1869.

    d. Frank[5] S. Castner b. 9-12-1874 in Jefferson Co., OH and d. 5-17-1886 in Jefferson Co., OH.

    e. Martha[5] Edna Castner b. 1876 and d. 8-22-1880 in Jefferson Co., OH.

B. Rhoda[4] Castner b. 5-7-1838 and d. 12-26-1906 in Jefferson Co., OH.

C. †John[4] Adams Castner b. 8-31-1840. He belonged to Company H, First Ohio Volunteer Infantry. Enlisted at Steubenville, OH, 2-11-1862. John was wounded at *Mission Ridge* 11-25-1863, and d. at Chatanooga, TN 12-22-1863 and was buried there in the military cemetery.

D. †Edwin[4] A. Castner b. 1-11-1844 and d. 4-2-1912 in Newark, OH. m. 1st Mary Josephine Stone 2-20-1868 and 2nd Dema Hebbell on 11-4-1908. He belonged to Company H, First Ohio Volunteer Infantry. Was mustered in at Corinth, MS by Capt. Smith. Discharged 3-1-1864, by order of Secretary of War. (See Ohio Roster, Vol. 2, p. 24).

†Rasillas Castner, widower of Permelia[4] Rex, had 4 other sons named Paul, Roderick, Nimmie and Eli by a second marriage. The father of Rasillas Castner had lived in or near Philadelphia and bought a beautiful tract of land adjoining that of Jonas Rex. Belonged to a Company called "The Silver Grays." Was mustered out of the Army in 1863. d. 2-19-1883 and was buried at Steubenville, OH.

3. William[3] Rex (3rd child of Jonas[2] and R. M. Rex, George[1]) b. Jefferson Co., OH 7-11-1813. He m. Harriett Beall Johnson in Jefferson Co., OH 3-20-1846. She was given the middle name Beall for her uncle, General Rezin Beall of Wooster, OH. She d. 12-21-1880. He d. 4-8-1886 in Richmond, OH. Both buried in Two Ridge Cemetery, Richmond, OH. 4 sons.

A. Homer[4] Rex b. 9-3-1847, Jefferson Co., OH near Richmond. He attended Mt. Union College to prepare for the ministry and while there d. 9-27-1873. m. Martha Simpson of Richmond, OH, 9-14-1868.

a. Margaret[5] Simpson Rex m. Edward Ward. They had one child.

(1) J.[6] Charles Ward. She and child d. soon after his birth.

b. William[6] E. Rex m. Aggie Caine. They lived in East Liverpool, OH. 2 daughters.

(1) Ethel[6] Rex.

(2) Hilda[6] Rex.

B. Joseph[4] Burson Rex, b. 7-3-1850 m. Nettie C. Campbell 9-16-1876. Was for a time a druggist in Philadelphia, PA. d. 9-16-1898 in Harrisburg, PA. In 1900 his family was living in Harrisburg, PA. 4 children.

a. Ruby[5] Rex b. 1879 m. W. Fred Adams, 1904. She was an Eastern Star and he a 32° Mason. Reside Cleveland, OH. 3 children.

(1) Dorothy[6] Dean Adams b. 6-30-1905, school teacher, Lakewood, OH.

(2) Edith[6] Marie Adams b. 3-26-1908 m. at Lakewood, Glenn E. Green 9-10-1926. 2 children.

+Glenn[7] E. Green, Jr. b. 6-21-1927.

+David[7] Roland Green b. 9-23-1930.

(3) Jane[6] Louise Adams b. 4-28-1916.

b. Marie[5] Rex b. 1881 m. at Newark, NJ 1902, Homer W. Allen. He d. 11-1-1919, Columbus, OH. 4 children.

(1) Janice[6] Marie Allen b. 10-4-1903. Librarian, Columbus, OH.

(2) Virginia[6] Allen b. 3-19-1905. Clerking.

(3) Katherine[6] Allen b. 7-6-1909. m. Wesley Davis, 1925. 1 daughter.

+Jacqualine[7] Davis b. 12-30-1929.

(4) Martha[6] Rex Allen b. 2-24-1912. Clerking.

c. Ethel[5] Rex b. 1885 m. Frank Baynard, 1909. She d. 5-1915. 1 daughter.

(1) Jeanette[6] Bayard b. 8-4-1911, Chagrin Falls, OH. School teacher and member Congregational Church, Warren, OH

d. Sylvanus[5] Rex b. 1885 d. 1902, Newark, OH.

C. Rezin[4] Rex b. 2-20-1853 and d.____. He was a dentist and lived in Philadelphia. m. Annie Rebecca Donaldson 5-25-1876. 2 children.

a. Allen[5] Rex.

b. Nancy[5] Rex. She lived in Steelton, PA.

D. Orlando[4] Gladden Rex b. 12-9-1853 d. 9-17-1905. m. Emma Eliza Cooper 10-1-1880. Had a livery business at Freeman's Landing across the river from Toronto, OH. 1 son.

a. Charles[5] Moreland Rex m. Lola Sanderson 12-27-1909. Is a dry goods merchant in Toronto, OH. 1 son.

(1) George[6] S. Rex b. 11-20-1910 who was in Postal Service, Toronto, OH.

4. Mary[3] Rex (4th child of Jonas[2] and R. M. Rex, George[1]) b. at Richmond, OH 9-7-1815. m. Aaron Gladden 12-24-1840. She d. 2-16-1893. 2 children.

A. Rhoda[4] Rex Gladden b. 11-1-1841 m. William H. Beebout 10-5-1871. He d. 2-18-1910 and she d. 2-21-1910. They had a double funeral and were buried in the same grave. 3 children.

a. Aaron[5] Gladden Beebout b. 10-27-1874. m. Alice Barton, Wheaton, IL. She d. 6-30-1922. 1 son.

(1) William[6] H. Beebout, Jr.

b. Permelia[5] Beebout b. 7-28-1876. m. J. R. Simpson 1896. 2 sons.

(1) Harry[6] E. Simpson b. 12-21-1896. d. 8-18-1906.

(2) Fred[6] R. Simpson b. 1-9-1898. m. Edith Townsend. 1

daughter.

  +June[7] Simpson b. 6-13-1929.

  c. Constance[5] Beebout b. 7-12-1878 m. Thomas Hobson 9-26-1900. 3 children.

    (1) Rachel[6] Rex Hobson b. 11-21-1902 and d. 10-16-1992. m. James Hanlin 12-1922. 4 children.

    +Virginia[7] May Hanlin b. 10-3-1923.

    +Constance[7] Hanlin b. 1-17-1926.

    +James[7] Robert Hanlin b. 9-20-1927.

    +Eleanor[7] Janet Hanlin b. 1930.

    (2) James[6] Robert Hobson b. 1-10-1906 d. 1-11-1905.

    (3) William[6] B. Hobson b. 3-13-1906.

  B. Permelia[4] Gladden b. 12-31-1842 d. 7-10-1913. Never married.

5. Margaret[3] Jane Rex (5th of Jonas[2] and R. M. Rex, George[1]) b. Richmond, OH 5-14-1818 and d. 4-12-1889. m. David Johnson 2-10-1841. He b. 5-19-1813 in Washington, PA and d. 2-9-1883 in Steubenville, OH. He was a man of means and an Elder in Two Ridge Church. 4 children.

  A. Walter[4] Johnson m. Julia Blinn, Steubenville, OH.

  B. John[4] Johnson, prominent physician in MI, m. twice.

  C. Permelia[4] Johnson m. Madison Weldy, Jefferson Co., OH. 3 children.

    a. Madison[5] Weldy.

    b. William[5] Weldy.

    c. Martha[5] Margaret Weldy.

  D. Mary[4] Alice Johnson never m. and lived for years in Steubenville with the wife of Walter and d. at age of 60 or more years. She was very intelligent and capable and had traveled abroad several times.

6. John[3] Styles Rex (6th of Jonas[2] and R. M. Rex, George[1]) (Figure 68) b. at Richmond 5-7-1821. He spent his life in Richmond and d. there on 11-20-1898. m. Rachel Scott, daughter of John and Elizabeth Scott, 3-23-1848. She was also a native of Richmond, b. 11-7-1826 and d. Steubenville, OH 10-31-1819. Parents of 7 children. The Rex homestead on which they lived belonged to the family from 1815 to 1900. (Old Jonas Rex place, three miles S. E. of Richmond). John S. Rex was a farmer, a very tall man, very industrious and had very strong reli-

Figure 68. John Styles Rex.

gious convictions.

His picture and following were taken out of a book, History of Two Ridge Church: "John Rex was b. May 7-1821 on the farm where he died November 20, 1898. For forty years Mr. Rex was a consecrated follower of the Master. He was in every sense of the word a good man. He was naturally quiet and reserved. A former pastor who knew him well says of him: 'My recollections of Mr. Rex are very pleasant. As a citizen, he had positive views on things political, but not abusive of those who differed with him. As a neighbor he was ever ready to lend a helping hand. As a husband and father of a large family, he was ever kind and loving. But I knew him best as an Elder. He was noted for his strong convictions of right and duty, from which he could not be easily turned aside. He was a champion for the religion of his ancestry, which was strictly Pauline. To me he was a spiritual father, a wise counseler, the preacher's friend. In the days of his strong manhood he was a man of power in prayer, but the closing years of his life were clouded by physical infirmities, brought about by numerous light paralytic strokes. God granted him up to the last well-balanced, clear mental faculties, and a short time before he died he requested of the writer to sing that grand old hymn *How Firm a Foundation, Ye Saints of the Lord*, which request was granted, and soon he passed away resting secure on that foundation.' He was elected and installed as Elder of Two Ridge Church, April 24, 1864, and remained as such until the day of his death as recorded above."

"Probably the most marked characteristics of my father, John Styles Rex, were his unceasing industry and his strong religious convictions. He was especially strict in his ideas of Sabbath observance. This is illustrated quite well by an incident which occured shortly after the writer, his youngest son of 21 years of age, had taken over the management of the home farm. That spring I decided to tap a few maple trees that were on the farm and connected some pans with an old-fashioned fireplace in the basement of the house where the sap was boiled into syrup. The sap as gathered was stored in barrels outside and was run from there into the basement as fast as it could be boiled down. It so happened that on Saturday we had an immense run of sap. Father told me at noon it would be useless for me to gather more sap than could be boiled down before midnight because there could be no Sunday boiling on his premises. Nevertheless, I gathered and stored all the sap that flowed and at midnight was boiling away at full sped. A few minutes after the clock struck twelve, I was not greatly surprised to see father's tall form come slowly down the inside cellar stairs clad only in the scanty garments of slumber hours. Without pause he passed across a corner of the basement to the outside cellar way and disappeared into darkness. He made no comment upon the situation or explanation of his mission other than to ask me rather sternly as he passed if I did not know it was the Sabbath. Only a few seconds after his disappearance into the night, I heard the sound of wood striking wood, followed quickly by the merry gurgle and swish of sap released from the confines of the barrels. One after another, as all my raw material was on its way to Cross Creek and the Ohio River, there was absolutely nothing for me to do but shut down and go to bed."

Albert Rex.

A. Edwin[4] Rex b. 2-17-1849 near Richmond, Jefferson Co., OH. d. 11-3-1931. m. Caroline Matilda Heizer 1-25-1870 at Kossuth, Des Moines Co., I. by the Rev. Alex. Scott. She is a daughter of Frederick and Margaret Heizer and d. 10-5-1928 at Ames, IA. They belonged to the Congregational Church. Following notice from Ames paper: "Edwin Rex, 83, one of the pioneers of Story Co. and for a quarter of a century a resident of Ames passed away at 8:15 A. M. Thursday at the home of his son Edwin on his old homestead, two and a half miles west of the Iowa State College dairy farm. Mr. Rex was stricken with a heart attack last Wednesday. He was a farmer, retiring many years ago. At one time he served on the County Board of Supervisors and during his earlier years in Ames lived on the present site of the State Highway Commission headquarters. His son conducts his old farm. Mrs. Rex died three years ago and Mr. Rex is survived besides his son, Edwin, by four other sons, Clarence of Boone Co., John living on a farm in South Dakota; Fred living in Watertown, S. D.; and Larry, living in Colorado Springs, Colo. He also leaves four brothers: David of Pittsburgh, PA, John, California; Albert and Scott living in Ohio."

a. Frederick[5] S. Rex b. near Ames, Story Co., IA. 11-2-1872. (A twin of John). He m. Jessie Kogle, daughter of Charles Kogle, 6-25-1902 near Henry, SD. For fifteen years they lived on a farm. Became a merchant in Watertown, SD December 1915. No children.

b. John[5] Rex b. near Ames, IA 11-2-1872 (Twin of Frederick). m.

Ida May Mather 12-22-1909 at Watertown, SD. Lived at Elrod, SD. 10 children.

    (1) John[6] Wilbur Rex, b. 8-10-1910 d. 1910.

    (2) Virgil[6] Edwin Rex, b. 1-4-1912.

    (3) Wilma[6] Frances Rex, b. 12-30-1912.

    (4) Ethel[6] Caroline Rex, b. 4-1-1914.

    (5) Maynard[6] Leroy Rex, b. 5-2-1918 d. 10-3-1989.

    (6) Lorain[6] Denton Rex, b. 9-30-1919.

    (7) Rachel[6] Eileen Rex, b. 1-21-1921.

    (8) Margaret[6] Doreen Rex, b. 6-19-1922.

    (9) Dale[6] Levern Rex, b. 7-19-1924.

    (10) Donald[6] James Rex, b. 2-21-1927.

  c. Harry[5] Rex b. near Ames, IA. 6-10-1875. m. Alma McColly 2-4-1903 at Des Moines, IA. She d. 1912. Parents of a daughter Nellie, and three sons.

  d. Rachel[5] Elizabeth Rex b. near Ames, Story Co., IA 12-23-1876. d. at Ames, 9-11-1926. Single.

  e. Clarence[5] Rex b. near Ames, IA 7-2-1880. m. Maude Thomas 2-27-1904 at Ames, IA. Lived near Ames and was a successful farmer and stock grower. 4 children.

    (1) Charles[6] Russell Rex, b. 1-18-1906 in Ames, IA. Bank clerk at Ames.

    (2) Grace[6] Margaret Rex b. 6-13-1908 in Ames, IA. Employed Extension Dept. Iowa State College.

    (3) Carroll[6] Thomas Rex b. 12-19-1910 in Ames, IA.

    (4) Doris[6] Laura Rex b. 8-28-1914 in Ames, IA.

  f. Edwin[5] Rex b. near Ames, IA 4-8-1882. m. Carrie Freed 4-6-1900. He is an Agriculturist and profitable stock raiser.

B. David[4] Johnson Rex (Figure 66) b. 1-7-1851 in Steubenville, OH and d. 9-7-1946 in Ingram, Allegheny Co., PA. In 1871 removed to Pittsburgh where he has always lived. m. Harriet Elizabeth Reed 1-6-1876. Had 9 children. She was b. 4-27-1853 and d. 2-28-1924. Mr. Rex has been much interested in the family history and has given valuable assitance in compiling it. He furnished the pictures (2nd generation of his Grandmother Rhoda Milliken Rex and Sally Rex Cloaky Day who was a sister of Jonas Rex and he

Figure 69. David J. Rex.

was the husband of Rhoda M. R.) Also Mr. Rex has the original Jonas Rex bible of which he furnished the pictures, etc. He is manufacturer of paper boxes in Pittsburgh. In Pittsburgh Sun-Telegraph, 7-28-1932, his picture appeared 'D. J. Rex, 82, first Burgess of Ingram, who will take part in the Borrough's thirtieth anniversary.'

  a. John^5 Scott Rex b. in Pittsburgh, PA 10-3-1876. m. Nellie T. Rhodes of Pittsburgh, 6-4-1889 where they resided. 4 children.

    (1) David^6 Ford Rex, b. 11-11-1900 in Ingram, PA and d. 6-9-1978 in Pittsburgh, PA. m. Johanna E. A. Winter 7-19-1923. She b. about 1899. 4 children

      +Ruth^7 Rex m. White.

      +Audrey^7 J. Rex b. 10-10-1924. m. Mursch.

      +Joan^7 Rex b. 7-19-1926. m. Dean.

      +Vera^7 Rex b. 2-5-1928. m. Neleppa.

    (2) Helen^6 T. Rex b. 12-30-1903 m. William Whitney White 6-14-1928.

    (3) Harriett^6 E. Rex b. 7-14-1907 m. Robert Nieman 8-14-1928.

    (4) John^6 Stewart Rex b. 10-16-1913 and d. 10-2-1994 in Ingram, PA. m. Phyllis. 2 children.

      +Marilyn^7 B. Rex.

      +Claire^7 H. Rex.

  b. Eleanor^5 Reed Rex b. in Pittsburgh 11-27-1879 and d. after 1972.

  c. Frank^5 Clyde Rex b. in Pittsburgh 8-3-1882. m. Florence Anna McNary of Pittsburgh 10-25-1906. She b. 3-7-1885 in Hickory, PA. 2 children.

    (1) Charles.^{6} E. Rex b. 6-1910.

    (2) Mary^6 Jane Rex b. 9-28-1914.

  d. Edward^5 Geary Rex b. 7-9-1884 m. Margaret Harper also a native of Pittsburgh 11-12-1908. 6 children.

    (1) Lois^6 Eleanor Rex b. 12-30-1909. m. Stirling.

    (2) Ola^6 Meredith Rex b. 9-28-1912. m. Gordon.

    (3) Edward^6 Geary Rex b. 9-18-1914 and d. 12-1-1985. m. Elizabeth Kern. 4 children.

      +Edward^7 Geary Rex.

      +Marty^7 Rex.

      +Karen^7 Rex.

      +Bruce^7 Rex.

    (4) Frank^6 Harper Rex b. 12-6-1920.

(5) Myrtle[6] Mary Rex b. 5-12-1922 d. 3-27-1927.

(6) Donald[6] Frederick Rex b. 11-13-1926.

e. Rachel[5] Mary Rex b. 1-23-1886 in Ingram, PA, and d. 5-1974. m. 6-14-1911 in Ingram, PA to Guy N. Rumbaugh also of Pittsburgh. He b. 10-19-1881. 3 children.

(1) Anna[6] Herriett Rumbaugh b. 11-12-1912.

(2) John[6] Rex Rumbaugh b. 2-15-1914.

(3) Guy[6] Neely Rumbaugh b. 10-2-1915 and d. 9-1980.

f. Samuel[5] Miller Rex b. 10-22-1888 and d. 2-19-1972. m. Mary McNary also of Pittsburgh 6-27-1914. She b. 7-7-1889 in Hickory, PA. 2 children.

(1) Ruth[6] Rex, b. 5-15-1916.

(2) Marylin[6] Rex, b. 12-3-1923. m. Bennett.

g. Harriett[5] Elizabeth Rex b. 1-9-1891 in Ingram, PA and d. 9-1981 m. 9-4-1912 William F. Aull. He b. 7-17-1899 in Pittsburgh, PA, and d. 1-1965. 4 children.

(1) Elizabeth[6] Rex Aull b. 2-24-1915.

(2) Jane[6] Irwin Aull b. 6-19-1916.

(3) William[6] Aull b. 1-22-1922.

(4) Helen[6] Frances Aull b. 12-9-1926.

h. Laura[5] Margaret Rex b. 3-20-1892 and d. after 1924.

i. †David[5] Johnson Rex, Jr. b. 9-3-1894 and d. 8-26-1977 in Mckees Rocks, Allegheny Co., PA. Service record of David[5] J. Rex, Jr., 87 Berry St., Ingram, PA. says he b. 9-3-1894. Serial No. 1828002. Sept. 20, 1917. Inducted into service at McKee's Rock, Allegheny Co., PA Sept. 21, 1917. Arrived at Camp Lee, Petersburg, VA Sept. 26, 1917. Assigned to Co. L. 319th Infantry, 80th Division Oct. 13th 1917. Appointed "Corporal." April 1918, placed on detached service with Headquarters 3rd Battalion, 319th Infantry as member of Battalion Intelligence, Section (Snipers, Observers and Scouts). Remained with Bn. Hdqtrs. until after the signing of the Armistice. May 17, 1918 sailed from Norfolk, VA on U.S.S. Leelandia. May 31, 1918 arrived St. Nagairre, France.

"Activities."

June 17 to June 24, 1918 on special duty with the 52nd British Div. in trenches (front) at Vimy Ridge. June 24 to July 15, 1918, attended British First Army S. O. & S. School at Linghem, France. July 17 to Aug.18, 1918 two tours of duty in front line and two tours in reserve line Somme Front. Sept. 12 to

Sept. 16, 1918 St. Mehiel. Sept. 22 to Sept. 25, 1918, Verdun Front. Sept. 26 to Sept. 29, 1918, Meusse Argonne, advance, (Bethincourt to Meusse). Sept. 29 to Oct. 6, 1918 in reserve in Montfaucon District. Oct. 6 to Oct. 12, 1918 Meusse Argonne advance between Nantillois and Cunnell. Oct. 30 to Nov. 7, 1918, Meusse Argonne, Advance Somerance to Buzancy. Nov. 11–Armistice Day–organization had been relieved and were on way back from lines for rest. Were on march which ended at Florent. Dec. 15th relieved from detached service with Co. A, First Provisional Regt. A. E. F. University, Beaune, Cote D'Or. Returned to original organization about May 1, 1919. May 20, 1919, sailed from Brest, France, U. S. S. "Graf. Waldersee." June 2, 1919 arrived at Hoboken, N. J. Entrained for Camp Dix. Arrived at Camp Dix. Transferred to Camp Sherman at Chillicothe, Ohio with organization June 12, 1919. Discharged at Camp Sherman, Ohio. Never sick or injured. Commanding officers during active service: Maj. Gen. Adelbert Cronkhite, 80th Division. Brig. Gen. Lloyd M. Brett, 160th Brigade. Cols. Frank N. Cochne and Lore, 319th Infantry. Capt. Gerald Egan, Company Commander and Battallion Commander during action. After his discharge he went home and m. Evangeline Hazel Reno, 9-25-1919. 2 children.

    (1) David[6] J. Rex, 3rd, b. 9-7-1920.

    (2) Harold[6] Reno Rex, b. 9-1-1926.

C. Frank[4] Rex b. 6-15-1853 d. 12-18-1856.

D. Rhora[4] Rex b. 12-24-1859.

E. John[4] C. Rex b. 9-1-1860 near Richmond, OH. m. 9-19-1882 to Louella Winter by Nixon B. Stewart, Steubenville, OH. They moved to Ames, IA and then to Los Angeles, CA. 6 children.

    a. Earl[5] Gladden Rex b. at Story City, IA 12-23-1883. m. Jennie Elser 1-10-1909.

    b. Evelyn[5] Rex b. Story City, IA, 11-14-1886. m. David W. Barclay 7-30-1905.

    c. J.[5] Winter Rex b. Story City, IA 7-29-1889. m. Verda Seeley 10-1-1914.

    d. Don[5] Shane Rex b., Ames, IA 11-7-1891. m. Mary Lord 4-20-1916.

    e. Blanch[5] Roshel Rex b. at Ames, IA 10-26-1893. m. Rutherford Green 6-22-1918.

F. Scott[4] Rex b. near Richmond, OH 9-10-1865. m. Agnes May

Crismore in Wooster, OH 8-9-1887. Ceremony by Rev. Ewitman. (Her parents were Wesley D. and Hannah Dillier Crismore). She b. Wooster OH 1-22-1868. 5 children. Bank of Italy Bldg. Stockton, CA.

     a. Helen[5] May Rex b. St. Paul, MN, 9-16-1889 m. to Elmer Smith 10-12-1915. Address New Bedford, OH.

     b. Maude[5] Jeannette Rex b. at Wooster, OH. 4-19-1891. m. to P. Sheridan Ohmstead 7-30-1910. Lived in New Philadelphia, OH.

     c. Ruth[5] Gertrude Rex b. in Duluth, MN 6-22-1893 m. Otto F. Selle 7-5-1917. Lived in Kapowskin, WA.

     d. Dorothy[5] Alice Rex b. 8-1-1899 at Grand Forks, ND and d. 12-1972. m. to Edward Sullivan 6-20-1919. Lived in Pierre, SD.

     e. Scott[5] Theadore Rex b. in Grand Forks, ND. 8-14-1904. Lived in Sookston, MN. Single.

G. Albert[4] Rex b. 12-24 1871, Richmond, OH. m. Jennie Reed 12-25-1895, near Reed's Mills, Jefferson Co., OH. Ceremony by Rev. Henry Webb. Her parents were George W. and Nancy Welday Reed. She b. at Bloomfield, OH 6-15-1871 and d. 1-17-1922 near Medinah, OH. 2 daughters. Both school teachers before marriage as were their parents.

     a. Dorothy[5] Rex b. in Steubenville, OH 4-27-1899. m. Foster Kindig 10-22-1921. He d. 11-28-1928.

       (1) Robert[6] Rex Kindig, 9-13-1922.

     b. Florence[5] Rex b. 10-29-1900 in Medinah, OH d. 1-1-1990 in Akron, OH. m. Loyal H. Geisinger, 9-10-1927.

7. Eliza[3] Rex (7th of Jonas[2], and R. M. Rex, George[1]) (Figure 67) b. Richmond, OH 9-6-1824 and d. 3-4-1856. m. 3-3-1840 James F. Snowden and they resided in Wheeling, WV. Were parents of 4 children. In her picture, the baby in arms is supposed to be John Snowden, her second child. James F. Snowden b. 3-23-1818 d. 1-5-1896 of apoplexy at Cornwall, MO. He had a second wife.

Figure 70. Eliza Rex Snowden with child.

A. Martha[4] Eudora Snowden b. 6-17-1841, Knowville, OH. d. 6-12-1916, Mariatta, Ohio of paralysis. m. Bernard Masterson 11-21-1861. He. d. 4-12-1893. 7 children.

     a. Elizabeth[5] Rex Masterson b. 10-3-1862. m. John Howarth 10-3-1881. 2 children.

(1) John[6] Howarth, Jr. Single.

(2) Mattie[6] Snowden Howarth m. D. C. Sullivan of Huntington, WV. He is a druggist and they have a son.

+Wayne[7] Howard Sullivan.

b. John[5] Thomas Masterson b. 6-7-1864 d. 1927. m. Mary Stephens 11-5-1896. 1 daughter.

(1) Alice[6] Masterson m. H. C. Daniels, Chatanooga, TN. 2 daughters.

+Louise[7] Daniels, b. 6-17-1916.

+Dorothy[7] Daniels, b. 7-4-1927. Huntington, WV.

c. Ray[5] Masterson b. 9-13-1866 d. 1898. m. Rosalie Bryan 9-12-1894. Both school teachers. 2 daughters.

(1) Bertha[6] Pearl Masterson b. 8-30-1895 d. 11-16-1916.

(2) Anna[6] Eudora Masterson b. 3-3-1897 m. Anthony Gebhart 10-7-1913. d. 11-5-1918.

d. Georgia[5] Ann Masterson b. 12-28-1868 m. John Sherrer 11-16-1911. No children.

e. Homer[5] Gillett Masterson b. 11-27-1870. m. Myrtle Harbor 7-17-1893. 9 children.

(1) Bernard[6] Clinton Masterson b. 6-12-1896 m. 2-22-1914 Ollie Hensley who was b. 9-18-1898. 5 children.

+Frank[7] Shirley Masterson b. 12-18-1914 d. 1-4-1918.

+Russell[7] Ray Masterson b. 5-15-1917 d. 1-1958.

+Arthur[7] Lee Masterson b. 1-8-1920.

+Mabel[7] Louise Masterson b. 12-31-1921 d. 5-9-1923.

+Ruby[7] May Masterson b. 10-5-1926.

(2) Mattie[6] Masterson b. 11-24-1909 d. 6-28-1914.

(3) Anna[6] L. Masterson b. 2-25-1911.

(4) James[6] Herschel Masterson b. 2-20-1913.

(5) George[6] Masterson b. 2-7-1915 d. 1-1-1930.

(6) Marjorie[6] Helen Masterson b. 4-7-1917.

(7) John[6] Edward Masterson b. 10-1-1919 d. 1-11-1922.

(8) Virginia[6] Dare Masterson b. 11-28-1921.

(9) Charles[6] Ray Masterson b. 2-25-1923 d. 8-27-1924.

f. Clara[5] Emma Masterson b. 1-5-1877 m. William E. Neal, he d. 7-15-1898. 2 daughters.

(1) Pauline[6] Rex Neal b. 4-20-1897. (H. S. teacher, Williamstown, WV) A. B. and M. A. Marrietta College, Post Grad. Ohio State and U of M., Ann Arbor, MI.

(2) Willie[6] Estelle Neal (teacher Parkersburg, WV. H. S.) A. B.

Marietta College. Post Grad Ohio State U. and Middleburg College, Middlebury, VT.

m. 2nd Herschel V. Brown 18-1900. 2 daughters.

(3) Neva[6] Ray Brown b. 9-2-1902 m. W. W. Ankenlrant, Supt. of Schools, Athens, OH. She was critic and teacher in the college at Athens. No children.

(4) Ruth[6] Louise Brown b. 3-9-1904 m. W. J. Blume, resides Marietta, OH.

g. Walter[5] Lionel Masterson b. 3-1-1881 m. Eva Rust 5-22-1906. 1 son.

(1) Ray[4] L. Masterson b. 5-13-1908. Is a druggist, Parkersburg, WV. Marietta H. S. Grad. and Ohio Northern U.

B. †John[4] Snowden. See Ohio Roster, Civil War Vol. 2, p. 23. 1st O. V. I. Co. H.

C. Lucy[4] Snowden d. of paralysis, Chestnutfield, OH 1889. m. Edwin P. Worrall, 1874. 1 son.

a. Snowden[5] Worrall b. 8-27-1881. Is in Olivet College, Olivet, MI. m. Emma R. Omsey of Delaware, OH 12-25-1907. 1 daughter.

(1) Dorothy[6] Louise Worrall b. 11-27-1915.

D. William[4] Edwin Snowden b. 2-19-1859 d. McKees Rocks, PA 5-15-1919. m. Sarah Keips 7-4-1897. 4 children. Mrs. Sarah Keip Snowden-Merscher (has married second time) has the black ebony silver-headed cane which belongs to James F. Snowden. Is inscribed 'Presented to J. F. Snowden by the pupils of the 3rd Ward School of Wheeling, WV June 80, 1870.' On a silver band where the cane was once broken is June 1895 when the father gave the cane to his son, William Edwin.

a. James[5] Francis Snowden b. 9-12-1898.

b. Martha[5] Elizabeth Snowden b. 6-9-1901 m. John E. Cooper 12-24-1921. 1 son.

(1) John[6] E. Cooper, Jr. b. 11-10-1922.

c. William[5] Orrin Snowden b. 10-2-1904 m. Margaret Shannon 2-1926. 2 children.

(1) William[6] Edwin Snowden b. 4-1927.

(2) Elizabeth[6] Jane Snowden b. 11-16-1928.

d. Milton[5] Arthur Snowden b. 5-30-1908.

8. Martha[3] W. Rex (8th of Jonas and R. M. Rex, George[1]) b. Richmond, OH 5-1-1827 and d. 3-8-1833.

9. Joseph[3] Burson Rex (9th of Jonas[2] and R. M. Rex, George[1]) b.

Richmond, OH 10-20-1829 and d. 3-10-1833.

10. James[3] Rex (10th of Jonas and R. M. Rex, George[1]) b. Richmond, OH 4-5-1832 and d. 4-1-1895. He never m. and lived with his brother, John S. Rex on the Jonas Rex homestead.

Chapter 9

Hannah[2] Rex (7th child of Margaret Kepler and George Rex[1]) (Figure 71) was b. 7-16-1787 in Mifflin Co., PA, d. 12-25-1866. She and husband Isaac Shane both are buried at Bacon Ridge near Richmond, OH. Isaac Shane b. 12-26-1782 and d. 7-31-1880. Isaac Shane and Hannah Rex were m. 10-8- 1805 at her home, Jefferson, Greene Co., PA. They were the parents of ten children. "Isaac Shane was the son of James Shane who emigrated from N. J. to Washington Co., PA in 1774 and settled 4 miles west of Monongahela City where Isaac was b. In 1798 his father located on the headwaters of Mills Creek. Isaac lived here till 10-8-1805 when he m. Hannah Rex, daughter of George Rex of Greene Co., PA and in 1810 moved to what is known as the "Red Mill" property. In 1812 he removed to N. E. quarter of Sec. 19, Range 3, township 11, where he remained, clearing a large farm and rearing a large family. The children all m. but Margaret who d. in infancy. Mr. Shane was industrious. At one time he and his sons owned 1,000 acres of land in Ross Township. He was elected Justice of the Peace in 1817 and held this office until 1827. He was in the Legislature in 1843. He was a Republican and a Presbyterian until he was 97 yrs. old. Retentive memory – all faculties. Dictated Bacon Ridge Church History in this book." (This from *History of Belmont and Jefferson Counties* O. J. A. Caldwell Pub. 1880.)

Figure 71. Hannah Rex Shane.

Figure 72. Gravestone of Hannah Rex Shane.

Following is an article from the Steubenville Herald:
"Cemetery Association Granted Ohio Charter. Ross Township Group takes Over Pioneer Burying Ground. Name is changed.–As a result of renewed interest in a pioneer burying ground in Ross Township, a gathering was called of friends and relatives of those buried there. A committee was appointed and a charter was obtained from the state for the Mt. Lebonon Cemetery Association. Title of the two tracts in the

cemetery was transferred to the new corporation, and the cemetery will hereafter be known as "Mt. Lebonon Cemetery." There are a number of good lots still available in the plot. Miss Frances Sutton is given credit for her efforts in bringing about the new organization. The incorporators are A. M. Shane, W. R. Scott, W. V. Wallace, John L. McClelland, R. W. Sutton. The original plot for burying ground purposes was given to the community by Isaac Shane, a pioneer of Bacon Ridge in Ross Township. Mainly Scotch pioneers and their descendants rest there as the markers indicate. There are Suttons, Shanes, Scotts, Baresfords, Crabbs, Rexs, Ryans, Kerrs, McClellands, Wallaces, Williams, Browns, Fraziers, Wycoffs and many other families buried there. In later years as the cemetery was nearly filled up, additional ground was purchased by William R. Lyle of Bellingham, Washington, whose parents, John and Sara Lyle, are buried there and this was donated to the cemetery association. A grandson of the pioneer is John R. Shane of Miami, Florida, a former resident of Steubenville."

To Mrs. Anna B. Scott is due the credit for much of the information for Line VII, also for the pictures of her grandmother Hannah Rex and her aunt, Kitty Burson, those of the graves of Hannah and Isaac Shane, and of the lovely old brick home (Figure 73) which they built in 1829, which is yet in good repair. I will say, if on every line there were one person as energetic and conscientious as Mrs. Scott, this would be a most complete genealogy. After our lengthy correspondence, it was with pleasure indeed for my son, Dan Rex, and I to meet her in her Ohio home. She is what is called "The salt of the earth" and knowing her, I feel repays much of the effort put forth in compiling

Figure 73. Hannah Rex and Isaac Shane home near Steubenville, Ohio.

this history. In connection with this Line VII, I will also say we drove in our car as far as Eliot, Maine, to met Mrs. Aline Shane Devin, who has been much interested in the family.

In writing in 1930 Mrs. Scott says "My brother B. F. Shane and I both remember distinctly our Grandmother Shane as a large woman and in her early days, strong and resolute, a famous housekeeper and one who looked to the ways of her household. Of her father, George[1] Rex 1st, I have always heard he was settled in PA and had money, plenty for those days. He came (over the mountains) with his family and settled in Greene Co., PA. Grandmother often told how the family came in wagons. She said she walked all the way only as she would swing on behind one of the wagons with her feet drawn up. She came to Jefferson Co. OH to visit her sister, Mattie Rex Winters, and there met Isaac Shane. When her first child was several months old, she went back to Greene Co. PA to visit her parents. She rode horseback, carrying the child on her lap. Grandfather went with her and helped her across the Ohio River at Wells Riffles (below Steubenville, OH.) Then he came back and she made the rest of the journey alone. When her first son was born and was named George Rex Shane, his grandfather Rex came to see him and brought him a complete suit like the British Soldiers wore,–red." Hannah Rex Shane is remembered as she always appeared when dressed in stiff black silk.

1. Martha[3] Shane (1st child of Isaac and Hannah[2] Rex Shane, George[1]) b. 7-5-1807 d. 1866. m. James G. Allen, he d. 1883, no children.
2. Ellza[3] Shane (2nd of Isaac and Hannah[2] Rex Shane, George[1]) b. 2-1-1809. m. 1st William Walker and they had 2 children.
   A. †William[4] Walker enlisted in the 12th Iowa, and was killed in battle. He was m. and left 1 son,
      a. Edwin[5] Walker, who is also d.
   B. Hannah[4] Walker b. 1830 m. John Wallace Scott 1849. 8 children.
      a. Lucinda[5] Scott b. 1851, d. infant.
      b. Eloria[5] Scott b. 1852, d. 1867.
      c. William[5] W. Scott b. 1854 d. 1898 m. Anna B. Scott.
      d. Robert[5] E. Scott b. 1856 d. 1906 m. Agnes Clark.
      e. Eliza[5] May Scott b. 1858 d._____m. John S. Umensetter, Richmond, OH. She has 6 teaspoons marked "H. S.", same as large one Mrs. Scott has (H. S. means Hannah Shane) and also a corner cupboard, this H. S. used. 1 child:
         (1) Agnes[6] Umensetter b. 10-1894 m. Clarence Hendrix 1915. 5

children.
    +Helen[7] Hendrix b. 1917.
    +Thelma[7] Hendrix b. 1918.
    +Warner[7] Mills Hendrix b. 1922.
    +Doris[7] Mildred Hendrix b. 1924.
    +Grace[7] Louise Hendrix b. 1927. Prosperous farmers, Methodists. Resided near E. Springfield, OH.
f. Alexander[5] Scott b. 1860 d. 1873.
g. Melton[5] Scott b. 1867 m. Mary L. Pyles 1893 and have 6 children. Resided Barterton, OH.
  (1) Walter[6] Scott b. 1896 m. Myra_____.
    +1 child b. 1923.
  (2) Syrilla[6] Scott b. 1897 m. Mr. Shultz, Canton, OH.
  (3) Paul[6] Scott b. 1899.
  (4) Robert[6] Scott b. 1901.
  (5) William[6] Scott b. 1904.
  (6) Lloyd[6] Scott b. 1905.
h. Myrtle[5] H. Scott b. 1869 m. John W. Frazier 1891. 5 children.
  (1) Altha[6] M. Frazier b. 1892 m. Clarence Ault. 6 children.
    +Hazel[7] Ault b. 1914.
    +Marjorie[7] Ault b. 1917.
    +Billy[7] Ault b. 1919.
    +Jack[7] Ault (twin) b. 1924.
    +Jean[7] Ault (twin) b. 1924.
    +Barbara[7] Ann Ault b. 1929.
  (2) Letha[6] Frazier b. 1893 m. Donald Weber. 2 children.
    +Arline[7] Weber b. 1926.
    +Donald[7] Weber b. 1930.
  (3) Hannah[6] Frazier b. 1900 m. Albert Johnson 1926. 2 children.
    +Virginia[7] Johnson b. 1926.
    +Eugene[7] Weber Johnson b. 1929.
  (4) Charles[6] Frazier b. 1906 m. Alice Reichenbaugh, no children.
  (5) Mary[6] Frazier b. 1907. Family resides Canton, OH. Presbyterians.
Eliza[3] Shane m. 2nd Alexander Morrison and they had 8 children.
  C. Isaac[4] Morrison (1st child of Eliza[3] and 2nd husband Alexander Morrison, Hanah[2], George[1]) m. Jennie Miser and had 4 children.
    a. Mary[5] Morrison m. Wynn Cox. 6 children.

(1) Morris[6] Cox.

(2) Mordecai[6] Cox.

(3) James[6] Cox.

(4) Ben[6] Cox.

(5) Charlotte[6] Cox.

b. Stanley[5] Morrison m. Mattie Smyth. Presbyterians, Hershey, NE. 1 child.

(1) Myron[6] Morrison.

c. Laura[5] Morrison m. Arthur Fritz. 1 child. Later m. Tom Ingram, E. Springfield, OH.

(1) Stanley[6] Fritz.

d. Ida[5] Morrison m. Robert Campbell. 1 child.

(1) Frederick[6] Campbell, Pittsburg, PA.

D. Hamilton[4] Morrison d. in infancy.

E. Harriett[4] Morrison.

F. Katherine[4] Morrison m. William Cox in Hershey, NE. 5 children.

a. Anna[5] Cox m. Charles Becker. 7 children.

(1) Fred[6] Becker m. Belle Ware. 4 children.

+Helen[7] Becker.

+Marjorie[7] Becker.

+Elizabeth[7] Becker.

+Bonnie[7] Becker.

(2) Stanley[6] Becker m. Bessie Calonay, no children.

(3) Dan[6] Becker m. Hazel Dickerson, no children.

(4) Otto[6] Becker m. Jean Maxwell, no children.

(5) Mabel[6] Becker m. James Calonay. 4 children.

+Eldon[7] Calonay.

+Geneva[7] Calonay.

+Gail[7] Calonay.

+Charles[7] Calonay.

(6) Jessie[6] Becker m. Cecil Crider. 3 children.

+Jean[7] Crider.

+Beverly[7] Crider.

+Robert[7] Crider.

(7) Norman[6] Becker, single.

b. Mattie[5] Cox m. Allen Jared. 6 children.

(1) Harold[6] Jared.

(2) Ernest[6] Jared.

(3) Homer[6] Jared, single (1933).

(4) Dorothy[6] Jared m. Herman Kalloff. 1 child.

+Ada[7] Kalloff.
(5) Alice[6] Jared m. Lenard Montgomery. 5 children.
+Gertrude[7] Montgomery.
+Mildred[7] Montgomery.
+Wilma[7] Montgomery.
+Lilia[7] Montgomery.and another.
(6) Ada[6] Jared m. Jack Kalloff, no children.
c. Wynn[5] Cox.
d. Jennie[5] Cox.
e. Frank[5] Cox.
G. George[4] Morrison m. Ida White. 1 child.
a. Hershel[5] White Morrison, Chicago, IL.
H. Mary[4] Morrison m. Orville Allen. 3 children.
a. Ada[5] Allen m. Harry Snell, 2 children. Phillip and a daughter.
b. Hattie[5] Allen m. James Butler. 2 children.
c. Frank[5] Allen. No information.
I. Martha[4] Morrison d. 11-1929 m. Silas Blazer. 1 child.
a. Daisy[5] Blazer m. Frank Dotts. 2 children.
(1) Erma[6] Dotts.
(2) Ina[6] Dotts m. Paul Abel and have 4 children.
+Frank[7] Abel.
+Myron[7] Abel.
+John[7] Abel. Carrolltown, OH.
+_____Abel[7] Carrolltown, OH.
J. James[4] Morrison, d. in infancy.
3. Mary[3] Shane (3rd of Isaac and Hannah[2] Rex Shane, George[1]) b. 10-31-1810 m. Abraham Crabb and had 10 children. Mr. Crabb d. 2-22-1891, aged 85 years 6 mo. 13 days. Both in Bacon Ridge Cemetery near Richmond, OH. On other side of stone "Mary C. wife of Abraham Crabb d. Jan. 28-1897, aged 86 yrs. 3 mo. 4 days."
A. Isaac[4] Crabb m. Mary Miser. 6 children.
a. Maggie[5] B. Crabb m. Samuel Byers, 1880. Now a widow, New London, IA.
b. Frank[5] Crabb, d. as infant.
c. George[5] Crabb m. 1st Alice Herrington, she d. leaving 1 son. He was adopted by his aunt Maggie and husband, Samuel Byers. Is m. and has a son, Benjamin,[6] and lives in Madison, IA. 2nd wife of George Crabb, Susie Lymand and they had 3 children.
d. Dr. A.[5] A. Crabb m. Jessie Signs, no children. Traer, IA.
e. Benjamin[5] Scott Crabb, single, New London, IA.

f. Lillian[5] L. Crabb m. Edward Kunath, had 3 children. A widow in Washington, IA.

B. Annie[4] Crabb m. †John Scott, Colonel Civil War, Mexican War veteran, Nevada, IA. Auctioneer, stock raiser, Senator from Story Co., and Lieut. Gov. of IA. 2 children.

C. Hannah[4] Crabb d. at age of 4 years.

D. Martha[4] Crabb d. at 25 yrs.

E. Sarah[4] Crabb b. 11-1-1837 d. 12-17-1930. Sarah and husband buried in Evergreen Cemetery, Victor, IA. m. Bateman Beresford, Benton Co., IA. 6 children.

  a. Howard[5] Leon Beresford b. 4-22-1856 m. Leah Margaret Williams. She b. 1860. Went to IA, 1863. 7 children.

    (1) Cecile[6] Aline Beresford b. 9-27-1881 m. Arthur Auld, Vinton, IA. 5 children as follows:

      +Emory[7] Auld.

      +Leland[7] Auld.

      +Byron[7] Auld.

      +Howard[7] Auld.

      +James[7] Auld.

    (2) Ethel[6] Beresford b. 1884 m. J. T. Porter, Mason City, IA. 2 children.

      +Rex[7] Porter.

      +Phillip[7] Porter.

    (3) Rex[6] Beresford b. 12-18-1885 Vinton, IA. m. Mary Blodgett 9-26-1912, Mt. Pleasant, IA. 5 children. Rex Beresford, 839 Brookridge, Ames, IA. Extension Prof. Animal Husbandry, Iowa State College.

      +Robert[7] Beresford b. 6-17-1914, Ames, IA.

      +Donald[7] Rex Beresford b. 8-23-1918, Ames, IA.

      +Bruce[7] Comstock Beresford b. 10-5-1919, Ames, IA.

      +Mary[7] Ruth Beresford b. 3-8-1921, Ames, IA.

      +Kenneth[7] Charles Beresford b. 12-14-1923, Ames, IA.

    (4) Frank[6] Beresford b. 1893 m. Nellie Patterson. 2 children.

      +Frank[7] Beresford.

      +Helen[7] Beresford.

    (5) Hobart[6] Beresford b. 12-6-1897 m. Lorene Kling.

    (6) Helen[6] E. Beresford b. 1-5-1900.

    (7) Howard[6] C. Beresford b. 9-2-1902 m. Vivian Brand.

  b. Alexander[5] M. Beresford b. 1-5-1858 d. 11-16-1930. m. Lottie Treat. 8 children.

(1) Robert[6] Beresford.
(2) Elizabeth[6] Beresford.
(3) Lester[6] Beresford.
(4) Paul[6] Beresford.
(5) Howard[6] Beresford.
(6) Kenneth[6] Beresford.
(7) Theodore[6] Beresford.
(8) Stewart[6] Beresford.
 c. Emory[5] S. Beresford b. 1860, d. young.
 d. Abraham[5] Beresford b. 1862, no children.
 e. John[5] S. Beresford b. 1865. 5 children as follows:
  (1) John[6] Lawrence Beresford b. 1890. 4 children.
  (2) Carl[6] Beresford, 8 children.
  (3) Byrl[6] Beresford, 6 children.
  (4) Verne[6] Beresford, 1 child.
  (5) Harold[6] Beresford, 2 children.
 f. Mary[5] E. Beresford b. 1867 m. E. G. Moon. 1 child.
  (1) Zella Moon.
F. Hannah[4] Mariah Crabb m. Isaac LaRue. No children.
G. Mary[4] Crabb m. Frank Shane. Had 1 daughter Mrs. Parr.
H. Eliza[4] Crabb m. Dennie Jackman. No children.
I. William[4] Henry Crabb m. Mary Wallace 1876, had 6 children. d. 1924.
J. James[4] Harvey Crabb d. 1929 m. Sarah Ellis 1883, had 3 daughters.
 a. Lauchee[5] Crabb m. John Hanlon, no children.
 b. Ada[5] Crabb m. W. L. Hales. 2 sons,
  (1) Donald[6] Hales.
  (2) Kenneth[6] Hales.
 c. Floy[5] Crabb m. John Peterson. (All live in Stark Co., OH.)
4. George[3] Rex Shane (4th of Isaac and Hannah[2] Shane, George[1]) b. 7-22-1813 m. Susan Markle. 2 children.
 A. Abraham[4] Shane m. Louise Kepling, Salem, OH. 2 sons.
  a. Myron[5] Holly Shane d. 3-1931, aged 69 yrs.
  b. George[5] Shane, Canton, OH.
 B. Gustavus[4] Shane m. Kate Rinehart. 1 son.
  a. Frank[5] Shane, M. D., Cleveland, OH.
5. Susanna[3] Shane (5th of Isaac and Hannah[2] Shane, George[1]) b. 12-1-1816. m. 8-16-1835 Joseph Shane b. 2-23-1811. Joseph, son of Benjamin Shane, Justice of the Peace 1861, County Commissioner

1867-70. (Mrs. Anna Scott, her daughter has a cup and saucer of her mother's wedding dishes.) 7 children.

A. †Isaac[4] Henry Shane, b. 1836. m. Louisa Maria Ross 1861, both of Jefferson Co., OH. Moved to Wisconsin in Spring of 1862 and in 1864 Isaac H. Shane enlisted in Co. K. 5th Wisconsin Reg. 6th Army Corps and served until the close of the war. Was under Gen. Sheridan in the wilderness campaign and was present at the surrender of Lee. While in the service, his wife with their six month old child returned to Ohio and remained there until the husband returned in the Spring of 1866. They returned then to Wisconsin, settling at Eau Claire. He entered the Shaw Lumber Co. and continued until his death in 1891. Members of Congregational Church and family raised in that faith. Had 4 sons.

  a. Joseph[5] Edgar Shane b. 1864 d. 1922 m. Laura Bean 1891. 3 children.

    (1) Shirley[6] Shane, b. 1894 m. Emma Annette Olson 1916. V. Pres Chippewa Food Products, Eau Claire, WI. 1 child.
    +Phyllis[7] Jane Shane b. 1918.

    (2) Villa[6] Marie Shane b. 1896 m. Christopher Remol in 1924. Address, Chippewa Falls, WI. 1 son.
    +John[7] Shane Remol. b. 1926.

    (3) De Alton[6] R. Shane b. 1904. Traveling Salesman, single, lived with his mother, 222 Harvard St., Minneapolis. MN.

  b. Alonzo[3] Dorsey Shane b. 1866 m. Olive M. Garret 1888. Railroad engineer and killed on duty, 1915. 1 child.

    (1) Lyle[6] Emerson Shane b. 1890 m. Edith H. Peterson. In Auditing Dept. Northern Ry., Minneapolis, MN. 2 children.
    +Doris[7] Marie Shane b. 1918.
    +Russell[7] E. Shane b. 1923.

  c. Charles[5] E. Shane m. Emma Cromwell, no children.

  d. Royal[5] Ross Shane killed while playing ball.

"The descendants of Isaac Henry and Louisa Shane still live in Wisconsin and Minnesota, and all are thrifty and useful citizens."

B. Helen[4] Shane b. 12-1838 m. John L. McLean 1858. 8 children.

  a. Joseph[5] E. McLean b. 1861. Grad. Eastman College, taught school m. Lottie Guy, Poughkeepsie, NY. 1 child.

    (1) Blanche[6] Helen McLean b. 1892 m. 1st Griggs. Had 1 son. m. 2nd Spracklin, Jersey City, NJ. Mrs. Spracklin was a magazine writer.

  b. James[5] F. McLean b. 1863. Taught school all his life. m. Allie

Goodlin. 4 children. Two sons d. pneumonia in World War I, remains brought back to America and buried in cemetery, Toronto, OH. Methodists.

(1) †Ray[6] Lemuel McLean b. 1891 d. France.

(2) †Paul[6] McLean b. 1893 d. Belgium.

(3) Helen[6] McLean b. 1888.

(4) Frances[6] McLean b. 1896.

c. Nina[5] S. McLean b. 1868 m. Ed. Jones (R.R. Carpenter). 2 children.

(1) Edgar[6] Jones m. Drowned while fishing in IA. Left 3 children.

(2) Alice[6] Jones in CA.

d. Mansfield[5] McLean b. 1871, Jefferson Co. OH. m. Emma Burnett of NY. He taught school, went to NY, and studied at Eastman College. Postmaster; in Uappingers Falls, NY. Then fine position in NY City Customshouse. 1 son.

(1) John[6] McLean b. about 1905 m. 1927, resided NY City.

e. Blanche[5] McLean b. 1874. Successful school teacher. m. W. H. Long who d. in a few years. 2 children.

(1) Dewey[6] Long d. infant.

(2) Irma[6] Long m. Methodist Minister J. L. McQueen (Both Grads. Asbury College, KY.) Live in Steubenville, OH.

f. John[5] S. McLean b. 1876. Taught school, now cashier bank of Magnolia, OH. Was a fine violinist. m. 1905 Maz Blazier who d. 1927. Lutherans. 1 son.

(1) Dwight[6] McLean b. 1913, H. S. Grad.

g. Eulalia[5] McLean d. young.

h. Conrad[5] McLean d. in middle life. m. Nannie Anderson. 5 children.

(1) Edna[6] McLean m. Wiley Johnson, Bergholz, OH. 2 children.

+Ruth[7] Johnson.

+Kenneth[7] Johnson.

(2) Blanche[6] Nina McLean, Canton, OH.

(3) James[6] McLean, single, Alliance, OH.

(4) Ruth[6] M. McLean, married, 2 children.

(5) McClellan[6] McLean, single, Alliance, OH.

C.†Charles[4] Rex Shane b. 12-1842 Ross township Jefferson Co., OH. Enlisted in Co. K. 2nd 0. V. I. 9-1861. Served in KY and TN Campaigns under Rosecrans, Thomas and others. Just missed

Sherman's march to the sea as his enlistment was about to expire, was turned back northward guarding trains and supplies on the way until 9-16-1866, when he was honorably discharged. m. Emily Critser, 1870. Was a farmer and elder in the church of his fathers, Presbyterian. d. 4-22-1926 in his 84th year. His wife d. 7-31-1927. Buried Center Chapel Cemetery, Island Creek township Jefferson Co. OH. 6 sons.

  a. Anson[5] C. Shane b. 9-1871. Oil operator and is single.

  b. Scott[5] S. Shane b. 1874 m. Ella Faweet 1904. Presbyterians. Live near Salem, OH. 2 children.

    (1) Ethel[6] Mae Shane b. 1910.

    (2) Charles[6] Shane, Jr. b. 1905 m. lives in Michigan.

  c. Joseph[5] C. Shane b. 1877 m. Jessie Mills, Jefferson, OH. 4 children.

    (1) Florence[6] Shane.

    (2) Elwood[6] Shane.

    (3) Joseph[6] Shane.

    (4) Wanda[6] Shane.

  d. Leonard[5] Shane (twin) b. 1880 R. R. Engineer. d. 1919.

  e. Leroy[5] Shane (twin) m. 1st Eliza Ault. 3 children.

    (1) Elizabeth[6] Shane, Secy. Rev. Hugh T. Kerr, Pitts. PA.

    (2) Agnes[6] Shane m. Mr. McMillen. 2 sons.

      +Charles[7] McMillen.

      +William[7] McMillen, Pittsburg, PA.

    (3) Albert[6] Shane.

  m. 2nd Jewel Duckworth. (Southern). 1 child.

    (1) Leroy[6] B. Shane, Jr. Indianapolis, IN.

  f. Jay[5] R. Shane b. 1890, single.

D. Hannah[4] Shane (named for her Grandmother, Hannah Rex) b. 1846. Said to be very bright and good student. Much opposed to slavery. A friend to all who wore the blue uniform and did her bit for the Union Cause. Was never very rugged and in winter of 1866-67, went to church and took a heavy cold with chills, went into quick consumption. d. 6-10-1867. She was a strong Christian, is buried in Bacon Ridge cemetery in Ross Township, Jefferson Co., OH.

E. Benjamin[4] F. Shane b. 1852 d. 1-14-1931 m. 11-28-1881 Essie M. George. Benjamin F. enjoyed playing the violin and old fashioned country dances. 2 children.

  a. Eileen[5] Shane b. 3-2-1884 m. 1st Paul Wells 1913 and moved to

Cleveland, OH where Mr. Wells d. in 1924. m. 2nd Tom Sharpe, Cleveland, 1925.

b. A.^{5} G. Shane b. 1-25-1888. Professional telegraph operator. With Western Union, Pittsburg. m. Olive Sproul, 1919, Pittsburg, PA. Presbyterians. 2 children.

(1) Robert^6 Shane b. 10-15-1919.

(2) Constance^6 O. Shane b. 12-15-1921.

F. Anna^4 B. Shane b. 1857 Ross Township Jefferson Co., OH. School teacher. m. William. W. Scott 9-1879. (Scott and Shane lines have mingled for 5 generations, W. W. S. being the great grandson of Hannah Rex.) Presbyterians. 10 children.

a. John^5 Wallace Scott b. 1880 m. 1910 Celia Owings. R. R. Engineer. Steubenville, OH. 3 children.

(1) John^6 Wallace Scott, Jr. b. 1913. Was in H. S. band.

(2) Hugh^6 Ryland Scott, d. infant.

(3) Anna^6 Wanda Scott, b. 1916.

b. Joseph^5 Shane Scott b. 1882. Electrical Engineer. m. Edyth M. Phipps of Canada. Lived in Salinas, CA. Presbyterians. 2 children.

(1) Anna^6 Mae Scott b. 1924.

(2) Joseph^6 Reid Scott b. 1926.

c. Whitelaw^5 Reid Scott b. 1884. Progressive farmer near Steubenville, OH. m. Etta Usher Gault. Presbyterians. 6 children.

(1) Mary^6 Elizabeth Scott b. 1910 m. Frank Riddle 8-23-1931.

(2) Jessie^6 Shane Scott b. 1914.

(3) Emma^6 Gault Scott b. 1914.

(4) William^6 Reid Scott b. 1916.

(5) Bernice^6 Margaret Scott b. 1919.

(6) John^6 Edwin Scott b. 1921.

d. Susanna^5 Scott b. 1886. School teacher. m. L. E. Gorham, Ashland Co., OH. 1910. Lived at Leroy, OH. Mr. G. principal Chippewa School. Methodist 5 children.

(1) Lewis^6 Armstrong Gorham b. 1913.

(2) Anna^6 Genevieve Gorham b. 1915.

(3) David^6 Scott Gorham b. 1918.

(4) Joyce^6 Lavinia Gorham b. 1921.

(5) Richard^6 Leon Gorham b. 1924.

e. Mary^5 Edna Scott b. 1888. School teacher. m. John E. Grimm, both of Winterville, OH. 1911. Farmer and Timber Dealer, La

Fayette, OH. Methodists. 11 children.
    (1) Frederick⁶ Hugh Grimm b. 1911.
    (2) Phillip⁶ Rex Grimm b. 1912.
    (3) Donald⁶ Scott Grimm b. 1913.
    (5) John⁶ E. Grimm, Jr. b. 1915.
    (4) Martha⁶ Louise Grimm b. 1917.
    (6) Edwin⁶ Paul Grimm b. 1918.
    (7) Stanley⁶ S. Grimm b. 1919.
    (8) Perry⁶ H. Grimm b. 1920.
    (9) Marian⁶ Grimm b. 1922.
    (10) Harold⁶ Victor Grimm b. 1924.
    (11) Roderick⁶ Nealy Grimm b. 1925.
 f. Jessie⁵ Louise Scott b.____m. Henry M. Eft of Winterville, OH.
1910. Farmer and Dairyman. Presbyterians. 9 children.
    (1) Virginia⁶ Edna Eft b. 1911.
    (2) Helen⁶ Louise Eft b. 1913.
    (3) John⁶ Scott Eft b. 1915.
    (4) Clarice⁶ Irene Eft b. 1917.
    (5) Grace⁶ Shirley Eft b. 1919.
    (6) Paul⁶ Eft (twin) b. 1922.
    (7) Pauline⁶ Eft (twin) b. 1922.
    (8) Anna⁶ Lois Eft b. 1924.
    (9) George⁶ Frederick Eft b. 1929.
 g. Hannah⁵ Rex Scott b. 1892 m. Grover C. Grimm, Wintersville,
OH. 1914. Congregationalists. (She had the large silver spoon
and cup and saucer which belonged to the first Hannah Rex
Shane). 3 children.
    (1) Wilbur⁶ Reid Grimm b. 1917.
    (2) Elizabeth⁶ Vivian Grimm b. 1923.
    (3) Wilma⁶ Gene Grimm b. 1919.
 h. Irene⁵ E. Scott b. 1894 H. S. and College Grad. Teacher. m.
John G. Swickard (Grad O.S.U.) Farmer and Dairyman. 2 children.
    (1) John⁶ Grafton Swickard b. 1919 d. infant.
    (2) Drennen⁶ Wallace Swickard b. 1928.
 i. Hugh⁵ Parker Scott b. 1897 d. age 2 months.
 j. Wilma⁵ Walker Scott b. 1898 d. 1910.
G. Dr. Jessie⁴ F. Shane b. 1859. Educated Richmond College and
Hopedale Normal. Successful teacher. Studied Medicine, grad.
Western Reserve College, Cleveland, OH. Successful practitioner.

d. Steubenville, OH. 1914. Rests in Center Chapel Cemetery, Jefferson, OH.

6. James[3] H. Shane (6th of Isaac and Hannah[2] Rex Shane, George[1]) b. 11-18-1817 d. 1-2-1888. m. three times. 1st 9-7-1843 to Eliza Mills and had 3 children.

A. William[4] Shane d. as infant.

B. Nancy[4] Shane d. as infant.

C.†Cyril[4] Stanley Shane b. 1-5-1845 enlisted 52nd O. V. I. in 1862 d. Nashville, TN. Buried Shane Cemetery, Ross Township Jefferson Co., OH. Age 18 yrs.

m. 2nd Lucinda Scott 10-28 1852. 1 child.

D. Elizabeth[4] N. Shane.

m. 3rd Charlotte (Lottie) Rinehart 2-25-1854. 2 children.

E. John[4] Shane b. 11-10-1856.

F. Eliza[4] M. Shane b. 3-13-1859. (Lida) Mrs. Jay Northrup, 1738 S. 32nd Ave., Omaha, NE.

7. Isaac[3] Shane 2nd (7th of Isaac and Hannah[2] Shane, George[1]) b. 10-22-1819. m. twice. 1st Hannah Baird and had 9 children.

A. George. E. Shane.

B. Robert[4] A. Shane.

C. Henry[4] A. Shane.

D. Isaac[4] Rex Shane N. St. Paul, MN.

E. Nannie[4] E. Shane m. 1st John F. Parks, 7 children.

a. Rena[5] W. Parks m. William Ruthenburg.

b. Henry[5] I. Parks m. Elizabeth Phillips.

c. Charles[5] R. Parks d. as an infant.

d. William[5] G. Parks m. Marguerite Ford.

e. Hazel[5] J. Parks m. Rev. Winfield Harman.

f. Margaret[5] H. Parks m. John Allensworth.

g. Mary[5] B. Parks m. Prof. Stanton Crawford.

E. Nannie[4] E. Shane-Parks 2nd m. Simeon G. Rutledge. No children. E. Springfield, OH.

F. Hannah[4] L. Shane.

G. Pera[4] J. Shane.

H. Mary[4] Shane.

I. Birdie[4] Shane.

Isaac Rex Shane and Nannie E. Shane-Parks-Rutledge are the only ones living (1933).

m. 2nd Alice Lucas had 2 children.

A. Otto[4] Shane. d.

B. Mabel[4] Shane d.

8. †Judge John[3] Shane (Figure 74) (8th of Isaac and Hannah[2] Shane, George[1]) b. 5-26-1822. m. 1st his first cousin Hannah Goudy (Figure 75) of Linn Co., IA. b. 4-1824 in OH, d. 1879. Educated at Jefferson College, PA. Taught, then studied law in office of Edwin M. Stanton. Moved to Iowa before Civil War, raised a company of volunteers, enlisted in Co. G. 13th Iowa Inf. Elected Capt. Promoted to Major, to Lieut., to Col. Bore Distinguished part in battle of Shiloh, and before Atlanta. After his return, Gov. Kirkwood appointed him Dist. Judge, 1876. Nominated and elected in 1882 but partial paralysis caused him to resign. Invalid a dozen years. d. 9-18-1899. Was twice State Senator from IA. 2 children by this marriage.

Figure 74. Judge John Shane.

Figure 75 Hannah Goudy Shane (Mrs John Shane)

A. Sarah[4] Ann Shane (Called Annie) b. 1850 d. 1910. m. O. L. Cooper b. 1848 d. 1915. 4 children.

   a. Fred[5] Cooper (Always known as Fritz) b. 8-30-1870 m. 1898 to Olive. Injured in a railroad accident and d. about 1906.

   b. Alice[5] Cooper b. 6-18-1872 m. in Chicago to Elmer Northrop, 855 E. Beach St., Pass Christian, MS. No children.

   c. Harriet[5] Ambrose Cooper b. 4-25-1875 m. Frank Smead King, Maryville, MO in 1896. Mrs. King much interested in the Republican Party. 3 children.

     (1) Donald[6] Cooper King b. 1898.

     (2) Alsamene[6] King.

     (3) Shane[6] Hastings King m. has a daughter.

   d. Hannah[5] Shane Cooper b. 7-25-1880 m. Harry Benjamin Sprague in Omaha 10-6-1906. No children. Lived at 120 Primrose Rd., Burlingame, CA.

B. Ida[4] Shane d. 1852 (called Aline) m. Mr. Devin who was accidently killed many years ago when stepping from a boat while duck hunting. Aline S. D. is highly educated and is much traveled, having been around the world twice, etc. Spends her summers at

Eliot, ME, where she lives in a delightful house built to her liking on oriental lines and filled with treasures of her trips. Lives in the winter with her neice, Mrs. Northrop, in Pass Christian. Her hobby is writing and such high class publications as the Boston Transcript use her short stories. She has a Hammond typewriter, so is interchangeable, using one type for her writings and the other for French. Has no children of her own but has a French God Child with whom she has visited many times in France.

Judge John Shane m. 2nd 1881 Mrs. Carrie Lynch. He survived her by several years.

9. Margaret^3 Shane (9th of Isaac and Hannah^2 Shane, George^1) d. as infant.

10. Henry^3 Shane (10th of Isaac and Hannah^2 Shane, George^1) b. 2-7-1826. m. Martha Taylor. 9 children.

  A. Hannah^4 Ellen Shane m. Mr. Crabb. He d. No children.

  B. James^4 Taylor Shane, d. young.

  C. Elizabeth^4 Wilhelmina Shane (Called Will and Willie) m. Charles A. Jack, 1873, Tekamah, NB. 9 children.

    a. Charles^5 H. Jack.

    b. Clifford^5 Jack.

    c. Ruth^5 Jack, Tekomah, NB.

    d. Margaret^5 Jack, Boise, Idaho.

    e. Arthur^5 H. Jack.

    f. Nellie^5 J. Jack.

    g. Hattie^5 Jack-Adams.

    h. Carrie^5 Jack-Hopewell.

    i. Fred^5 Jack, died.

  D. Martha^4 Shane m. Wallace. 3 children.

    a. Charles^5 W. Wallace, Wenotahea, WA.

    b. Roy^5 Wallace, Tekomah, NB.

    c. Alice^5 Wallace, CA.

  E. Carrie^4 Shane m. F. A. Hopkins, West 1408 Dalton Ave., Spokane, WA. 6 children.

    a. Nellie^5 Hopkins m. Houston. 1 daughter.

      (1) Esther^6 Houston m. Hendrickson. 3 children.

        +Ruth^7 Hendrickson.

        +Ralph^7 Hendrickson.

        +Cleveland^7 Hendrickson.

    b. Stanley^5 Hopkins, d.

    c. Ralph^5 Hopkins, d.

    d. Edgar^5 A. Hopkins, Whitefish, MT. 2 sons.
      (1) Roger^6 Hopkins.
      (2) Donald^6 Hopkins.
    e. William^5 Henry Hopkins, Wilbur, WA. 3 children.
      (1) Faye^6 Hopkins.
      (2) Phyllis^6 Hopkins.
      (3) Catherine^6 Hopkins.
     f. Ruth^5 Hopkins.
F. Esther^4 Shane (called Hetty) m. Clark, d. 1 child.
    a. Keith^5 Clark d.
G. Stanley^4 Shane 1140 N. Garfield, Pocatello, ID. 4 children.
    a. Bonnie^5 Shane, Pocatello.
    b. Wayne^5 Shane, Pocatello.
    c. Cleve^5 Shane, Los Angeles.
    d. Louise^5 Shane m. Holmes, Twin Falls, ID.
H. Margaret^4 Shane m. Rogers. She d. 2 children.
    a. Jean^5 Rogers, NE.
    b. Esther^5 Rogers, Los Angeles, CA.
I. Blanche^4 Shane m. Scully, Mansfield, WA.

Chapter 10

Margaret[2] Rex (Peggy, 8th child of Margaret Keppler-Rex and George[1]) was b. in Mifflin Co., PA in the year 1790 and was the youngest child when the family left for Greene Co., PA. May 1, 1808. m. William McCullough. We have no record of the birth or death of William McCullough nor the date of their marriage, however, the marriage took place in Greene Co. at her father's home and must have been during the year 1807. In New Jefferson, PA, Greene Co. Cemetery are the Rex graves among which is a sort of tan colored slab which reads "In memory of Margaret McCollough, consort of William McCollough, deceased May 1st, 1808, aged 18 years 5 months 22 days."

> "Unveil thy bosom Faithful Tomb
> Take this new treasure to thy trust
> And give these Sacred Relics room
> To seek a Slumber in the dust
> Nor pain nor grief nor anxious fear
> Invade thy bonds no mortal woes
> Can reach the Lovely Sleeper here
> And Angels watch her Soft Repose."

Mrs. Anna R. Scott (Line VII) has a lock of hair of this Margaret's and a piece of her silk wedding dress and remembers well her son George[3] McCullough visiting at her home about 1869 or 1870. He was then a fine looking man with gray hair, from Tuscarawas Co., Ohio. Her 1 son as follows:

1. George[3] McCullough, was born at the time of his mother's death and was raised by her brother, Benjamin Rex, although Benjamin was not married until 8 years after his sister died. They both made their home with Benjamin's parents and it is said that Benjamin took complete charge and care of the child up to the time he was married and left home. The boy lived for a number of years with a family by the name of Vantros. (Location not given.) After leaving there, he went to another part of Ohio and on May 31, 1829, he wrote a letter to his uncle, Benjamin Rex, which is yet preserved.

Chapter 11

Benjamin[2] Rex (9th child of Margaret Keppler and George[1] Rex) was the first of their
children born in Greene Co., PA 1-9-1792. He d.
Wintersville, Jefferson Co., OH, 9-17-1854. He
is buried at Two Ridge Presbyterian Church
Cemetery (Figure 76). (This church is about a
mile from their old home and his first wife is
buried beside him). Anne Barclay-Rex was b.
4-20-1795 in Fayette Co., PA and d. in Wintersville, 6-7-1838. Benjamin Rex and Anne Barclay were married in Fayette Co., PA 1-23-1816
by Thomas Hughes, Esq. They moved from
Fayette Co., PA to Jefferson Co.,
OH in 1830. They were the parents
of 11 children.

Figure 76. Benjamin
Rex gravestone.

On Dec. 3, 1839, Benjamin
Rex m. his second wife, Martha
Thompson, who was b. 10-6-1806
at Richmond, Jefferson Co., OH.
Marriage was by Rev. William
Lorimer. She d. 8-17-1886. She is
buried at Richmond United Pres-
byterian Church Cemetery (Figure

Figure 77. Martha Rex gravestone.

77) beside her father, James Thompson. Benjamin Rex and Martha
Thompson-Rex were the parents of 4 children.

Benjamin Rex was a man of sterling character and one of the
kindest hearted men of the community in which he lived. His grand-

Figure 78. Benjamin Rex home near Richmond Ohio.

daughter, Catherine Farnam, says of him, "I remember grandfather as small, with large head of beautiful curly locks and deep blue eyes."

Helen Dance speaks of the old home near Richmond, OH (Figure 78), saying the buildings were erected by Benjamin Rex, the grandfather of her mother. "The home was so interesting, at one time a fine mansion, brick with hand carved mantels, solid brass doorknobs and sun-mark on windowsill. The stone under the barn had the name B. Rex carved upon it and date, June 11, 1843 (Figure 79)." (It yet remains clear and easily read). Grace Steinwehr, in speaking of this beautiful home mentions, "(It contained) The old candle sticks, dishes, silverware and so many lovely things I used to stand and gaze at and admire as a little girl."

Figure 79. Benjamin Rex barn cornerstone.

Benjamin Rex settled on this farm near Two Ridge Church, which was a full section of uncleared timberland. He was one of the administrators of the will of his father George Rex 1st.

Figure 80. Benjamin Rex barn.

Figure 81. Benjamin Rex barn interior showing beams and peg construction.

The parents of Anne Barclay Rex, first wife of Benjamin[2] Rex, were Hugh and Ann Darrah Barclay. Hugh Barclay b. 8-24-1763, in Philadelphia, was a gentlemen who wore satin knee breeches and silver buckles. His wife, Ann Darrah, was also of Philadelphia and they had 9 children as follows: Mary, Margaret, Harriet, Sarah, Ann, Hannah, James, Hugh and Henry. Anne Barclay's grandparents were retired merchants of Philadelphia, PA. Their summer residence was about 12 miles north of Philadelphia. George Washington had his headquarters at one time during the Revolutionary War at this Barclay summer home. (U. S. History, Boys of 1776, pg. 256, speaks of Lydia

Darrah's home in S. Phila.) Ann Darrah Barclay, wife of Hugh, was b. 6-16-1770. The parents of Anne Barclay were Henry and Anne Jameson Darrah. Anne Jameson Darrah was the daughter of Henry Jameson and Mary Stewart, born in Warrick, Bucks Co., PA. Married in 1760.

Children of Capt. Henry and Ann Jameson Darrah:
- James Darrah b. 1764, d. 2-17-1842. m. Rachel Henderson.
- William Darrah b. 1767 d. 7-11-1838.
- Ann Darrah b. 1-16-1770 m. Hugh Barclay about 1788.
- John George Darrah.
- Margaret Darrah.

Henry Darrah was the third son of Thomas Darrah and Agnes Thompson Darrah b. 1726 at New Brittain, PA. d. 6-1782 in New Brittain and is buried at Deep Run. Thomas Darrah (father of Henry) was of Scotch Irish descent. He came from Ireland in 1725 and settled at Deep Run, PA. He raised a family of 5 sons and 3 daughters. Henry Darrah was a Captain in the Revolutionary War. Commissioned Lieutenant 1776, promoted to Captain, 1777. He served as Captain of Militia under General Lacey and was probably in the Amboy Expedition in 1776. He served under Col. William Roberts, 1778. In 1780, he commanded the Eighth Company, Bucks County Militia. The family has a tradition that Gen'l Washington stopped several times with Henry Darrah and on such occasions the children were sent to the neighbors that he might not be disturbed with their noise. This is a proven Revolutionary Line and we quote from a Pennsylvania newspaper clipping:
"LYDIA DARRAH NOT A MYTH. Really Gave Alarm to American Troops, Frankford Historians Hear. Lydia Darrah was no myth, Henry Darrah told the Frankford Historical Society last night, but actually warned the American troops at Whitemarsh of an attack planned by Howe, thus probably saving from annihilation the American troops at Valley Forge. Mr. Darrah showed by a map, made by the Survey Bureau, that Lydia made her way from 2nd and Spruce Sts., where she lived, to an old mill, on Frankford Creek, by way of Nicetown lane, using as a subterfuge a bag of grain, which she carried the whole distance of more than six miles, ostensibly to have it made into meal at the mill." There is more on Darrah in *The Lives of Eminent Philadelphians* by Henry Simpson, Pub. 1859, pg. 286-7.

Darrah in *Bucks Co. History*, by Davis, and *The Jamesons in America* may be interesting reading.

Martha Thompson, second wife of Benjamin[2] Rex (Figure 82), was a devout member of the United Presbyterian Church. She is buried in the cemetery of that church. The following was sent to Leda Rex on the Thompson Line, by Mrs. Carrie G. Arnold, Cadiz, Ohio, also a member of the family:

"This book is the property of James Thompson (Figure 83) who was born in the County Tyrone, Ireland, 1st day of February A. D. 1776 and emigrated to the United States in A. D. 1793. Married Rebecca Ramsey of Fayette County A. D. 1800, who was born 30th of April, 1780; and after her death was married to Agnes Glasgow the 4th of April, 1819, being at that time living in Jefferson Co., Ohio, and after her death in October 1822, was married to Margaret McCary of Fayette County, PA the 22nd of April 1823. She was born the 20th of April A. D. 1789 and is now living at this time, the 5th August 1831 with his said wife Margaret in Jefferson Co., OH."

Figure 82. Martha Thompson Rex.

Figure 83. James Thompson, father of Martha Thompson Rex.

Births

William Thompson was born the 16th March, A. D.1801.
Matthew Thompson was born the 12th June A. D.1804.
Martha Thompson was born 6th October A. D.1806.
Mary Thompson was born the 29th April A. D. 1809.
Elizabeth Thompson was born the 5th September A. D. 1811.
Rebecca Thompson was born the 14th June A. D.1814.
(The above were the children of James and Rebecca, his wife.)
John McCray Thompson was born the 28th April A.D. 1824.
Rebecca Glasgow Thompson was born the 29th May A. D. 1825.
Sarah Jane Thompson was born the 13th January A. D. 1829.

Marriages

Elizabeth, daughter of James and Rebecca Thompson was married the 8th September A. D. 1831 to Moses Allen.

Martha, daughter of James and Rebecca Thompson was married to Benjamin Rex, December 3rd A. D. 1839.

Mary, daughter of James and Rebecca Thompson, was married to Robert Kirkwood the 16th October A. D. 1838.

Deaths

Rebecca, daughter of James and Rebecca Thompson departed this life the 11th July A. D. 1816.

My wife, Rebecca Thompson departed this life the 8th July A. D. 1818.

My wife, Agnes Thompson, departed this life the 1st October A. D. 1822.

John McCray, son of James and Margaret Thompson, departed this life July 5, A. D. 1833.

James Thompson died of infirmities of age on November 29th, 1854, aged 79 years.

Rebecca G. Thompson died (of typhoid fever) on the 3rd of March, 1855, in the 30th year of her age.

1. George[3] Darrah Rex, (1st child of Anne Barclay and Benjamin[2] Rex, George[1]) was b. near Jefferson, Greene Co., PA 11-10-1816. He first married Martha Swan 11-12-1840, at Uniontown, PA and moved to one of his two farms near Knoxville, OH where they lived until 1855. His father, Benjamin, had recently died so he purchased his farm, on which he lived until his death. The old two story and basement brick house with the spring at the foot of the hill back of the house and the big bank barn with heavy hardwood timber (pegged together) and stone foundation still stand away back up from the road and will be there for several generations unless some calamity befalls them. Martha Swan Rex was b. in Uniontown, PA 8-24-1819 and d. 5-8-1845 at Knoxville, OH. Buried at Two Ridge Church. They were the parents of three children.

George D. Rex married 2nd, Rebecca Jane Ross (widow of Aaron Ross, whose son Edwin Ross, married Mary McCoy and they had a son Mason, and daughter Jessie who married Coe Boyd) ne Porter, daughter of James Porter of Jefferson Co., OH in 1846. She was b. 1819 d. 1852 and was buried at Island Creek Church. They were the parents of three children.

George Rex m. 3rd, Mary Jane Winters, (daughter of Elizabeth and Isaiah Winters). Mary's brother, John Winters m. Lucy Brooks and William Winters m. Nan Maxwell) in 1855 at Island Creek Parsonage, Jefferson Co., OH. Ceremony by Rev. A. J. Parkinson. No issue.

"George D. Rex was a small man, perhaps 5 feet, 5 inches in height, well built, muscular and active. Was industrious, methodical, conservative and of few words. Was of strict integrity, upright and an earnest Christian. Was highly respected by all who knew him. Died 3-12-1890 and buried at Two Ridge Church, Jefferson Co., OH. Martha Swan was the daughter of Thomas Swan and Eleanor Anderson Swan. Thomas Swan b. 11-13-1781 d. Fayette Co., PA 4-11-1845. Was the third son of Colonel Charles Swan and Sarah Van Meter. Charles Swan, son of John Swan No. 1 and Elizabeth Van Meter. John Swan No. 1, son of Joshua Swan and Elizabeth Lucas. Joshua Swan was b. in 1700, was the son of Robert Swan who emigrated to America in 1650."

This was taken from the family record of John Swan of Greene Co., PA from which Martha Swan descends and also she descends from Charlemagne, the French Emperor born A. D. 742. Further reference to John Swan (md) Captain of the Third Continental Dragoons, 26th April 1777. Taken prisoner at Tapen 28th Sept. 1778. See Heitmans Historical Register of Continental Army 1775-1783. Pg. 528-9. John Swan was Major of First Continental Dragoons 21st Oct. 1780. Retained in Baylors Regiment of Dragoons 9th Nov. 1782. Served until close of War. PA Archives, 5th Series, Vol. 6, Pg. 277-8, Border Warfare, Pg. 125. Auditors accounts XII, Pg. 271, Illinois Papers D 51 War Vol. 4, Pg. 20.

John Swan married Elizabeth Lucas in 1743. Their oldest child was John Swan, b. about 1744. He married Elizabeth Van Meter and three of his brothers also married girls by the name of Van Meter.

A. Charles[4] Swan Rex b. 1-11-1842 on a farm near Knoxville, Jefferson Co., OH. He first m. Ann Eliza Payne at Mt. Pleasant, IA 1-10-1865. She is the daughter of John Wesley and Lydia Caulk Payne. Charles S. Rex went West to St. Louis in 1880 where he was a street car conductor for a short time. 12-2-1862 he went to Mt. Pleasant, IA where he engaged in farming and sheep raising for 6 years. In 3-1867, he left Burlington by boat for St. Louis; thence to Kansas City; then to Lawrence, KS. He then moved with his wife and one child to a farm 6 miles west of Lawrence. There was nothing but sickness, trouble and sorrow for them in Kansas. In the spring of 1869, he returned to Mt. Pleasant with his two children and his sick wife, who d. 7-13-1869. After her death, he disposed of his Kansas farm and on 8-2-1870, settled in Creston, IA where he remained until his death, 5-12-1917.

On 11-11-1873 he returned to Mt. Pleasant and m. Sarah Kitchen. She was b. 1840, d. 10-21-1929. To this union five children were born. He was an influential man in the community and an active member of the Congregational Church. It was about 1885 that he became interested in genealogical research and later began compiling statistics for this record. For ten years prior to his death, his health would not permit much research although he always took pleasure in writing letters and talking with relatives about this family history. He was engaged in the mercantile business the greater part of his life and was especially fond of horses. He was the father of seven children.

a. Mattie[5] Blanche Rex b. 1866 Mt. P. IA. d. 1878.

b. George[5] B. Rex (Figure 84) b. 11-16-1867, Lawrence, KS. Educated at Shenandoah, Creston and Des Moines. Engaged in Lumber business, Des Moines, until 1890. Went to Phillips, WI with a sawmill business. While thus engaged went to Selma, OH, 1890, to m. Anna Kitchen (Figure 85), she d. Creston, IA 12-3-1931. In June 1891, left Phillips, WI, returned to Iowa to engage in the retail lumber business at Newmarket. In 7-1894, sold this yard and moved to Council Bluffs, IA and bought a yard which he ran until 12-1898. Spent nearly a year at Tacoma, WA. Returned to Creston, IA as a partner in the home yard in the wholesale lumber business. They have one son.

(1) George[6] Robert Rex (Figure 86) b. 3-24-1901, Creston, IA

c. Anna[5] Grace Rex b. Creston, IA 8-26-1874. She graduated from Creston High School. Had some years of college and then

Figure 84. George   **Figure 85.** Anna   **Figure 86.** George
B. Rex   Kitchen Rex.   Robert Rex.

a grad. nurse. m. at Creston to Alexander Burtch Clark, 12-23-1903. Lived two years in Oklahoma, two years in Utah and then to Clarinda, IA.where Mr. Clark was Postmaster. 3 children.

(1) Talton[6] Rex Clark b. 12-28-1905, Tishamingo, OK.

(2) Noel[6] Burtch Clark b. 12-23-1911, Clarinda, IA.

(3) Joseph[6] Embry Clark b. 7-10-1916, Shelly, Idaho.

d. Harry[5] Noel Rex b. in Creston, 7-11-1876. Grad. of Creston H. S., Knox College, Galesburg, and State School of Mines, Rolla, MO. m. Mary Burtch Howard of Columbus, NE 5-14-1914, her father was an editor and United States Senator from NE. 3 children.

(1) Edgar[6] Howard Rex b. 11-16-1916, Creston, IA.

(2) Helen[6] Anne Rex.

(3) Mary[6] Elizabeth Rex.

e. Sarah[5] Edna Rex b. Creston, IA 10-23-1877. Grad. of Creston High School, attended Knox College, Galesburg, Grad. from St. Mary's College. Immediately after her marriage at Creston to Harry Alvin Parkin of Elgin, IL, on 6-26-1901, they left for the Phillipine Islands under U. S. Government contract as instructors in the schools there. Upon their return from the Phillipines, after three years service, they completed a trip around the World and located in Chicago where Mr. Parkin was a successful lawyer and judge. 3 children.

(1) Margaret[6] Parkin b. 2-21-1905, Chicago, IL Grad. Smith College 1928 m. William Lewis Ninters, Physician. Resided Highland Park, IL.

(2) Richard[6] Rex Parkin b. 10-14-1906, Chicago, IL Grad. Yale 1929. Northwestern Law School 1932.

(3) Henry[6] Alvin Parkin b. 9-28-1911, Chicago, IL. Junior at Yale College (1933).

f. Charles[5] Sherman Rex b. Creston, IA 2-5-1880. Attended public school, Creston and Commercial School in Chicago, a good businessman and a shrewd financier. m. Estella P. Schaible who was a minister's daughter at Burlingame, KS 4-19-1905. No children of their own but have adopted a son.

g. May[5] Rex b. Creston, 5-26-1882. She was a beautiful young woman and well educated. Attended three colleges, finishing at Smith. m. Edmund David Adcock of Galesburg, IL, who was a lawyer in Chicago and held the position of chief council for the Chicago Drainage Board for years. Parents of 2 children.

(1) William[6] Henderson Adcock b. 6-23-1915 d. an infant.

(2) Edmund[6] Rex Adcock b. 8-28-1911. Resided at Galesburg, IL.

B. Eleanor[4] Rex b. 9-1-1843 d. before 1845.

C. Thomas[4] S. Rex b. 10-8-1844 d. 3-24-1846.

D. Darwin[4] Rex (Figure 87) b. 7-5-1847 near Knoxville, Ohio. He d. 2-7-1901 at Harriman, TN. His picture and the article out of the church paper *History of Two Ridges Church*:

"Darwin Rex was born at Knoxville, Jefferson County. Ohio July 1847. He united with Two Ridges Church January 13th, 1865. He removed from the bounds of the congregation for a few years. He moved within the bounds again in 1875, and on the 8th of June

Figure 87. Darwin Rex.

was elected Elder and installed in Two Ridges church June 20th, 1875. He was elected clerk of the Session and held this position until his removal to Steubenville. He next moved to Harriman, TN, in 1892. He died February 7th, 1901, and is buried in the Emory Gap cemetery near his home in Tennessee."

He m. Elizabeth A. Cole 2-27-1872 at Richmond, OH. Ceremony by Rev. Alex Scott. She is the daughter of George and Jane Speedy Cole of Steubenville, OH. She b. 7-5-1850 and lives in Los Angeles, CA. 6 children, all b. near Wintersville, OH.

a. Emma[5] Grace Rex b. 11-29-1872. m. Charles F. Steinwehr, 9-1-1904. He was a photographer, d. 5-13-1929. Lived in Rockwood, TN and Los Angeles, CA. 3 sons.

(1) Rex[6] Christian Steinwehr, b. 8-7-1905.

(2) Charles[6] Leslie Steinwehr, b. 7-29-1907.

(3) Richard[6] Roland Steinwehr, b. 11-25-1913. Lived in Los Angeles, CA. Presbyterians.

b. Hugh[5] Gladden Rex b. 7-12-1874 d. 1891.

c. George[5] Ernest Rex b. near Wintersville, OH 5-27-1876. m. Jennie Baumgartner of Harriman, TN 9-1903. He was employed by the Southern Pacific R. R. as electrician. They lived in Los Angeles, CA and have 2 children.

(1) Stanley[6] Cole Rex b. 9-1-1904.

(2) Mildred[6] Scott Rex b. 5-14-1906.

d. Myrtle[5] Alice Rex b. 1-1-1880. Single.

e. Charles[5] D. Rex b. 1-8-1882. m. Sarepta Ewing Jackson 1-17-1923. No children. Employed by the Cincinnatti Southern for many years, rising to Superintendant of the Signal Division with headquarters at Cincinnatti, OH.

f. Anne[5] Gertrude Rex b. 12-29-1884. m. Frederick Victor Millar 6-1916. He is an Englishman b. Shirehampton, England. Was connected with the movie business in Los A., CA. 3 sons and live in Venice, CA.

(1) Charles[6] Rex Millar b. 8-10-1918.

(2) Frederick[6] Victor Millar, Jr. b. 2-10-1920.

(3) Edmund[6] deLaunay Millar b. 11-12-1923.

E. Elizabeth[4] Ann Rex (Figure 88) b. 3-1-1849 near Knoxville, OH. d. at Wintersville, Ohio 12-20-1922. m. Benjamin Rex Dance 6-24-1880. His parents were Jacob and Harriet Love Dance of Jefferson Co., OH. They were m. at the home of her father by the Rev. John C. McCracken. 4 children.

Figure 88. Elizabeth Ann Rex Dance.

a. Lindsey[5] Porter Dance b. 3-16-1881. m. Beatrice A. Lockett 4-17-1922. No children, live at Tucson, AZ where he was employed by the Mountain States Telephone and Telegraph Co. as construction and repair foreman.

b. Hubert[5] Jacob Dance b. 9-30-1885 m. Anna Belle Strayer 8-13-1910. Five children and are the fourth generation of the Dance family to live on the same farm.

(1) Benjamin[6] Rex Dance 2nd b. 9-20-1911.

(2) Walter[6] Strayer Dance b. 8-2-1912.

(3) Charles[6] Hubert Dance b. 12-26-1913.

(4) Mary[6] Ann Dance b. 2-12-1916.

(5) Joseph[6] Calvin Dance b. 4-13-1918.

The Dance and Rex families were friends and neighbors in PA. Benjamin Rex Dance being named for Benjamin Rex (son of George Rex 1st) and in turn the sister of Benjamin Rex Dance (Ann Dance, Mrs. Rezin Beall Johnson) named her son Hubert Rex Johnson for her brother (Benjamin Dance). This is another double line for as H. R. Johnson says, "Harriet Johnson married William Rex who was the son of Jonas, son of George Rex 1st." Hubert Rex

Johnson, D. D. b. Pekin (now Island Creek) Jefferson Co., OH. 7-1-1858. A self made man, even paying back to his grandfather for his first term of school. Has been a successful teacher, lecturer and minister. Always in poor health, he retired from the pastorate, Chevy Chase Presbyterian Church, Washington, D. C., a beautiful thriving church where we had the pleasure of seeing (among the first) a lifesize oil portrait of him–the gift of one of the members of his congregation. He has written many books on mathematics and when he must spend his days flat on his back, makes mathematical puzzles and has written several genealogies. Has just finished one for the Johnsons–I will refer you to this work for much interesting information. Rev. Dr. Johnson deserves great thanks for his assistance and encouragement in this Rex genealogy.

F. Hugh^4 Barclay Rex b. 1851 d. young.

2. Margaret^3 Rex, (Figure 86) (2nd of Benjamin^2 and Anne Rex, George^1) b. near Jefferson, Greene Co., PA 2-5-1818. m. 5-29-1842 in Jefferson Co., OH to James Frazier. (Ceremony performed by Rev. William Lorimer.) He d. in Pittsburg, PA 3-28-1873 and she d. in Wayne, PA 4-23-1902. They were the parents of four children.

A. Ann^4 Catherine (Kate) Frazier b. 7-23-1844, Richmond, OH. m. William Farnam 1-16-1879 Allegheny City, PA. (Now Pittsburg). There were no children but she lived with a devoted step daughter in Wayne, PA. At the age of 88, was still alert and perfectly capable. A remarkable woman, most refined and a joy to meet.

B. Mary^4 Minerva Frazier (Figure 89) b. 6-9-1846, Richmond, OH, d. Erie, PA 11-20-1924. Buried in West Laurel Hill Cemetery, Phila. PA. m. Elliott Bard 4-23-1872 at Allegheny, PA. Parents of 2 children.

Figure 89. Both sides of the family including four generations. Baby Catherine Bard, her mother, Anna Johnson, her mother, Laura Cochran, and her mother Phoebe Schimer; father of baby, James Frazier Bard, his mother standing, Mary Minerva Frazier and her mother sitting with cap on her head, Margaret Rex.

a. James^5 Frazier Bard (Figure 89) b. in Allegheny, PA 5-4-1874. m. Anna Coleman Johnson in Wayne, PA 5-19-1898. He was a mechanical and electrical engineer, a grad. of the U.of PA, class 1896. Spent 18 years in South America in the employ of the Western Electric Co., the last eight years as Chief Engineer in the Argentine Republic. Lives in Wayne, PA and has an interesting family of 3 children living. m.

(1) Catherine[6] Frazier Bard b. 4-2-1899, Wayne, PA. (Figure 89) Educated in Cuba and Argentina. Studied art in Buenos Aires. Twin of:

(2) Laura[6] Bard, who d. as infant.

(3) Richard[6] Johnson Bard b. 12-12-1900, Wayne, PA.

(4) Elliot[6] Bard, 2nd b. 12-12-1902 at Wayne, PA. Educated in Cuba, Westtown School, PA and Buenos Aires. Lived in Buenos Aires, was consulting Engineer. m. 12-12-1926, Delia Ribault de Toledo. Had an adopted daughter.

b. Margaret[5] Carson Bard (Figure 90) b. Allegheny, PA 5-14-1877. m. Gustave Faure of Paris, France, 10-7-1902 at Wayne, PA. They lived in Erie, PA and were the parents of 3 children. A beautiful and refined family. Presbyterians on both sides. Mr. Faure, Elder in Erie church and his father and brother are ministers in the French Calvanist Church. He was with the Burke Elec. Co.

Figure 90. Gustave and Margaret Bard Faure at Summer home on Lake Erie.

(1) Audre[6] Melville Bard Faure, b. 8-13-1903, Paris, France.

(2) Rene[6] Bard Faure b. 4-23-1905, Erie, PA. While at Culver Military Academy was Indiana State A.A.U. swimming champion in both 220 yard breast stroke and 440 yds. Grad. Columbia U., N. Y. Pres., Phi Kappa Sigma.

(3) Mary[6] Aline Faure (Figure 91) b. 11-20-1914, Erie, PA. Studied a year in France and visited her paternal grandmother. Very athletic, expert swimmer and fine student.

Figure 91. Mary Aline Faure.

C. Emma[4] Frazier b. 9-16-1853, Steubenville,

OH. She d. 11-10-1886. Buried West Laurel Hill Cemetery, Phila. m. William H. Black 4-30-1885, Phila., PA. Had no children.

D. Sallie[4] Frazier b. Steubenville, OH 10-8-1856. d. 5-14-1895, Phila. Buried West Laurel Hill Cemetery, Phila. m. Burriet H. Sawyer at Allegheny, PA. Parents of 2 children.

     a. †John[5] Mills Sawyer b. in Allegheny, PA 8-12-1878. Grad. of Harvard, Columbia and Beaux Artes, Paris France. m. in Paris, Camille. Has a daughter Sarah[6] Sawyer. Highly educated in English and French. At beginning of the World War I, employed in American Embassy in Paris and when U.S. entered this war, was commissioned Lieut. in U.S. Army and served as Liason officer. Received French Cross of Legion of Honor for his services in the war.

     b. Burriet[5] Frazier Sawyer b. Phila., PA 4-27-1895. m. 1st June Gingell 6-16-1919 at West Pittston, PA. 3 children of this union. He m. 2nd Sarah A. Harkins at Phila., PA. 11-14-1925. They have no children.

         (1) Warren[6] Davis Sawyer b. 4-8-1920, Philadelphia, PA.

         (2) Theodore[6] Gordon Sawyer b. 8-24-1921, Phila., PA.

         (3) George[6] Culmer Sawyer b. 7-18-1923, Philadelphia.

3. Mary[3] Rex (3rd of Benjamin[2], and Anne B. Rex, George[1]) b. near Jefferson, Greene Co., PA 9-23-1819. She was drowned in the spring at the home of her grandfather, George Rex 1st, 8-9-1922. Her mother was weaving and the child went to the spring for water for her mother and fell into the spring. This happened the year after the death of George Rex 1st. Buried Jefferson, Greene Co., PA.

4. Hugh[3] Barclay Rex (Figure 89)(4th of Benjamin[2], and Ann Rex, George[1]) b. in Greene Co., PA 11-18-1821. m. 6-6-1855 Mary Jane Roberts (Figure 90) in Steubenville, OH. Ceremony by Rev. William

Figure 92. Hugh Barclay Rex.

Figure 93. Mary Jane Roberts Rex.

Figure 94. Benjamin and Adelaide Rex.

B. Reed. He d. 4-23-1883, in Aiken, SC and was taken to St. Louis, MO for burial 4-27-1883. 2 children.

 A. Benjamin[4] F. Rex (Figure 91) b. 6-15-1899 St. Louis, MO where he was a Patent Atty. His book on Patent Law, *Duties of Notaries* is yet an authority. 2 children.

  a. John[5] Rex. 3 children.

   (1) Benjamin[6] Rex.

   (2) Jean[6] Rex.

   (3) Michael[6] Rex, Berkley, CA.

  b. Helen[5] May Rex, Nun Sacred Heart Convent, Villa Duchesne, St. L., MO.

 B. Adelaide[4] (Addie) Louise Rex (Figure 94) m. in 1883, George B. Preston, deceased. She lived in Pittsburgh, PA and d. there 1890. 1 daughter.

  a. Marguerit[5] Preston m. Lawrence M. Willson, resided in St. Davids, PA.

5. Anne[3] Rex (5th of Benjamin.[2], and Anne Rex) (Figure 96) b. near Jefferson, Greene Co., PA 9-25-1823. She d. 1-17-1904 near Bonapart, IA. On 3-31-1847 in Jefferson Co., OH m. to Jacob G. Vale (Figure 95) who was b. 7-7-1821 and d. near Bonapart, IA 2-17-1875. Jacob Vale was the son of William, son of Robert Vale. Jacob G. and Anne Vale were the parents of 6 children and adopted 2 children.

Figure 95. Jacob Vale

 A. Benjamin[4] Rex Vale (Figure 96) b. 6-4-1848 at Smithfield, OH. d. 4-3-1915, Bonaparte, IA. He m. Nancy Van

Figure 96. Anne Rex Vale with son, Benjamin Rex Vale, and two daughters: top, Martha M. Vale-Downie, and bottom Lydia A. Vale-Leffler.

Figure 97. House in which Anne Rex and Jacob Vale began housekeeping, Smithfield Ohio, 1847.

Julia Biddle 2-12-1874 at Monmouth, IL. She d. 5-31-1923. He was reared on a farm near Bonaparte, IA. Grad. of Monmouth in 1873, A. B. and A. M. Successful career as farmer, business man and politician. Was elected to the State Senate in 1887 and reelected in 1891. Serving in the 22nd, 23rd, 24th and 25th General Assemblies. President of the Farmers' and Traders' Bank at Bonaparte, IA, and highly esteemed by all. At the time of his death he was an Elder in the Presbyterian Church of Bonaparte. 4 children.

a. Anna^5 Regina Vale b. in Bonaparte, IA 11-4-1874. m. Howard Tedford 6-4-1902. They lived at Mt. Ayr, IA where Mr. Tedford was Postmaster. No children.

b. Mary^5 Biddle Vale b. at Bonaparte, IA 10-17-1876. Is single. Cared for her parents as long as they lived and adopted:

  (1) Evelyn^6 H. Reeder b. 1909 d. 1928. m. A .W. Miller 9-11-1926. Had a son.

  +Jean^7 Miller b. 11-20-1927.

c. Margaret^5 Emma Vale b. at Bonaparte, IA 8-15-1878. m. Albert G. Roberts of Bonaparte 8-15-1900. 2 children.

  (1) Vale^6 Roberts b. 1-26-1904 m. Robert Winslow 4-1-1930.

  (2) Rex^6 Albert Roberts b. 1-6-1913.

d. Bruce^5 Rex Vale b. on the home farm at Bonaparte, IA 3-30-1888. m. Emma Nicholson 8-20-1914. They lived on the old home farm. No children.

B. George^4 Hussey Vale b. 10-2-1850 d. 10-23-1850.

C. Another son, b. 12-29-1851 d. same day.

D. Lydia^4 Anne Vale (Figures 96 & 98) b. in a log cabin 11-8-1853 near Primrose, IA (Lee Co.) d. Ames IA 8-17-1924. m. Andrew Jackson (A. J.) Leffler, 4th son of Mansuit and Irene Caven Leffler. He was born at the Leffler home 2 miles west of Harrisburg Church, 2-6-1847, d. at the home of his daughter, Mrs. Lee Forman, at Ames, IA 3-25-1932, aged 85 yrs. 1 mo. 19 days.

Figure 98. 1. Lydia Elizabeth, 2. Ann Irene, 3. John Mansuit, 4. Jacob George, 5. Mary Myrtle, 6. Robert Wallace, 7. Martha Mable, 8. Lydia Vale, 9. Andrew Rex, and 10. Andrew Jackson Leffler. Leffler Family portrait taken in 1902.

A little book published by Lydia Vale's family after her death has quite a record of her life. In it, she says,

"On January 1, 1878, I was united in marriage with A. J. Leffler and a few weeks later we began housekeeping on Cedar Flat farm in Cedar township, five miles from my childhood home and six miles from his. There we lived and raised our eight children, removing to Ames, October 4, 1912. When sixteen years old (1869), I made a public profession of faith in the Second United Presbyterian Church of Monmouth, IL. Dr. Alexander Young was pastor."

Lydia Leffler had written many poems and compiled at least one geneaology and was said of her she could do well four things at one time. As an illustration it is said it was not unusual to find her rocking the old-fashioned wooden (butter) churn with one foot, rocking the cradle which contained one of the sleeping twins with the other, and in her left arm the other twin, while with the right hand would be writing a bit of verse. She completed the course at Monmouth College in two and a half years at eighteen years of age with the highest honors of a class of forty-five. Her brother, Benjamin Rex Vale, said of her: "She is a woman of strong individuality; strong physically and intellectually. She has left the lasting impress of her personal character in every stage of her life,–as daughter, sister, wife, mother and friend."

Mrs. Leffler was one of the real Marthas in working for this book (first edition) and since her death, her daughter, Martha Forman, has continued in the same faithful manner. Mattie Downie and Mary Vale also assisted.

a. Jacob[5] George Vale Leffler b. on the home farm near Stockport, IA 6-26-1879. Grad. Iowa State College, 1904 in Animal Husbandry. He was a Master Farmer, Master Swine Breeder, District Director in the Farm Bureau. d. 3-9-1962. m. 8-28-1912 Lucretia Roberts b.4-1-1882 at Keosauqua, IA and d. 10-18-1948. She attended Drake U. in Desmoins IA. She daughter of Wyatt Roberts and Carolyn Gustin. One son.

(1) †Gustin[6] Vale Leffler b. 3-11-1916. Graduated Iowa State U. in 1941 in Forestry. served in WW II, then worked in Soil Conservation until he settled on the home farm in Van BurenCo., IA. m. 11-16-1946 June Burlington b. 6-27-1917 and d. 12-20-1996. She attended Graceland College in Lamoni, IA. She daughter of Wallace Burlington and Lucille Wilson of Independence, KS. 2 adopted children: Robert Wallace Leffler and Nancy Lynn Leffler.

b. Ann[5] Irene Leffler (Figure 98) b. on home farm near Stockport, IA 4-2-1881 and d. 7-13-1972. Attended Iowa S U, taught Home Economics in Lead, SD. After Earl d. she was director of Dining Halls at Denison U. Granville, OH. Then was Assistant in Food Services in Women's dormitories at ISU in Ames, IA. m. 6-1-1908 at Stockport to Earl H. Wells. He b. 11-11-1875 and d. 7-13-1932. He graduate in law at Wisconsin U. taught school in Huron and Lead, SD and Cleveland,OH. Lived Cleveland, OH and had 1 son.

   (1) Ronald[6] Vale Wells b. 8-16-1913 in Cleveland, OH. Education: Iowa State College 31-33; Denison U. 33-35, A.B. Degree; Crozer Theological Seminary 35-38, B.D. degree; Columbia U. 38-42 Ph.D in philosophy. Author of many books and articles. Multiple teaching positions in Universities and Seminaries. Honorary Degrees from: Denison U., Bucknell U., Brown U., Colby College, Franklin College, Widener College. m. 6-20-1938 in Chester, PA to Helen Patricia Woodburne b. 6-29-1913 in Kodaikanal, India. Lived in Bridgeport, CT. Her parents were A Stewart Woodburne and Helen White. He was Minister. 2 children.

      + †David[6] Woodburne Wells b. 10-26-1939 in Denver, CO. Graduated Dartmouth Medical School Internship and Residency in pediatrics at McGill University in Montreal, Canada. Entered US Army rising to rank of Col. MC was head of Adolescent Medical Dept at Fitzimmons Hospital in Denver. m. Madge Grace. 2 children
         ^Kiersten[7] Wells.
         ^Ian[7] Wells.
      +Robert[6] Vale Wells b. 7-19-1943 in Bridgeport CT. Received Ph.D. Columbia University. Professor of American History and Demography and head of Department of History Union college, Schenectady, NY. Author of 4 books. m. Cathie Marie Anderson. 2 children.
         ^Lisa[7] Wells.
         ^Vanessa[7] Wells.

   c. Andrew[5] Rex Leffler b. on home farm near Stockport 8-4-1883. m. Dorothea Steen 6-26-1910. She b. 12-11-1886. Route 1, Vinton, IA. Five children.

      (1) †Robert[6] Wayne Leffler b. 4-30-1912 at Bonaparte, IA and d. 6-29-1992 at Council Bluffs, IA. m. 6-17-1944 to Olive

Emilie Burton b. 11-4-1918 at Peterborough, England, and d. 2-4-1997 at Council Bluffs, IA. Both served in WW II. He was in reserves until 1966. She daughter of William Henry Burton and Susan Albion. She served as Subaltern from July 1942 to July 17 1945 in England. Members of Episcopal Church. 2 children.

+Susan[7] Jane Leffler b. 10-21-1947 at Council Bluffs, IA m. 9-27-1970 in Ames, IA to Robert Stephen Weinbeck. 2 sons.

^Christopher[8] James Weinbeck b. 3-26-1970 at Albuquerque, NM.

^Stephen[8] Wayne Weinbeck b. 3-26-1970 at Albuquerque, NM. m. 12-28-1996 in Brockport, NY to Corrine Margaret Dilcher.

+Charles[7] Wayne Leffler b. 4-11-1953 and d. 10-12-1953 at Council Bluffs, IA.

(2) Allan[6] Theodore Leffler b. 3-25-1914 in Bonapart, IA and d. 6-11-1985 in Ames, IA Graduated ISU in Agronemy. Employed by Pioneer Seed Corn Co. and Acco Seed Co. in IA. m. 9-1-1939 to Josephine Brown b. 5-9-1916 in Ames, IA Grad of ISU in Child Development and worked in nursery school. 4 children.

+Allan[7] Theodore Leffler b. 9-10-1940 in Lexington, KY. m. 1st 6-7-1964 at Hartsdale, NY to Martha Jane Bradford b. 9-12-1943. Both graduated Johns Hopkins Medical School. He specializes in Pediatrics and she in Ophthamology. both divorced. 3 children.

^Katherine[8] Elizabeth Leffler b. 8-24-1996.

^Christopher[8] Theodore Bradford Leffler b. 7-7-1968. m. 1st Susan Andrew Theodore b. 1996. m. 2nd Melissa Carpenter 6-13-1981. 1 child.

^Margaret[8] Jane Leffler b. 1-4-1973.

m. 2nd Melissa Carpenter.

+Harry[7] Rex Leffler b. 9-20-1942 in Renselaer, IN. m. 12-11-1972 in Champaign to Nancy Kamman b. 5-3-1946. She daughter of Prof. and Mrs. James Kamman. He grad ISU in 1964 and received Ph.D. Purdue U 1968. 3 children.

^Suzanne[8] Leffler b. 1974.

^George[8] Andrew Leffler b. 1978.

^John[8] Douglas Leffler b. 1979.

+Thomas[7] Brown Leffler b. 3-6-1946 in Ames IA. m. 9-27-1988 to Judith Lynne Anderson b. 1942. He graduated ISU in 1968. Taught mathematics in Phillippines with Peace Corps.

+Mary[7] Ellen Leffler b. 10-7-1947 Ames IA. m. 12-29-1993 to Ron Hilliard. She grad. ISU 1969 and did post-graduate work at SUI. 2 children.

(3) Beatrice[6] Dorothea Leffler b. 6-16-1916 near Bonaparte, IA m. 8-18-1937 to Orin Bolin b. 10-10-1910. She studied horticulture at ISU. He grad in Agronomy ISU. 4 children

+Helen[7] Bolin b. 8-18-1938 at Urbana, IL m. 1st 6-14-1958 to Dick Lewis b. 4-11-1938. 3 children.

^Sandra[8] Lynn Lewis b. 8-25-1959.

^Kendra[8] Suzanne Lewis b. 12-28-1960.

^Warren[8] Eugene Lewis b. 8-24-1965.

m. 2nd Rodney Parkinson 2-5-1965.

m. 3rd 11-18-1978 to William DuFour b. 5-14-1924.

+Robert[7] Stuart Bolin b. 2-1-1940. m. 4-11-1959 to Nancy Lee Scmidt b. 8-1-1943. 3 children.

^Linda[8] Lee Bolin b. 5-1-1960.

^Robert[8] Stuart Bolin b. 6-28-1961.

^Roger[8] Scott Bolin b. 1-31-1964.

+Dorothy[7] Ellen Bolin b. 6-10-1941 and d. 9-19-1957 in an auto accident.

+Janet[7] Carol Bolin b. 12-24-1945. m. 9-19-1966 to Don Gilfillan b. 9-4-1945. 2 children

^Jason[8] Gilfillan b. 5-5-1970.

^ Carrie[8] Gilfillan b. 1981.

(4) Mary[6] Lydia Leffler b. 9-26-1919 in Fairfield, IA. m. 9-11-1947 in Ames, IA to Oscar Theodore Cook II. She attended ISU before becoming a SPAR in WW II. 7 children.

+Oscar[7] Theodore Cook III b. 7-7-1948.

+Mary[7] Elizabeth Cook b. 7-28-1949. m. 4-4-1970 to Charles Frederick Driggs b. 2-15-1945. 1 daughter.

^Elizabeth[8] Driggs.

+Kathleen[7] Vale Cook died at birth.

+Carol[7] Lynne Cook b. 6-21-1952.

+Rex[7] Owen Cook b. 8-1-1953.

+Christopher[7] Vale Cook b. 4-4-1955.

+Michael[7] Anthony Cook b. 7-16-1960.

(5) Owen[6] Rex Leffler b. 1-22-1922 in Vinton, IA and d. 1984. m. 9-17-1948 Dows, IA to Katherine Oleson. Both were graduates of ISU. 4 children.

+Robert[7] Owen Leffler b. 2-23-1950. m. Denise Gray. 2 children.

^Nicole[8] Marie Leffler b. 1981.

^Brett[8] Owen Leffler b. 1983

+Katherine[7] Ann Leffler b. 7-13-1951. m. 1983 to Mark Secosh. 1 son.

^Peter[8] Andrew Secosh b. 1982.

+Sarah[7] Faith Leffler b. 3-13-1954. m. 1976 to Robert Lee Paterson b. 1948. 3 children.

^Anna[8] Peterson b. 1982

^Drew[8] Peterson b. 1984

^Elissa[8] Peterson b. 1988.

+Elizabeth Jane Leffler b. 6-26-1957. m. 1991 to Mark Snyder b. 1945.

d. John[5] Mansuit Leffler b. 6-15-1885 on home farm near Stockport, IA and d.8-23-1973. Grad ISU in Animal Husbandry in 1910. Farmed in Ban Buren Co., IA for 37 years, and was declared by the county agricultural agent to be the "best farmer in Ban Buren County." He kept very detailed records. m. 9-21-1927 Mrs. Ruby Newham Galland b. 4-15-1891 and d. 7-2-1967. She daughter of Thurston Newham and Mary Ann Grotz. No children.

e. Mary[5] Myrtle Leffler (Figure 98) (Twin of Martha Mable) b. 5-20-1887 on home farm near Stockport. m. George Marius Nelson 2-14-1911. He b. 8-17-1883 and d. 10-19-1943. Grad. Iowa State College 1910. Presbyterians, lived Eagle Grove IA. 5 children.

(1) Winston[6] Vale Nelson b. 4-14-1914 in Goldfield, IA. m. 4-25-1942 in St. Paul, MN to Virginia Elizabeth Bradley. She b. 8-1-1923 in Hartley, IA. She was daughter of Alfred Martin Bradley and Elizabeth Celena DeKing. Lived Omaha, NE. He received BS Degree in Agronomy from Iowa State U. Worked as seed corn breeder, mink rancher, and zoo employee. She attended Stephens College, MO and Iowa State U. worked as bookkeeper and in Civil Service as contract specialist for Corps of Engineers. Live in AZ. 4 children.

+Ingrid[7] Elizabeth Nelson b. 3-14-1944 in LeMars, IA. Attended Morningside College, IA and Iowa State U., Cochise College, Sierra Vista, AZ, AAS in Computer Science with a certificate in network management. Worked as newspaper reporter, billing clerk and in computer lab, and computer lab manager for adult education. She provided outstanding assistance with the entire Leffler line for this Second Edition of the *George Rex Genealogy*. m. 9-28-1968 in Sioux Falls, SD to Harold H. Baillie. He b. 8-12-1943 in Sioux Falls, SD. Son of Charles Royce Baillie and Helen Eileen Lias. Lived Ames, IA. He received BS Degree in Physics and Math from Augustana College, SD, and worked on Ph.D. Iowa State U. in physics. Worked as instructor of Computer Science, Luther College, Deiorah, IA. Defense Contractor at Offutt AFB, NE and then Ft. Huachuca, AZ. 4 children.

^Sarah[8] Vale Baillie b. 2-11-1969 in Ames, IA. Education: Iowa Western Community College, IA, BS Degree in Nursing, U of Nebraska Medical Center. Gateway Community College, Phoenix, AZ, Transition to Surgery Nursing course. Profession: Mother and Child nurse at Sierra Vista Community Hosp., AZ and Surgery nursing at U. Medical Center, Tucson, AZ. m. 8-12-1994 in Omaha, NE to John Andrada. 1 daughter.

~Jackie[9] Marie Andrada b. 6-3-1995 in Omaha, NE.

^Samuel[8] Royce Baillie b. 4-3-1971 in Ames, IA. BA in Music U. of Nebraska at Kearney, NE. Profession: Suzuki violin teacher, furniture refinisher, and bartender. m. 1st 7-31-1992 in Kearney, NE to Sharon Levett Mitchner.

^Joshua[8] Lee Baillie b. 2-1-1977 in Omaha, NE. Student at Northern Arizona U, Flagstaff, AZ in political science and history.

^Matthew[8] Nelson Baillie b. 9-4-1979 in Omaha, NE. Student at Arizona State U in Phoenix, AZ with major in geology.

+Andrea[7] Phyllis Nelson b. 5-16-1945 in LeMars, IA. BA in Spanish from U of S.D. 1967. m. 1st 10-31-1970 in Reno, NV to Daniel Cleve Bell b. 9-2-1949 Imperial Valley, CA. 1 daughter.

^Christine[8] Jacqualine Bell b. 6-23-1971 French Camp, CA. m. 4-26-1992 Sierra Vista, AZ to Robert Michael Kelsey, b.1-23-1971 Berlin, Germany. He son of Baerbel

Wlodarczak and James Kelsey.

m. 2nd to Jeffrey Schwarz b. 3-30-1951 in Ericsville, OH. He son of of James Schwarz and Rose Patterson.

+Kathleen[7] Vale Nelson b. 8-11-1946 in Soux Falls, SD. BS Degree in Textiles and Clothing Merchandising Iowa State, and MS in Computer Science from Southern Polytechnic State U. in GA. She is Senior Systems Engineer at Home Depot, Inc. Atlanta. GA. m. 6-14-1969 in Grenada Hills, CA to James Alexander Hadfield b. 10-10-1946 Chicago Heights, IL. BS Degree Aerospace Engineering Iowa State U. Employed as Site Manager, F-22 Airframe Integrated Product team, Lockheed Martin in Atlanta GA. He son of Walter Hadfield. 2 sons.

^Ian[8] Walter Hadfield b. 1-1-1976 Panorama City, CA. Attended Auburn U then DeVry Institute in Atlanta, GA.

^Andrew Winston Hadfield b. 2-3-1978 Panorama City, CA. Attending Georgia Tech..

+Vikki[7] Denice Nelson b. 3-23-1955 in Soux Falls, SD. Education: U of Nebraska then Bellevue College with BS in Human Resources. Profession: Billing. m. 6-4-1974 in Bellevue, NE to Gregory Wayne Buhr b. 6-13-1955. He son of Wayne Buhr and Barbara Allen. 2 children.

^Nicholas[8] Wayne Buhr b. 7-10-1980 Denver, CO.

^Amanda[8] Vale Buhr b. 4-1-1983 Papillion, NE.

(2) †Lewis[6] Andrew Nelson b. 6-19-1917 Goldfield, IA and d. 5-11-1996 in Salem, OR. Farmer and served in Army WW II. m. 4-22-1944 St. Paul, MN Margaret Annabelle Lyons b. 1-13-1922 Des Moines, IA. She daughter of Harry Floyd Lyons, and Elizabeth Enlow. She received BS in Science from Drake U. Was teacher. Live Goldfield, IA. 3 daughters.

+Pamela[7] Lou Nelson b. 5-31-1945 Des Moines, IA. Education: BA 1966 from Buena Vista College, IA; MA in Spanish 1969 Arizona State U. Profession: counselor, eating disorders. m. 1st 6-4-1967 in Goldfield, IA to Lynn Elwood Nagel b. 7-10-1945 Des Moines, IA. 1 daughter. m. 2nd Phillip Stephen Kenney.

^Jacqueline[8] Cara Nagel b. 8-31-1969.

+Jacqueline[7] Margaret Nelson b. 2-11-1947 Lanesboro, MN. Education: BA Degree U. of Iowa, Masters and Ph.D. in Clinical Psychology U of Victoria, Victoria BC, Canada.

Profession: Senior Policy Maker, Attorney General, British Columbia, Canada. m. 1st 10-10-1972 to Robert Seens. Divorced 1989. m. 2nd William John Stanley Wilcox III. He son of William John Wilcox II and Martha Joan Stanley.

+Regina^7 Gaye Nelson b. 9-12-1950 Fairfield, IA. Education: U of Missouri, Nursing degree. Profession: occupational therapist. m. 7-12-1975 in Goldfield, IA to Stephen Charles Tackett b. 7-20-1949. He son of Ray Tackett and Roxielee Morgan. He is Doctor of Psychology. 3 children.

^Sarah^8 Grace Tackett-Nelson b. 9-9-1978.

^Matthew^8 Morgan Tackett-Nelson b. 1-7-1983.

^Christopher^8 Lewis Tackett-Nelson b. 11-18-1986.

(3) †George^6 Marius Nelson, Jr. b. 3-18-1923 d. 8-5-1944 in Laurel, NE in airplane collision during WW II. Was 2nd Lt. m. 4-24-1943 to Gloria Richards b. 8-21-1923. 1 child.

+David^7 George Nelson b. 5-3-1945.

(4) Ruth^6 Elizabeth Nelson. b. 1-3-1927 d. 2-16-1927.

(5) Mary^6 Mildred Nelson b. 5-1-1928 Goldfield, IA. m. 4-30-1949 in Goldfield, IA to Kenneth Wayne Axon b. 2-25-1927 in Goldfield, IA. He son of Clifford Fred Axon and Luella McCutcheon. 4 daughters.

+Sonna^7 Lou Axon b. 7-8-1950 Fort Dodge, IA. m. 12-9-1972 in Goldfield, IA to James Robert Johnson b. 4-24-1946 Hampton, IA. Occupation: Air traffic controller. He son of Willard Johnson and Ruth Pederson. 3 children.

^Christopher^8 Wayne Johnson b. 11-3-1974 Des Moines, IA. m. 11-8-1997 Sonya Kay Routh b.

Figure 99. 1. Dean Schipull, 2. Jayne Axon Schipull, 3. Julie Axon Burzacott, 4. Jon Burzacott, 5. Christopher Johnson, 6. Sonna Axon Johnson, 7. James Johnson, 8. Suzanne Axon Skadburg, 9. Donald Skadburg, 10. Cassie Schipull, 11. Kenneth Axon, 12. Mary Axon, 13. Jessica Johnson, 14. Stacy Schipull, 15. Corey Skadburg, 16. Erika Skadburg, 17. Erin Johnson.

1978. Daughter of Larry N. Routh, Sr and Deloris Routh.
^Erin[8] Michele Johnson b. 4-7-1978 Clarion, IA.
^Jessica[8] Ruth Johnson b. 5-20-1982 Clarion, IA.
+Suzanne[7] Mary Axon b. 12-9-1952 Clarion, IA. m. 6-5-1976 in Goldfield, IA to †Donald Gene Skadburg b. 1-1-1952 Clarion, IA. US Army 1970-2. Occupation Consultant. He son of Norris Skadburg and Esther Moss. 2 children.
^Erika[8] Lynn Skadburg b. 1-22-1980 Vinton, IA.
^Corey[8] Alan Skadburg b. 4-25-1982 Clarion, IA.
+Jayne[7] Luella Axon b. 11-29-1957 Clarion, IA. m. 9-1-1979 in Goldfield, IA to Dean Charles Schipull b. 6-4-1956 Clarion, IA. He son of Donald Walter Schipull and Kristine Wetterhus. 2 daughters.
^Stacy[8] Lee Schipull b. 4-26-1984 Clarion, IA.
^Cassie[8] Jo Schipull b. 10-20-1989 Clarion, IA.
+Julie[7] Mar Axon b. 10-26-1964 Clarion, IA. m. 4-16-1994 in Goldfield, IA to Jon Michael Burzacott b.10-2-1956 Des Moines, IA. Occupation: respiratory therapist. He son of Jack Leroy Burzacott and Vera Gleason.
f. Martha[5] Mabel Leffler (Figure 95) b. on home farm near Stockport, IA 5-20-1887. m. Lee W. Forman 6-15-1910. He b. 3-17-1881. Her N.S. D.A.R. No. 221989 Ancestor was Capt. Henry Darrah. P.E.O. Chapter A.A. Iowa. L.W.F., graduate Iowa State College 1909. M.S. Degree 1913. Since 1909 Chief in Soils Fertility Experimental Station, Iowa State College. Boy Scout Veteran, Pres. Ames Library Board, Rotarian, Member Congregational Church, S.A.R. IA. No. 1167 Natl. 49967. Member Phi Kappa Phi, Gamma Sigma Delta, Phi Lambda Epsilon and Alpha Phi Omega. He b. near Lenox, IA, son of Ruth Ann Vare and Lewis Willets Forman. Parents of 3 children. 419 Lynn Ave., Ames, IA.
(1) Loren[6] Verne Forman b. 10-24-1912 Ames, IA and d. 9-12-1977. Education: Chemical engineering degree Iowa State 1934; MS and PhD degrees from Institute of Paper Chemistry in Appleton, WI 1936 and 1940. During WW II worked at the Institute as coordinator of applied research for the wartime program. He joined Scott Paper Co in 1950. He climbed through the ranks to VP for research and engineering, and then in 1967 to having primary responsibility for environmental concerns, one of the first corporate executives to have

such a position. In 1970 he was the recipiant of the Professional Achievement Citation in Engeneering from the College
of Engineering for outstanding leadership in research, development and environtology in the paper manufacturing industry. m. 8-4-1939 Miriam Richardson b. 12-26-1915. 4 children.

+George[7] Lee Forman b. 5-11-1942. m. 12-17-1966 Patricia
Sparks b. 11-16-1945. 7 adopted children.

+Richard[7] Loren Forman b. 11-26-1943. m. 1st 11-19-1966
Carolyn Downing b. 9-24-1946. m. 2nd 1-29-1972 Cheri
Herdman b. 3-28-1948. 2 children.

^Andrew[8] L. Forman b. 1972.

^Jay[8] W. Forman b. 1976. m. Sandi Hubbard.

+Phillip[7] Robert Forman b. 2-18-1949. m. 4-8-1972 Kathie
Fisher b. 7-12-1951. 2 children.

^Valerie[8] L. Forman b. 1974.

^David[8] J. Forman b. 11-23-1978.

+Lori[7] Martha Forman b. 7-21-1958. m. Scott Davidson b.
1954. 2 children.

^Peter[8] L. Davidson b. 1981.

^Dawn[8] Davidson b. 1987.

(2) Mary[6] Gail Forman b. 2-9-1916. m. 1st 12-25-1936 to
Robert K. Davis b. 11-17-1911. 2 children. m 2nd John Mack
7-4-1947. Children were adopted in 1948.

+Richard[7] Forman Davis b. 10-14-1937. m. 7-21-1962 to Eva
Lanno b. 2-28-1940. 3 children.

^Peter[8] Alexander Mack b. 8-28-1965. m. 8-8-1987 to
Sharon Gibson b. 6-1-1966 divorced 12-90.

^John[8] Patrick Mack b. 3-21-1968. m. 11-30-1996 to Terri
Silhavy b. 11-3-1962.

^Daniel[8] Christopher Mack b. 5-26-1970. m. 3-5-1968 to
Lauren Joy Brooks.

+Roberta[7] Kaye Davis b. 5-22-1941.

(3) Wallace[6] Rex Forman b. 2-14-1924. m. 8-20-1960 to Mur-
ray Sarubin b. 8-12-1941. Divorced 1989. 2 children.

+Amy[7] Beth Sarubin b. 7-11-1961. m 5-2-1992 to Curtis
Olson b. 11-21-1959. 2 children.

^Jack[8] Alexander Olson b. 5-23-1994.

^Lily[8] Elizabeth Olson b. 5-18-1995.

+Daniel[7] Benjamin Sarubin b. 5-1-1967.

g. Lydia[5] Elizabeth Leffler (Figure 95) b. home farm 10-11-1889 d. single 2-24-1916.

h. Robert[5] Wallace Leffler b. old home farm 1-5-1893. m. Catherine Canfield Dale 6-21-1918. Grad I.S.C. 1916. In Dairy (Ass't Sales Mgr.), National Cheese Producers Federation, Plymouth, WI.

E. Mary[4] Jane Vale b. 2-15-1856 d. 2-18-1856.

F. Martha[4] Margaret Vale (Figure 100) b. 4-10-1857, Bonaparte, IA. d. 4-13-1908, Beaver Falls, PA. Educated at Monmouth College. Was badly injured in gas explosion which caused her death. A rare personality. Beloved by all who knew her. m. Robert M. Downie 11-23-1882 at Bonaparte, IA. He d. 10-1924. Their 6 children all b. at Beaver Falls, PA.

Figure 100. Martha Margaret Vale-Downie in youth.

a. James[5] Vale Downie b. 8-12-1883, m. Janett Tesdova Matheng 3-30-1909. 1 child.

(1) Theodora[6] Downie b. 9-7-1920.

b. Ann[5] Jane Downie b. 11-18-1885 d. single 2-24-1902.

c. Regina[5] Martha Downie b. 4-28-1889. Dr. Regina M. Downie, 20 E. Baltimore Ave., Lansdowne, PA.

d. Robert[5] Rex Downie b. 8-13-1894.

e. John[5] Lincoln Downie (Twin of Mary Lydia) b. 11-8-1895. Lost at sea 10-5-1918. Was in the U.S. Merchant Marine Service, Quartermaster Steamship San Saba which struck a German mine near the New Jersey Coast.

f. Mary[5] Lydia Downie (Twin of John Lincoln) b. 11-8-1895. m. John Thompson White 4-19-1924, Hickory, PA. Parents of one daughter.

(1) Martha[6] Alice White b. 11-29-1927.

6. Minerva[3] Rex (6th of Benjamin[2] and Anne Rex, George[1]) b. in Jefferson Co., OH 6-20-1825 and d. 10-16-1826. Choked to death on timothy seeds.

7. Charles[3] H. Rex (7th of Benjamin[2] and Anne Rex, George[1]) b. Jefferson Co., OH 4-18-1827. d. of Scarlet Fever 4-12-1833.

8. Benjamin[3] Kepler Rex (8th of Benjamin[2] and Anne Rex, George[1]) b. in Jefferson Co., OH 9-27-1829. d. of Scarlet Fever 4-10-1833.

9. James[3] Rex (9th of Benjamin[2] and Anne Rex, George[1]) b. in Jefferson Co., OH 8-10-1831. He. d. of Scarlet Fever 4-10-1833.

10. Martha[3] Rex (10th of Benjamin[2] and Anne Rex, George[1]) b. in Jefferson Co., OH 7-15-1833. d. 5-8-1866. m. John S. McGregor 9-25-1855. He b. 3-31-1825 and d. 9-15-1897. Four children.

A. George[4] Rex McGregor b. 10-11-1856 d. 7-11-1860.

B. Henry[4] Vale McGregor b. 6-21-1860 at Mt. Pleasant, IA. m. Mary Coates of Mt. Pleasant 11-4-1884, Rev. J. B. Blakeney officiating. She was b. 11-8-1862. He is a dentist at Mason City, IA. Children as follows:

   a. Helen[5] McGregor b. 9-20-1888 at Mt. Pleasant, IA. m. to William Vridenburg 6-10-1913. Ceremony by Rev. W. Parker of Eagle Grove, IA.

   b. Paul[5] McGregor (twin of Pauline) b. at Atlantic, IA 11-9-1893 m. Sarah Kelley at Mason City, IA 4-27-1918. 2 children.

      (1) Richard[6] Vale McGregor b. 9-24-1920, Mason City, IA.

      (2) Helen[6] Wick McGregor b. 2-6-1927, St. Petersburg, FL.

   c. Pauline[5] McGregor (twin of Paul) b. 11-9-1893. m. Frank D. Haddock at Calrian, IA. 12-6-1919. Have one child. Lived at Crawford, NJ (1933).

      (1) Channing[6] Haddock b. 2-25-1923, Mason City, IA.

   d. Jay[5] B. McGregor b. 2-24-1895. m. Helen Kelley at Mason City, IA 4-27-1918. Lived in Mason City. 2 children.

      (1) John[6] Kelley McGregor b. 4-7-1919.

      (2) Mary[6] Katherine McGregor b. 6-2-1922.

C. John[4] S. McGregor 2nd b. 6-21-1862 m. Josephine Patrick 11-22-1898. She b. 4-30-1878. 2 children.

   a. Mary[5] Madaline McGregor b. 12-20-1899 m. Robert H. Winn at Washington, D.C. 5-29-1926. No children.

   b. James[5] McGregor b. 11-3-1902 d. 7-19-1904.

D. Mary[4] Martha McGregor b. 5-4-1866 d. 7-3-1897. m. Arthur Cummings 11-1890. 3 children.

   a. Gladys[5] Rex Cummings b. 1-1-1892 m. M. G. Sollers 1-24-1925.

   b. Ernest[5] Linwood Cummings b. 5-11-1893 d. 3-1897.

   c. Malcolm[5] McGregor Cummings b. 4-19-1895. Lives in Fairhaven, MA. m. 12-25-1919 Emily Margeson. Three children.

      (1) Malcolm[6] McGregor Cummings, Jr. b. 6-17-1921.

      (2) Marjorie[6] Cummings b. 8-5-1922.

FEMALE SEMINARY,
STEUBENVILLE, O.

Miss Sarah I. Rex

Dr. For Boarding, Two Quarters; $50. .

Tuition, Junior Class;   14. ..

Washing;   4 74

Books 3.46   Music and use of Piano;
Station .85
$4.31   Drawing and Painting;   " "

French; Fire in Chamber   5. ..

" "

Advanced, as by account on margin,   4.31

78.05

Cr. Received in advance, $ " "

Balance due, $ 78.05

March 31st 1854. Recd Payment
Treasurer & Trustees
for C. C. Beatty

Figure 101. Boarding School Bill for Sarah Samantha Rex-Maxwell (Page 209) from the Steubenville Female Seminary.

Steubenville Female Seminary.

TERMS

THE year begins in the Spring, and is divided into two Sessions, with a vacation at the close of each, in the month of April and October: each Session being divided into two Quarters.

The respective charges are at the lowest point, consistent with preserving the comforts and maintaining the advantages heretofore enjoyed, and from them no deductions need be expected. The terms are stated upon the principle of advance payment.

REGULAR COURSE

Boarding, &c.,.........................Per Quarter $30 00
Tuition, Primary Class $5 00—Middle..   "   6 00
    "   Junior,........$7 00—Senior...   "   7 00

For these sums the pupil is entitled to Board, and all necessaries connected with it, such as furniture, room rent, lodging, fuel, &c., and to Instruction in the branches constituting the Regular Course of Studies, together with Calisthenics, and Vocal Music.

OPTIONAL COURSE

Extra charges to be made, PER QUARTER, for
Instruction in Music, Piano or Guitar, with use of
    Instrument.................................$10 00
Lessons in Drawing and Painting, or French....... 4 00
Heated Air in Chamber............................ 2 00
When Fire is required in sleeping room........... 4 00
Lectures on Physiology, or Chemistry, for course... 2 00
Washing, per dozen, 36 cents.

No extra charge for incidentals, as use of furniture or bedding, apparatus or library, fuel for school rooms, &c. Board during vacation to those who remain at the Seminary, will be at the same rate as during the session.

Books and Stationery, Drawing Materials and Music, when needed, are provided at the Book Store prices. When parents desire their daughters to be furnished with these, or clothing, &c., previous deposits will be expected. No advances for pupils will be made, but for articles absolutely indispensable, or by the particular intructions of parents or guardians, to the Principal.

Promptness and punctuality in the settlement of accounts are indispensable.

Bills will be rendered at the close of each session, and we require accounts then to be fully settled, or satisfactorily arranged before the Pupil is removed. Balances are considered on interest.

No deduction need be expected for such as are not punctual and regular in attendance, or withdraw before the examination, unless it be a matter of previous understanding with the Superintendent.

Figure 102. Brochure for the Steubenville Female Seminary attended by Sarah Samantha Rex-Maxwell (Page 209) in 1854.

(3) Bruce[6] Rex Cummings b. 12-13-1927.

11. Sarah[3] Samantha Rex (11th of Benjamin[2] and Anne B. Rex, George[1]) b. in Jefferson Co., OH. 2-20-1835. m. Hamilton Maxwell of Phila., PA. (See Figures 101 & 102) She d. 6-5-1905 in N.Y. City at the home of her daughter and taken to Philadelphia, PA for burial. 1 child.

    A. Emma[4] Louise Maxwell b. in Philadelphia., PA 3-28-1865. A very talented woman, studied art in Paris, Florence, Italy and Athens, Greece and has spent the greater part of her life abroad. She is an artist and teacher of languages. m. in Paris, France 8-1904, to Edward Lance de Parenty. No children. In 1926 lived in N.Y. City. Teacher of Languages, Columbia University.

12. †Ross[3] Edgar Rex (Figures 103 & 104) (12th of Benjamin[2] 1st of his second wife, Martha Thompson Rex) b. 12-10-1840, Jefferson Co., OH. Educated at Richmond College, OH. "A fine sincere man" as expressed by Anna Stevens. m. Mary Ann Betz 12-19-1865. Ceremony in MO by Rev. Marshall. He served as 4th Sergeant. Co. "G" 52nd Ohio Vol. Inf. Honorably discharged, 6-5-1865. More complete record in *Dan Cook's Regiment* by Nixon B. Stewart, Pg. 15; Official War Record. "The Record of a Soldier."

Figure 103. Ross Edgar Rex.

Ross E. Rex, enlisted from Jefferson County, State of Ohio, Aug. 16, 1862, Mustered into the United States service at Camp Dennison, Ohio, as a Corporal, to serve for a term of three years in Co. G. 52nd Regiment, Ohio Volunteers, Ohio Infantry under Captains James T. Holmes, 2nd Samuel Rothacker, and Colonel Daniel McCook.

    The regiment left the State for Lexington, KY Aug. 25, 1862, and was involved in the following battles and campaigns (in Italics): *Marched to the Relief of Gen. Nelson,* Aug 29, 1862; Engaged at *Richmond,* KY Aug. 30, 1862; *Kentucky River,* Aug. 31, 1862; *Lexington,* Sept. 2nd, 1862; *Battle of Berryville, KY* Oct. 8th, 1862; *Mitchelville, TN.* Nov. 5, 1862; *Stone's River,* Dec. 30, 31, 1862; Jan. 1, 2, 1863; *Chicamauga, GA.* Sept. 19, 21, 1863.

    He was attached to the 2nd Brigade, 4th Division, 14th Army Corps, Army of the Cumberland and fought in the following battles: *Chattanooga, Ringold Campaign,* Nov. 23 to Nov. 27, 1863; *Battles of Orchard Kud,* Nov. 23, 1863; *Look-out Mountain,* Nov. 24, 1863; *Mission Ridge,* Nov. 25, 1863; *Ringold, GA,* Nov. 27, 1863; *March to*

Relief of Knoxville, TN, Nov. 25, to Dec. 18, 1863.

He was then attached to the 3rd Brigade, 2nd Division, 14th Army Corps, Army of the Cumberland where he remained until the close of the war. He fought in the following battles under this command: *Demonstration on Dalton, GA*, Feb. 23 to 27, 1864; *Battles at Buzzard's Roost, and Tunnel Hill, GA* Feb. 25 to 27, 1864; *Atlanta, GA Campaign* from May to September, 1864; *Battles at Tunnel Hill, GA* May 6, 7, 1864; *Rockfaced Ridge*, GA May 8 to 11, 1864; R*esaca, GA* May 14, 15, 1864; *Rome GA* May 17, 1864. *Dallas, New Hope Church, and Allatoona Hills*, May 25 to June 5$^{th;}$ *Kenesaw Mountain*, June 9 to 30, 1864 including *Battles at Pine Hills, GA* June 11 to 14, 1864, *Lost Mountain*, June 15 to 17, 1864, *Golgatha and Assault on Kenesaw*, June 27, 1864; *Battle of Ruff's Station, GA* July 4, 1864; *Chatta-hoochie River, GA* July 6, to 17, 1864; *Peach Tree Creek*, July 19 to 20, 1864; *Siege of Atlanta, GA* July 22 to Sept. 2, 1864; *Utoy Creek, GA* Aug. 6, 7,

Figure 104. Ross Edgar Rex as Civil War Soldier.

1864; *Jonesboro, GA* Aug. 31, Sept. 1, 1864; *Lovejoy Station.* Sept. 2, 1864; *Capture of Atlanta, GA* Sept. 2, 1864; *March to the Sea*, Nov. 15 to Dec. 10, 1864; *Engaged at Louisville, GA* Nov. 30, 1864. *Savannah, GA* Dec. 10 to 21, 1864; *March through the Carolinas* Jan. to April, 1865. Engaged at *Averasboro, NC* March 16, 1865; *Bentonville*, NC March 19 to 21, 1865; *Advance on Raleigh, NC, Surrender of Johnston with his Army*, at Raleigh, NC April 26, 1865; *March to Washington, D.C.* April 29 to May 30, 1865. He was present at the Grand Review at Washington, D.C. May 23, 1865. Finally he received an Honorable Discharge, June 3rd, 1865, at Washington, D.C., By Reason of Close of the War." He was wounded many times and was promoted to Sergeant, March 1, 1863.

After their three children were born, lived most of their lives in Creston, IA, having gone first to Bonaparte for a short time from MO. He d. 1-3-1917, Seattle, WA, at the home of his sister, Mrs. Barrett. After cremation, the ashes were sent to Wichita, KS where they rest beside the remains of his son, Loren E. Rex, Wichita Mausoleum. Mary A. B. d. 12-21-1902, Omaha, NE where she is buried in Forest Lawn Cemetery. (Stone marked "Mysie," the pet name used for her by her little grandaughter, Halcyon Cotton). She the daughter of Mary

Ann Ball and George Betz, a soldier of the war of 1812. He d. 12-25-1874 and she 11-15-1859, Salem OH Cemetery. Abraham Betz, (Major, Rev. Berks Co. PA. Ref. PA Archives 5th series, Vol. 5, pg. 166) father of George, left an interesting will on file at Steubenville, OH. Probated 1-7-1821, in which he disposes of 10¼ sections and 650 acres of land; one ¼ section going to his son, George, who is named with two brothers as Executors. Eldest daughter given $175 and younger ones to have, upon leaving home,a bed, good bedding, a spinning wheel, etc., such as the other sisters had, besides their legacies; they and a younger brother to be kept and cared for with mother, educated, etc., etc. One section of land is to be sold to provide for what is needed, etc., and to build for mother, Eve Betz, after the death of her husband, Abraham, "A complete dwelling house on the home place." This plantation being willed to her, not included in other lands named, and after all debts paid. He names their 13 children: Mary, John, Elizabeth, Susannah, Catherine, Johnathan, George, Soloman, Phebe, Anna, Sarah, William and David.

Figure 105. Lillian Rex-Black. **Figure 106**. Charles E. Black. **Figure 107**. Halcyon (Hallie) Rex-Cotton and baby Halcyon.

A. Lillian[4] Rex (Figures 105, 108, 109) b. near Mt. Vernon, MO 9-29-1868 m. Charles E. Black (Figure 106) in Omaha, NE 2-25-1892. Their only two children died as infants.

B. Halcyon[4] Rex (Figures 107, 108, 109) b. near Mt. Vernon, MO 3-15-1870. m. Scott R. Cotton, both deceased, in Creston, IA 6-25-1890. She has painted many beautiful pictures and was an Interior Decorator in Chicago where she d. 1-12-1933. 1 daughter.

   a. Halycon[5] Cotton (Figure 107 & 109) b. 2-9-1894, Creston, IA. Educated Omaha, NE and Wellsley College, and a very capable musician.

C. Loren[4] Edgar Rex (Figure 108, 109, 110) b. on a farm near Mt. Vernon, MO 5-30-1872. d. 6-20-1917. Specialist Eye, Ear, Nose, and

Throat. Member Sedgwick Co. Medical Society, B.P.O.E., Masonic Lodge, Phi Rho Sigma, National Medical Fraternity. Joined Congregational Church in Creston, IA as a very young boy, in which choir he sang. Sang all his life from a child, had a beautiful tenor voice and did much choir and solo work where ever he lived. George B. Rex

Figure 108. Left to right: Hallie, Lily and Loren Rex.

says he had a paper route from about 10 years of age and we find some old checks, in his favor, from Creston Gazette, dated in the early eighties. His sister wrote, "Loren attended Creston public schools, carried papers from the time he was a very small boy, always just a dear manly helper. Loved baseball but never had much time to play, had a football he loved to kick around and a turning pole in the back yard on which we all had much fun. Had Plymouth Rock Chickens he much prized, and pigeons, two of which perched

Figure 109. Left to Right: Lily Rex Black, Hallie Rex Cotton, Mrs. Harry Black, Loren Rex, Dorothy Black, and Halcyon Cotton. Welcome to Loren Rex on summer vacation.

on the neighbor's roof who promptly shot them nearly breaking the boy's heart. He loved dogs and was always bringing home a stray. Raised "Vic" from a pup and trained him beautifully. This dog would tear around the house from the back porch to meet Loren when he heard him kissing mother, Lily and me goodbye and stayed all night with him at the ticket office, next morning returning with him carrying in his mouth his package of meat."

"With the railroad, Loren was in the freight and passenger offices and a car checker and then to Chicago in General Offices, but always had in mind wanting to be a doctor. When the opportunity came for him to attend Medical School in St. Louis, the officials told him he was a fool to leave because soon he would be at the top with the railroad." Writing to Dr. Parks Rex 1-17-1893, Charles S. Rex says, "Loren went to St. Louis, MO to educate and make a Dr. of himself and I have much confidence in his ability and energy to make a success in life." He had a scholarship and cared for a furnace to help on expenses.

After a year he had to stop and work again, and so on. His sister and husband, Mr. and Mrs. Charles Black, most kindly offered him a home

Figure 110. Loren Edgar Rex, M. D. "To live in the hearts we leave behind us is not to die." Husband of Leda Ferrel Rex, author of the First Edition of the *Rex Genealogy*. His untimely death at the age of 45 and the undying love and dedication of his wife is the reason this book exists.

GEORGE REX GENEALOGY
Line IX

Figure 111. Ferrell Home since June 1882, Wichita, Kansas, birthplace of Leda Ferrell Rex and her son Dan Rex.

Figure 112. Dan Rex, January 9, 1919.

Figure 113. Dan Rex.

Figure 114. Leda Ferrell Rex and son Dan on their home steps in Honolulu, December 1929.

with them in Omaha, so he then attended Creighton Medical School from which he graduated in 1899. Was recommended to Wichita by his work standard and became the first intern of St. Francis Hospital. Next he took office experience and then went for a number of terms to Manhattan Eye and Ear, (NY) in various positions as house surgeon, etc. Located in Wheeling, WV. His father, in writing to Lydia Leffler 5-24-1910 says, "I am very proud of my boy or my baby who is now 36. He has made a grand success of his profession and treats an average of over 62 patients per day. I am afraid he will ruin his health, scarcely ever gets out of his office at noon and sometimes no supper until 9 or 10 o'clock at night." 5-28-1914 m. Leda Marie Ferrell of Wichita, KS, and went abroad for a year of study and for the benefit of his health. The war disrupted these plans and he opened offices in 4th Natl. Bank Bldg., Wichita, where he dropped dead 6-20-1917, at which time their only child was six months old.

Leda M. Ferrell Rex (Figure 110 & 111) was b. 7-30-1882 (yet living [1933], in the same house) daughter of Tarsy S. Myers and Lloyd Bascom Ferrell. Member First Presbyterian Church (Since 1895) P.O.E. Chap. I, Thursday afternoon cooking Club, MA Society Colonial Dames of America, U.S. Daughters of 1812. Life member and serving on the boards of the following organizations: Saturday Afternoon Muscial Club (Pres. 1930-32) 20th Century Club, Art Association, Red Cross (Sedgwick Co. Chap.), N. A. D. A. R. (Wichita Chap. Regent 1932-34), Life member Y.W.C.A., Sedgwick Co. Pioneer Society, French Creek (WV) Pioneer Society, N. E. H. and G. Society, Magna Charta Dames, etc.

a. Daniel[5] Ferrell Rex (Figures 112, 113, 114, & 115) b. 12-4-1916. Finished at Punahou Junior Academy, Honolulu, T. H. 6-1930 (Figure 114). Wichita High School North 6-1933. Member First Presbyterian Church since 4-11-1926. Matthew Grant Chp. C.A.R. and a Sea Scout.

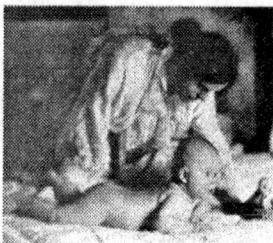

Figure 115. Leda Ferrell Rex and son Daniel Ferrell Rex age 6 months. This picture was taken as a surprise for Daniel's father, which he never lived to see.

"Dr. Loren E. Rex, my friend has passed away. I last saw Dr. Rex at one o'clock on the afternoon on which he died. As I left the office the last words he said to me were, 'Be sure and come to see me tomorrow.' But tomorrow brought to him the dark shadow and the angel of death who bore him away and away. Tomorrow brought to me the sunlight and wide o'er arching sky; but I saw and felt it not for it brought not to me the sound of the voice of my friend nor the warm clasp of his hand.

I first met Dr. Rex through the urging of a little child. And let me say that among the many fine traits of his character, none was sweeter, none more beautiful than his love for children, especially the boys. Every little newsboy on the streets knew that if a toe got hurt, Dr. Rex would tie it up; if a splinter got in a bare heel, he would take it out. He gave them just the same attention that he gave his most influential patients. It was in some such way my own little boy became acquainted with him and kept telling me about his friend until at last I went to meet him.

As I looked into his fine face and felt the clasp of his hand, I felt that he was my friend and I, too, soon learned to love him. One day my little boy was seized with a deadly disease and as I saw the splendid face of Dr. Rex bending over the sick bed, he seemed to me like some 'beautiful tall angel.' And what a comfort he was to me. After the boy was well, the Doctor and he became the closest of comrads; and I also got to going to his office almost daily if only for a few minutes for the sheer joy of his presence and the rest and comfort his companionship always gave me. No matter how often I went to see him, he always came and took me by the hand the same way. Even now as I go by the Bank Building, I turn unconsciously into the hall which leads up to his office above.

When I remember that he is not there, with sinking spirits I go away. Perhaps my footsteps turn down the avenue to where the waters of the Arkansas glide over the yellow sands toward the sea. The sun has gone down in the West far away beyond the river, leaving the sky all glorious with its golden light. The clouds are amber and orange and purple and rose, and the evening star shines like a far distant gem. The wind has died away until only a soft breeze comes from the green country far to the South. The cottonwood trees are sharply outlined against the sky and a night bird with outstretched wings seems to be slowly drifting away and away and away into the night. All is quiet and still and beautiful as such Summer evenings always are in June. But I suddenly think of the Doctor and my spirits sink. But I know somewhere he still lives. Perhaps far away in the West where the sun is still shining, he waits; and when I go will welcome me there with the same clasp of the hand as in the old days gone by. Dr. Rex is one and although I know his office rooms will never again know his step; his home will never again know the sound of his voice; his baby boy will never again feel the touch of his hand; although I saw the casket which held his earthly form buried beneath a hillock of flowers, I can not say, I will not say that he is dead, he's just away."

George D. Thompson.

13. Elizabeth[3] Barclay Rex (13th of Benjamin[2] and 2nd of Martha Rex) b. 7-18-1842 in Jefferson Co., OH. d. 1905 Wellsville, OH. Single.

Figure 116. Rebecca McCray Rex Barrett and husband James Barrett.

14. Rebecca[3] McCray Rex (Figures 116 & 117) (14th of Benjamin[2] and 3rd of Martha Rex) b. in Jefferson Co., OH 11-1-1844. d. 8-5-1927 in Seattle, WA. Cremated and ashes sent to Union Cemetery, Steubenville, OH beside her husband and son. m. James Barrett (Figure 116) 10-17-1864, ceremony by Rev. Peacock at Richmond, OH. d. 10-20-1869. Parents of three children.

Figure 117. Rebecca Rex Barrett in later years.

A. Martha[4] H. Barrett b. Richmond, OH 9-15-1865. Single. A real housewife, excellent cook, devoted to her mother through her long widowhood, possesses an even, cheerful disposition, a joy to those with whom she comes in contact. Lives with her sister, Mrs. Hagan in Seattle, WA (1933).

B. Mary[4] Rex Barrett (Figure 118) b. 2-2-1867 at Richmond, Ohio. m. at Eldorado, CA to Calvin H. Hagan 8-25-1891. They reside in Seattle, WA. She is very talented in art and literature and has had many of her poems published. She has the typical distinguished or queenly bearing of the Rex family. There are no children. As her modesty has kept Mrs. Hagan from selecting anything from her pen for this book, I am using the two little poems from a collection in my possession.

Figure 118. Mary Barrett-Hagan.

HEARTSEASE

When your poor heart aches and throbs,
With the weight of a new found sorrow,

When the future grows all dark
With never a light for the morrow,
When there's only a dull dark gray
In the stretch of your life's broad sky,
When the faded rose of your joy
Is thrown to the winds with a sigh;
Look, then, at the dark lives about you
Forgetting your own woes and strife,
While lifting the burdens of others
You bring back the color to life.
There's not such a Heartsease in Flower-land
As will grow in your life from the seed,
Sown in caring for others who sorrow
And binding the poor hearts that bleed.

MY CREED
I believe in a God So loving
That I feel His tender arms,
Bear me up when my feet would falter
And I shudder 'mid earth's alarms.
I believe in a tender Brother
Who has broken my thorny way,
With His own dear feet, so weary
Of that terrible earthly stay.
I believe in a calm sweet Spirit
That whispers but words of love,
That guides me with tenderest council
To the throne of my God above.

--From "Pictures from Puget Sound"
By Mary Barrett Hagan.

C. William[4] Parks Barrett b. 4-19-1869 at
Richmond, Ohio. d. 12-19-1881.
15. Parks[3] Rex (16th of Benjamin[2] and 4th of
Martha Rex) (Figures 119 & 120) b. 9-6-1847 in
Jefferson Co., Ohio. He was a physician (M.D.)
and lived at Wellsville, Columbiana Co., OH
where he d. 11-18-1912 and is buried. m. Emma
ElDora Gray 1-19-1881 at Richmond, Jefferson

Figure 119. Dr. Parks Rex.

Co., OH. Parents of four children.
   A. Margaret[4] Gray Rex (Figure 121) b. in Knoxville, OH 11-6-1881. m. Charles Everett Culp 6-2-1914 in First Presbyterian Church, Wheeling, WV. This family has given much assistance for this genealogy.

Figure 120. Ross (page 203) and his brother Dr Parks Rex.

      a. Charles[5] (Billy) Rex Culp (Figure 121, 122) b. 9-26-1916, Steubenville, OH. Much interested in Boy Scouts.
      b. Halcyon[5] ElDora Culp (Figure 121) b. 4-2-1918, Steubenville, OH. A very fine student.
   B. William[4] Parks Rex (Figure 122) b. Knoxville, Jefferson Co., OH 6-7-1883.
   C. Benjamin[4] Harold Rex b. 7-9-1888, Wellsville, Columbia Co., OH. d. 4-28-1907.

Figure 121. Margaret Rex Culp and children Billy and Halcyon.

   D. Martha[4] ElDora Rex (Figure 123) b. in Wellsville, OH. 8-21-1895. A trained nurse, resides with her mother and brother in Wellsville where she .holds the position of city nurse.

Figure 122. William Parks Rex and nephew Billy Culp

Figure 123. Martha ElDora Rex.

Chapter 12

Catherine[2] Rex (Figure 124), called Kitty (10th
child of Margaret Kepler and George[1] Rex) b.
near Jefferson in Greene Co., PA 12-25-1793
and d. at Richmond, OH 10-11-1873. m.
Joseph Burson at the old home place near
Jefferson, Greene Co., PA in the year 1814
and went to live in Richmond, OH. Joseph
Burson was b. 10-12-1790 and d. at Richmond, OH 6-18-1865, as the result of a gun
shot wound inflicted by a thief and a criminal
named Samuel Groff.

Figure 124. Catherine (Kitty) Rex.

The Honorable
Joseph Burson
had a wide cir-
cle of friends
and acquain-
tances and was
highly re-
spected by all
who knew him.

He was also a
Justice of the
Peace. Son of

Figure 125. Kitty Rex and Joseph Burson Home near Steubenville, Ohio.

Edward and Elizabeth Blackledge Burson, being the 5th child (of 10)
as follows: James, settled in Columbiana Co., OH; Thomas, resided in
Greene Co., PA, Member of Congress; David, settled in Columbiana
Co., OH; Levi, resided in Greene Co., PA; Joseph, resided in Richmond, OH; Isaac, Associate Judge of Greene Co., PA and resided
there; Abraham, m. 1st ____. Lived in Greene Co., m. 2nd Hannah
Crawford, Greene Co., PA; Elizabeth, b. 1-26-1799 m. Frederick Wise
b. 9-2-1793; Sarah m. John Johnson of Columbiana Co., OH; Margaret m. Joseph Burson of Guernsey Co., OH. Edward and Elizabeth
Blackledge Burson were among the earliest settlers of Greene Co.
They emigrated from Bucks Co., PA in 1789 and settled on a farm
near Clarksville, PA where Joseph was born. The Bursons were
Quakers tracing back to Joseph Burson who came from London,

Figure 126. Bible of Catherine Rex Burson, from her father, George Rex I[st.]

England to Philadelphia with William Penn's 1st colony of Quakers in 1681. The mother and grandmother, Mary Potts, was an aunt of Isaac Potts at whose house near Valley Forge, Washington had his head-quarters in the Rev. War (See Wise Family). We are glad to have a picture of aunt Kitty Rex Burson furnished by Mrs. Anna Scott, a grandniece, and pictures of the original Kitty Rex Burson bible (Figure 120) given to her by her father, George Rex 1st. Martha Leffler Forman says of Joseph and Kitty Burson, "He was a rather heavy set man and aunt Kitty was a dear old lady, rather large." We have pictures of their tombstones in Richmond at the United Presbyterian Church Cemetery. 1 daughter.

1. Elizabeth[3] Ann Burson b. 7-31-1815 d. 6-7-1868. m. Benjamin Shelly 12-28-1832 and they had 10 children. 3 died as infants. Benjamin Shelly was b. 10-13-1809, the son of John Shelly who was b. Lancaster Co., PA. Emigrated to OH in 1820, locating on Sec. 4 near Richmond where he lived the remainder of his life. See Cald-well's Hist. of Belmont and Jefferson Cos. Pub. 1880, p. 570.
   A. Catherine[4] Elizabeth Shelly b. 12-11-1833 d. 9-17-1920 m. John Wolf Lindley 10-9-1854. 6 children. He d. 12-16-1907.
      a. Amasa[5] Lindley b. 10-3-1855 d. 4-15-1923. Single.
      b. Joseph[5] Burson Lindley b. 10-17-1857 m. Margaret Ann Trim-ble 3-23-1882 b. 9-23-1855 d. 6-8-1919. He m. 2nd Mary Edith Hurst 9-27-1919. 3 sons by 1st marriage.
         (1) William[6] Cummings Lindley b. 3-1-1885 d. 11-16-1908.
         (2) John[6] Lindley d. few days after birth .
         (3) Joseph[6] Burson Lindley, Jr. b. 4-6-1894 m. Sarah Ruth Harris. 1 daughter.
            +Margaret[7] Ann Lindley b. 9-25-1930.
      c. Benjamin[5] Shelly Lindley b. 12-21-1861 d. 6-16-1926, single.
      d. Elizabeth[5] Lindley b. 12-13-1867 m. Frank Morton McMurry 12-20-1894 who was b. 7-2-1862. 2 daughters.
         (1) Katherine[6] Lindley McMurry b. 6-14-1896 m. Charles

Beverley Benson, he b. 12-6-1895. 3 children.

+Gwendolyn[7] Barbara Benson b. 7-26-1920.

+Page[7] Benson (daughter) b. 11-27-1926.

+Beverley[7] Benson (son) b. 2-19-1931.

(2) Margaret[6] Lindley McMurry b. 10-15-1903 m. 2-19-1926 Martin Haight Gambee. 2 children.

+Frank[7] McMurry Gambee b. 1-12-1927.

+Ann[7] Elizabeth Gambee b. 10-5-1929.

e. William[5] Lindley b. 7-9-1870 m. Lillian Eley 6-12-1898.

f. Anna[5] Lucinda (LuLu) Lindley b. 8-3-1873.

B. Sarah[4] Ann Shelly b. 4-26-1840 d. 2-11-1931 m. John McMillen 2-22-1860 who was b. 6-2-1836 d. 6-1-1924. 4 children.

a. Cordelia[5] Jane McMillen b. 6-24-1861 m. 6-6-1883 William E. McCandless b. 7-22-1859. 1 son.

(1) Walter[6] Floyd McCandless b. 6-21-1844 m. 2-27-1911 Maude Miller b. 12-15-1885. 3 daughters.

+Janet[7] Reta McCandless b. 4-29-1912.

+Betty[7] Jane McCandless b. 2-19-1917.

+Dorothy[7] Jean McCandless b. 9-27-1823.

b. Shelly[5] McMillen b. 9-30-1863 m. 1st Sarah Bell Stroud who d. 2-1921. m. 2nd Lillian Henness 11-17-1927. 2 sons 1st marriage.

(1) Harry[6] McMillen b. 1-12-1887 m. Pearl Stringham 8-4-1910. 2 children.

+Dena[7] Marie McMillen b. 3-6-1912.

+Shelly[7] Stroud McMillen b. 7-8-1913.

(2) Homer[6] Stroud McMillen b. 9-28-1889 m. 6-18-1917 Trean Loudermilk. 1 son.

+John[7] Stroud McMillen b. 8-23-1921.

c. William[5] McMillen b. 3-3-1868 m. Mettie Lippy 2-23-1897. She b. 7-16-1870 d. 2-4-1931.

d. Benjamin[5] Floyd McMillen b. 5-24-1876 m. Rosie Reader 7-1-1899.

(1) Clarence[6] M. McMillen b. 4-24-1900 m. 9-1-1922 Marie M. Roesch b. 5-10-1903.

C. Emma[4] Shelly b. 6-18-1842 d. 10-13-1923. m. 2-20-1862 John E. Irvine, a lawyer, Richmond, OH. b. 1830 d. 5-17-1869. 2 children.

a. Shelly[5] Irvine b. 8-14-1863 m. 12-30-1896 Jennie Cavitt b. 7-4-1873. 2 children.

(1) Olive[6] Lucille Irvine b. 4-27-1898 d. 11-2-1923.

(2) John[6] Elliott Irvine b. 5-14-1901.

b. James[5] Irvine b. 10-8-1865 m. 1st 12-20-1899 Elizabeth Borland b. 10-16-1869 d. 11-26-1908. 1 son.
  (1) John[6] Borland Irvine b. 11-5-1901 m. 2-10-1927 Mary E. Wardle. 1 child.
    +Juanita[7] Mae Irvine b. 11-24-1927.
  m. 2nd 4-24-1912 Wilma M. Crawford b. 9-13-1874. 4 children.
  (1) Emma[6] Crawford Irvine b. 1-20-1913, twin.
  (2) James[6] Crawford Irvine b. 1-20-1913, twin.
  (3) Mary[6] Hammond Irvine b. 7-1-1915.
  (4) Jimmy[6] Shelly Irvine b. 3-11-1917.
D. Martha[4] Maria Shelly b. 11-6-1844 d. 12-18-191 m. 6-30-1867 Rev. R. T. McCrea b. 8-3-1838. 6 children.
  a. Elizabeth[5] Burson McCrea b. 2-20-1870 m. 2-1890 J. H. Bailey b. 12-19-1864. 8 children.
    (1) Helen[6] R. Bailey b. 12-18-1890 m. 11-15-1923 Guy Hoyme. 1 child.
      +Lucille[7] Eleanor Hoyme b. 9-8-1924.
    (2) Gertrude[6] Bailey b. 11-27-1892.
    (3) Ross[6] C. Bailey b. 10-4-1894 m. 6-2-1920 Louise Munson b. 8-17-1895. 1 child.
      +James[7] H. Bailey b. 8-12-1923.
    (4) Frank[6] McCrea Bailey b. 1-26-1896 m. 1924 Barbara Sheppard. 2 children.
      +Frances[7] Lucille Bailey b. 10-19-1925.
      +Donald[7] Bailey d. 10-4-1928.
    (5) Martha[6] Lucille Bailey b. 7-4-1897 d. 8-2-1897.
    (6) Elizabeth[6] Bailey b. 8-21-1898 m. 2-26-1925 Will Shepperd.
    (7) John[6] Rex Bailey b. 11-10-1899 m. 6-3-1924 Helen Smith.
    (8) Mary[6] Bailey b. 5-12-1904 m. Richard Brownlee 6-4-1924. 1 son.
      +Robert[7] Eugene Brownlee b. 9-11-1928.
  b. Nancy[5] Fidella McCrea b. 4-17-1872 m. 3-4-1894. H. J. Keeley b. 9-22-1863. 5 children.
    (1) Robert[6] McCrea Keeley b. 12-17-1895 m. 12-7-1918, Clara Devine.
    (2) Maude[6] Keeley b. 12-29-1897 m. 9-15-1917 Horace Clark.
    (3) Martin[6] Keeley b. 10-4-1903, d. as infant.
    (4) William[6] Orrin Keeley b. 9-10-1906.
    (5) Martha[6] Keeley b. 7-28-1909.

c. William[5] Clark McCrea b. 1824 d. 1874, single.

d. Sarah[5] Edith McCrea b. 2-16-1876 d. 9-15-1909 m. 5-4-1898 J. B. Park. 3 children,

  (1) Laura[6] Madge Park b. 2-5-1899 m. 6-1918. Charles Corbett b. 9-12-1899. 3 children.

    +Mary[7] Edith Corbett b. 4-7-1919.

    +Charles[7] Corbett, Jr. b. 12-25-1920.

    +Helen[7] Catherine Corbett b. 8-1923.

  (2) Ross[6] McCrea Park b. 12-8-1900 d. 9-5-1913.

  (3) Ruth[6] Park b. 7-31-1902 m. 10-1-1921 Clyo Frodeliuns b. 7-1-1897. 1 child.

    +Pauline[7] Claire Frodeliuns b. 3-17-1923.

e. Thompsin[5] Porter McCrea b. 3-3-1886 m. 6-1-1908 Mable Park b. 7-8-1886. 6 children.

  (1) Robert[6] Park McCrea, b. 8-21-1909.

  (2) William[6] Ross McCrea b. 3-2-1912.

  (3) Joseph[6] Frederick McCrea b. 4-11-1917.

  (4) Mary[6] McCrea b. 3-20-1918.

  (5) James[6] McCrea b. 9-20-1920.

  (6) Thomas[6] Shelly McCrea b. 3-5-1923.

E. Samantha[4] Jane Shelly b. 2-22-1846 d. 1-12-1913 m. 8-22-1871 T. C. Harbourt, Coffeyville, KS. 2 children.

a. Charles[5] Ross Harbourt b. 6-17-1872 m. 10-25-1896 Lillian Ford.

  (1) Edith[6] May Harbourt b. 11-19-1902.

  (2) Ernest[6] Kane Harbourt b. 8-17-1906.

b. William[5] Westly Harbourt b. 9-18-1874 m. Lillian B. Mc-Queen.

  (1) Charles[6] Cook Harbourt b. 2-28-1904.

  (2) Florence[6] Mildred Harbourt b. 11-10-1908.

F. Anne[4] Elma Shelly b. 7-2-1855, twin, m. 4-14-1881, Joseph G. Cooper b. 5-6-1852. 3 children.

a. Benjamin[5] Clarington Cooper b. 3-16-1883 m. 10-11-1911 Jessie M. Price b. 9-5-1885. 4 children.

  (1) Frederick[6] Price Cooper b. 7-31-1912.

  (2) Robert[6] Clarington Cooper b. 5-9-1915.

  (3) Warren[6] Lindley Cooper b. 12-7-1917.

  (4) David[6] Kenda Cooper b. 12-29-1921.

b. Levina[5] Jean Cooper b. 12-28-1887 d. 7-21-1928 m. 6-10-1922 William R. Swickard. 1 son.

(1) Robert[7] Cooper Swickard b. 7-18-1928.

c. Emma[5] Cooper b. 24-1891 m. 2-19-1913 Raymond McClelland b. 8-12-1886. 4 children.

   (1) John[6] Burson McClelland b. 8-16-1914.

   (2) Mildred[6] Jane McClelland b. 3-26-1920. d. 4-9-1922.

   (3) Howard[6] Cooper McClelland b. 10-30-1922.

   (4) Francis[6] Marion McClelland b. 12-14-1924.

G. Harriet[4] Zelma Shelly, twin, b. 7-2-1855 m. 5-6-1875 Lew E. Whitman b. 12-17-1840 d. 8-4-1930. 5 children.

a. Claude[5] Shelly Whitman b. 10-18-1878 m. 2-18-1903 Pearl Cook b. 4-11-1886. 3 children.

   (1) Kenneth[6] Claude Whitman b. 12-18-1904 m. 12-2-1824 Ora Hedges.

   (2) Bennie[6] Hobart Whitman b. 10-24-1907.

   (3) Myrtle[6] Lee Whitman b. 2-16-1914.

b. Emmet[5] Burson Whitman b. 12-15-1886 m. Myrtle M. Maple b. 10-15-1894. 2 children.

   (1) Zelma[6] Irene Whitman b. 1-10-1917. d. 2-14-1920.

   (2) Clyde[6] Lester Whitman b. 5-11-1923.

c. Elizabeth[5] Borland Whitman b. 6-3-1889 m. 2-16-1927 Leroy W. Eshbaugh.

d. Joe Robert[5] Whitman b. 4-23-1893 m. 4-22-1914 Carrie De-Vore b. 11-25-1897. 3 children.

   (1) Lois[6] Madaline Whitman b. 12-7-1917.

   (2) Elizabeth[6] Harriet Whitman b. 5-9-1919.

   (3) Robert[6] DeVore Whitman b. 2-2-1924.

e. Orville[5] Shelly Whitman b. 4-23-1896.

Chapter 13

Sarah[2] Rex (Sally–11th child of Margaret Kepler and George[1] Rex) b. near Jefferson, Greene Co., Pennsylvania. Without actual dates we estimate that her birth was between 1793 and 1798. We have the least information about this branch of the family of any. We only know that her first husband's name was John Day and that he died and then she m. Samuel Cloaky and that they lived in Florence, Washington Co., PA in the 1860's. He was a second cousin to Reverend James Cloaky. She died without issue. Her old fashioned picture is interesting.

Figure 127. Sarah Rex Cloaky.

Chapter 14

Charles[2] Rex, (12th child of Margaret Kepler and George[1] Rex) was b. 6-1-1801 near Jefferson, Greene Co., PA on the home farm and lived there until his death on 9-13-1864 (This place is ½ mile east of Jefferson near Ten Mile Creek). His six children were also born on this farm. He was said to be very aristocratic. He played the violin. On 10-2-1831 he m. Mary Hickman, daughter of Solomon and Elizabeth McCombs Hickman, who was b. 1-19-1801 in Fayette Co., PA. They d. the same day 9-13-1854 (she at 7 P. M. and he at 9:30 P. M.) and were buried in the same grave. Their deaths were attributed to an epidemic of disentery. First buried on the home place, then in the Spring of 1895 were removed by their son, George Rex, to the Jefferson Cemetery. The parents of Mary Hickman-Rex were Eliza-beth McCombs, b. 8-11-1775 d. 12-24-1870, and Solomon Hickman, b. 11-10-1770 d. 6-29-1845. The Hickmans were parents of 7 children: Mary b. 1801; Elizabeth b. 1803; Sara b. 1805, d. 7-19-1887; Solomon; Eliza; Anna; and Experience. Charles and Mary Rex had 6 children.

Figure 128. Charles Rex Bible given to him by his father George Rex 1st.

1. Margaret[3] Kepler Rex (1st child of Charles and Mary[2] Rex, George[1]) b. 6-27-1832 d. 6-18-1904. m. 1st William Watkins 6-27-1850 who d. 10-1-1854, 28 yrs. 1 mo. 1 day (His grave is between Pera Hart and Mary Rex, daughter of Anna and Benjamin Rex, in Jefferson Ceme-tery). Their 2 children were:
 A. Virginia[4] Watkins d. aged 2 years.
 B. Richard[4] Watkins b. 6-24-1852 d. 10-11-1878. m. Mary Jackson of Mt. Pleasant, IA. 1 daughter.
  a. Richie[5] Watkins b. 6-2-1878, who m. Homer Cresop 6-22-

1910. 1 son.

   (1) Jackson[6] Cresop b. 2-7-1920.

m. 2nd †William F. Hughes 11-25-1857 and in 1865 moved to Henry Co. IA. W. F. H. mustered into service at Camp Howe, Pittsburg, PA 11-19-1862. He was 1st Lieut. of Co. A. 168. Discharged 7-25-1863. 5 children as follows:

  A. Thomas[4] R. Hughes b. 9-4-1858 Greene Co., PA. Single. d. 12-24-1884.

  B. Jessie[4] May Hughes b. 8-6-1862 Greene Co., PA. m. Neal Campbell 10-28-1885, Mt. Pleasant, IA. Their children 4 are:

    a. Clara[5] M. Campbell b. 10-31-1886 m. A. Walter 8-10-1912 of Knoxville, IA. 1 son.

     (1) Harold[6] Walter b. 11-25-1915.

    b. Will[5] Rex Campbell b. 8-11-1891 m. Jessie G. Cauming 10-27-1920 of Ottumwa, IA.

    c. †Ralph[5] C. Campbell b. 12-25-1893 m. Maud Calhoun of Keosoqua, IA 4-24-1919. Lieut. World War I, Air Div. 3 children.

     (1) Ralph[6] Calhoun Campbell b. 3-11-1920.

     (2) Laurance[6] Campbell b. 9-26-1921.

     (3) Julian[6] C. Campbell b. 2-27-1927.

    d. Mildred[5] Lucile Campbell b. 11-28-1905 m. Rollin S. White 3-20-1927 of Lamoni, IA. 2 children.

     (1) Jean[6] Anna White b. 2-25-1928.

     (2) James[6] Warren White b. 8-7-1929.

  C. John[4] Rex Hughes b. 7-18-1864, PA. d. 8-22-1922. Left a wife, Margaret, and 2 children.

    a. Rex[5] Campbell Hughes b. 3-24-1898.

    b. Elizabeth[5] Hughes b. 3-20-1908, m. Richie.

  D. Charles[4] R. Hughes b. 12-1868, Mt. Pleasant, IA. m. Clara Pressnell 10-16-1896. 1 son.

    a Theron[5] R. Hughes b. 4-22-1898 Mt. P., IA. m. DeEtta M. Pierce 10-9-1920. 1 son.

     (1) Theron[6] Rex Hughes, Jr. b. 2-2-1924.

  E. George[4] R. Hughes b. 7-3-1872 Mt. P., IA. d. 12-25-1873.

2. Elizabeth[3] Rex (2nd child of Mary and Charles[2] Rex, George[1]) b. 8-23-1834 d. 4-11-1877. m. Daniel Moredock 11-25-1849 who was b. 3-19-1820 d. 10-16-1906. He m. 2nd Rosa Stevens 1885. No children. Elizabeth and Daniel Moredock were parents of 10 children as follows:

A. Rex[4] Moredock b. 11-1-1850, Jefferson, PA and is buried there. d. 4-1-1929. m. 9-11-1878 Jennie McClenathan who was b. 2-14-1850 d. 11-30-1913. Lived at Khedive, PA and had 1 son.

  a. Earl[5] Thomas Moredock b. 8-16-1883 m. at Waynesburg, PA 5-29-1907 Anna M. Smith who was b. 6-25-1879 near Fordyce, Greene Co., PA. Parents of 6 children.

    (1) Charles[6] Rex Moredock b. 4-25-1908, Khedive, PA. m. Weatha L. Davis 5-19-1928. 1 daughter.

      +Alice[7] Mae Moredock b. 3-22-1929.

    (2) Albert[6] Earl Moredock b. 5-12-1910.

    (3) Ray[6] Smith Moredock b. 1-28-1913.

    (4) Dennis[6] McClenathan Moredock b. 6-28-1915.

    (5) Mary[6] Virginia Moredock b. 11-12-1917.

B. George[4] Moredock b. 4-3-1852 d. 2-26-1853.

C. James[4] A. Moredock b. 12-10-1853 d. 9-21-1854.

D. Margaret[4] Moredock b. 12-19-1855 m. Samuel Cox b. 9-23-1850 d. 1-9-1924, son of John B. and Maria Crayne Cox. No issue.

E. Emma[4] Moredock b. 2-12-1858 m. David Burson 8-29-1887. 2 children.

  a. Ray[5] J. Burson b. 2-20-1890 Murrietta, CA. m. Martha Gorshin 9-25-1919. 2 children.

    (1) Kenneth[6] David Burson b. 4-19-1922.

    (2) Francis[6] Mark Burson b. 12-14-1923, Murrietta, CA.

  b. Dora[5] E. Burson b. 9-21-1892, Murrietta, CA. m. Levi B. Johnston 4-27-1926.

F. Sarah[4] Moredock b. 3-16-1860 m. 1-18-1884 Anderson Moredock, at Carmichaels, PA. He was born Sept. 26, 1855, son of Mary Jane and Simon Moredock. 3 children.

  a. Elizabeth[5] Moredock b. 8-15-1887, m. John Fuller 10-5-1910, d. 11-19-1912. No issue.

  b. George[5] Rex Moredock b. 9-24-1889, single.

  c. Anna[5] Moredock b. 8-16-1893. m. Robert Hartley (son of Jane and Oscar Hartley) 12-30-1916. He d. 1926. 2 children.

    (1) Margaret[6] Jane Hartley b. 12-6-1918.

    (2) Sarah[6] M. Hartley b. 7-3-1922.

G. Anna[4] Moredock b. 2-12-1862 d. 1-2-1931. m. W. T. Daugherty 12-7-1886 Greensboro, PA. He b. 1-16-1861 d. 1-7-1916, son of Ross and Elizabeth Payne Daugherty. 3 children.

  a. Nellie[5] M. Daugherty b. 1-10-1888, Jefferson, PA. m. Dr. Charles H. Sherry 6-19-1920, Uniontown, PA. He b. 12-18-1887

Johnstown, PA. Son of Rachel Reichard and Joseph Sherry. 1 son.

(1) Charles[6] H. Sherry, Jr. b. 8-13-1924.

b. Daniel[5] R. Daugherty b. 12-10-1889 Jefferson, PA. d. 7-11-1893.

c. Sarah[5] E. Daugherty b. 9-12-1896 Brownsville, PA. m. Carlton G. Leonard 8-28-1916, he b. 11-13-1887 Brownsville, (son of Ettie Cox and Alvin G. Leonard.) 3 children.

(1) Janice[6] M. Leonard b. 10-12-1917 Brownsville, PA.

(2) Patricia[6] A. Leonard b. 8-6-1919, Brownsville, PA.

(3) Sara[6] E. Leonard b. 6-18-1925, Pittsburg, PA.

H. Edna[4] Moredock b. 6-4-1864 Jefferson, PA. m. 10-16-1889 Samuel Crans Faddis who was b. 12-23-1862, d. 10-11-1932, son of Isiah and Frances Ann Strohman Faddis. 5 children.

a. †Charles[5] Isiah Faddis b. 6-13-1890 Loudonville, OH. m. Jane Ely Morris, Waynesburg, PA., 1917, who was b. 1-16-1892, daughter of Gertrude Ely and Elijah Ephraim Morris. Cadet Corps PA State College 4 yrs. Capt. 1915, served with Co. K. 10th Pa. Inf. Big Bend Dist. 1916. 2nd Officers Training Camp Oglethorpe, GA, Commissioned Capt 1917. Assigned U.S. Inf. 4th Div. trans. 1918 4th Ammunition Train 4th Div. Sailed for France 4-1918. Participated in Aisne Marne, Champaign Marne, St. Meheil and Argonne Offensives. Promoted to Major Inf. 10-15-1918. Pro. Lt. Col. Inf. 11-13-1918. Cited by General Pershing for extraordinary, meritorious and conspicuous service at Runsur, Meuse, France. Served in Army of Occupation Luxemberg and Germany. Ret. U.S. Army Aug., 1918 discharged 9-1918. Joined Officers Reserve Corps, 1923. Executive Officer of 394th Inf. 99th Div. Col. Charles Faddis, a staunch Democrat, was elected to Congress Nov. 8, 1932 from the 25th Dist. of PA which is composed of Washington and Greene Counties. Jane and Charles Faddis had 3 children.

(1) William[6] George Faddis b. 5-1920, Waynesburg, PA.

(2) Jane[6] Morris Faddis b. 7-25-1922.

(3) Edna[6] Gertrude Faddis b. 6-17-1924.

b. Lucile[5] Faddis b. 8-27-1891.

c. Edna[5] Faddis b. 1-25-1897 Grad. Pa. College for Women, Pittsburg, PA and teacher. m. Robert M. Stephens 6-11-1924. 1 child.

(1) Elizabeth[6] Stephens b. 7-20-1928.

d. Samuel[5] Faddis b. 5-12-1903 m. Erba Long 7-3-1928.

e. Elizabeth[5] Faddis b. 2-1907.

I. Elizabeth[4] Moredock (called Tad) b. 6-12-1866 near Jefferson, PA, d. 3-26-1931 m. Samuel M. Smith at Carmichaels, PA 10-22-1890, who was b. 10-12-1865 at Jefferson, PA, the son of Louisa Crayne and Dr. S. Smith. 2 children.

a. Louisa[5] Crayne Smith b. 2-19-1894, Waynesburg, PA.

b. †Harry[5] S. Smith b. 10-21-1891 m. Ruth Lowry 7-27-1922. Second Lieut. Co. I. 9th U. S. Inf. Enlisted 9-18-1917. Discharged 6-2-1919. Decorated by Gen. Pershing with Distinguished Service Cross 12-6-1918 for extraordinary heroism in military operations against an armed enemy of the U. S. at Tuiierie Farm, France, 11-3-1918. Ruth and H. S. Smith parents of 1 son.

(1) Lowry[6] B. Smith b. 5-1924 d. 3 days later, Sharon, PA.

J. Austin[4] Moredock b. 8-11-1870 m. Elizabeth Smith 10-18-1900. She was the daughter of Louisa Crayne and Sylvanius S. Smith. He is an Atty. at Waynesburg, takes an active part in politics, and is a staunch Democrat. Have 3 children.

a. Albert[5] E. Moredock b. 1-12-1903, Waynesburg, PA.

b. Dora[5] Elizabeth Moredock b. 1-13-1909.

c. Daniel[5] Moredock b. 8-24-1901 d. 4-1902.

3. Experience[3] Rex (3rd child of Mary and Charles[2] Rex, George[1]) b. 10-12-1836 m. David Moffatt Hart 5-1-1856. She was called "Pera" and d. on her wedding trip at St. Louis, MO 6-18-1856 of typhoid fever. A very beautiful monument marks her grave in Jefferson Cemetery.

4. George[3] Rex (4th child of Mary and Charles[2] Rex, George[1]) b. 11-30-1838 d. 5-29-1897 at Jefferson. m. Mary E. Strickler, daughter of Catherine Heath and Isaac Strickler 12-8-1861. Mary S. b. 1-5-1843 Scottdale, PA. d. 4-11-1891. Ceremony by Rev. J. B. Solomon, Pres. Monongahela Baptist College, Jefferson. 10 children all b. at the old Rex homestead, Jefferson.

Bates History, Greene Co., PA. p. 744-745, gives:

"George Rex, farmer, P. O. Jefferson, is descendant of one of the pioneer families of the township and was b. 11-30-1838 on the farm where he and family now reside. He is a son of Charles and Mary (Hickman) Rex. His father was b. 7-1-1801 and was a son of George and Margaret Kepler Rex, the former a native of England and the latter of Germany. They emigrated to America and were m. in Pennsylvania.

settling in Greene Co. which at the time of their settlement was known as Washington Co. Here they remained until their deaths."
A. Mary[4] C. Rex b. 9-14-1862 d. 9-21-1863.
B. Charles[4] Rex 2nd b. 9-8-1864 d. 4-22-1899, single.
C. Ella[4] J. Rex b. 4-13-1867 d. 8-22-1899, single.
D. Edward[4] Bower Rex b. 2-24-1872 d. 8-14-1900, single.
E. George[4] Strickler Rex b. 4-22-1874 d. 8-8-1876.
F. Joseph[4] A. Rex b. 9-25-1876 d. 2-27-1904 m. Lizzie Davis 3-10-1898. A twin. No issue.
G. Georgiana[4] Rex b. 9-25-1876. Twin. m. Henry D. Bell 3-28-1896. He b. near Jefferson, PA 2-6-1868 (son of John R. Bell b. 4-12-1836 d. 7-4-1896 and Helen Davis Bell b. 7-23-1839 d. 9-12-1926.) They were m. at Waynesburg by Rev. P. F. DeLancy, Baptist Minister, that being their church. 2 children.
   a. John[5] Rex Bell b. 3-29-1899 d. 8-28-1921.
   b. Helen[5] Mary Bell b. 3-14-1897 near Jefferson, PA m. Andrew J. Frost (son of Mary Cox and George Frost) 8-6-1924. 1 son.
      (1) Richard[6] Bell Frost b. 9-21-1925, Pittsburg, PA.
H. Albert[4] Gallatin Rex b. 12-4-1879 m. Virginia G. Feitt 6-16-1904 who was b. 7-25-1884, Danville, VA. Ceremony at Jefferson by Rev. C. J. Feitt, M. E. Minister, father of the bride. As the oldest son in line, Albert G. Rex came into possession of the original bible of Line XII and furnished the picture of it in this book. 1 child.
   a. Virginia[5] Alberta Gallatin Rex. b. 6-25-1905. Los Angeles CA.
I. Martha[4] Mary Rex b. 4-21-1882 m. Harry P. Gallatin (son of Anna and William Gallatin) 10-13-1900 at Jefferson, PA. Ceremony by J. C. McMinn, M. E. Minister. They are Presbyterians and parents of 3 children.
   a. Ernest[5] Rex Gallatin b. 9-27-1901, Jefferson, m. Mary Gregg 2-14-1923 at Brownsville, PA. 2 sons.
      (1) Richard[6] Harry Gallatin b. 9-29-1924, Brownsville, PA.
      (2) Ernest[6] Rex Gallatin b. 8-1926, Brownsville, PA.
   b. John[5] Thomas Gallatin b. 1-16-1904, Jefferson, PA.
   c. Alvin[5] W. Gallatin b. 12-7-1905, Jefferson. PA.
J. Ernest[4] Walton Rex b. 5-23-1885 d. 4-16-1926. m. 12-18-1912 Ica Pearl Lemley, no children. Ernest was the last of the Rex name to be born at the Old Rex Homestead. He took a great interest in this genealogy and has given much assistance. Among other things, he furnished the picture of the old home appearing in this

book. He was in the Internal Revenue Service for 8 years, being especially posted on Law and Regulations in this work.

5. Mary[3] Rex (5th child of Mary and Charles[2] Rex, George[1]) b. 12-12-1842 d. as infant.

6. †John[3] B. Rex (6th child of Mary and Charles[2] Rex, George[1]) b. 4-6-1844 d. 1-21-1917, Shannon City, IA. m. Mary A. McMinn 12-31 1865 at Jefferson. PA. At birth is said J. B. was wrapped in the scarlet blanket, the same one used in the family for years back and that he grew into a stiff English gentleman adhering strictly to family traditions. Was attending a boy's school when the war started, which he promptly left, without ceremony and as so young entered as Bugler. Was much admired there for his fearless spirit and black glossy hair. Described as having very expressive, clear violet eyes, broad shoulders, erect carriage and exceedingly courteous. Distinguished in manner and appearance, as well as intellect. The family moved to Ill. and then to Des Moines and Shannon City, Iowa. 5 children.

A. Elizabeth[4] Rex b. 1869 d. 11-22-1932. Was teaching her S. S. class in Methodist Church and had a stroke and d. a few hours later. Single.

B. Margaret[4] Rex b. 1874. Deceased, single.

C. Derressa[4] Rex b. 1880, single, Shannon City, IA.

D. Anna[4] M. Rex b. 3-12-1872 at Jefferson, PA. Among other schools, attended Gouchen College, Baltimore. Speaks five different languages and a musician. At Shannon City 9-15-1904 m. Earl E. Stevens who is a Columbia Grad. and Mining Assayer and Electrical Engineer. They have traveled and lived in N. Y. City, Montana, Oregon and Central America.

E. William[4] M. Rex b. 1-29-1870 Jefferson, Pa. Grad. Northwestern and Chicago Law School, Attorney in Los Angeles, CA. At Des Moines 5-2-1907 m. Mary Louise McMinn (Oxford, Ohio Grad.) and are the parents of 2 sons.

a. John[5] Leonidas Rex b. 1-24-1909, Architecture class of 1931, University of Southern California. Kappa Alpha Fraternity.

b. Robert[5] M. Rex b. 2-13-1914.

Index of Names

Index of Names

Index of Names

Index of Names

Index of Names

Index of Names

Index of Names

Index of Names

*The number incorporated into the first name represents the generation of the individual. If no number appears, the person is not a direct descendant of George Rex, but rather a spouse or parent of a spouse. The number in the Line Column is self explanatory. If no number appears, the person is probably a parent of a spouse. Spouses of descendants are assigned the appropriate Line number.

Index of Figures

www.ingramcontent.com/pod-product-compliance
Lightning Source LLC
Chambersburg PA
CBHW070153310326
41914CB00097B/1669